Republicanism in the Modern World

*For
my mother and father
and
Cecilie*

Republicanism in the Modern World

JOHN W. MAYNOR

polity

First published in 2003 by Polity Press in association with Blackwell Publishing Ltd

Editorial office:
Polity Press
65 Bridge Street
Cambridge CB2 1UR, UK

Marketing and production:
Blackwell Publishing Ltd
108 Cowley Road
Oxford OX4 1JF, UK

Distributed in the USA by
Blackwell Publishing Inc.
350 Main Street
Malden, MA 02148, USA

A catalogue record for this book is available from the British Library.

Library of Congress Cataloging-in-Publication Data

Maynor, John W.
  Republicanism in the modern world / John W. Maynor.
     p. cm.
Includes bibliographical references and index.
  ISBN 0–7456–2807–9 (hc : acid-free)—ISBN 0–7456–2808–7 (pb : acid-free)
  1. Republicanism. 2. Political science—Philosophy. I. Title.
JC423 .M3795 2003
321.8′6—dc21

                                                                              2002013522

Typeset in 10.5 on 12pt Sabon
by Kolam Information Services Pvt. Ltd., India.
Printed and bound in Great Britain by MPG Books Ltd, Bodmin, Cornwall

For further information on Polity, visit our website: http://www.polity.co.uk

Contents

Acknowledgments

The seeds for this project were sown when I was working as a junior staffer in the Clinton Administration at the US Department of Agriculture. As part of my job I was extremely fortunate to be able to travel around the country working with state and local governments and talking to average citizens about the role of the federal government and its capacity to both help and hinder the normal goings on of everyday life. I became acutely aware of a real disconnection between the governed and the government, with each eyeing the other with trepidation and suspicion. I was also able to understand first-hand not only the important role that government can play in the lives of citizens, but also its limits. In my formative years growing up in Mississippi I had always thought that the US government and the people enjoyed a fruitful and close relationship. Now I was discovering that, for whatever reason, this was not necessarily the case. Through my many conversations with my fellow citizens I began to think about how it might be possible to rectify this development and change the way the government and the people related to one another by opening up the lines of communication and encouraging dialogue and discussion. One thing led to another and I decided to leave government service and apply myself to a philosophical research project involving civic republicanism and its potential to help bring about what I felt was a much needed change. I left Washington, DC for the medieval splendor of York, England.

At the University of York I had the privilege to work with some truly remarkable people who both challenged and inspired my research, and I owe them all a debt of gratitude. Both Duncan Ivision and Matt Matravers nurtured my raw ideas and helped me turn them into something intelligible. Matt in particular has read and re-read many different drafts of this present work, each time combining just the right amount of critique with constructive comments. Peter Nicholson also helped me improve my work and taught me a great amount about not only political philosophy, but education as well. Others at York I would like to thank include Sue Mendus, Alex Callinicos, and Mark Evans. Mark Philp deserves my thanks for examining my D.Phil and offering many helpful suggestions and comments.

Early drafts of the book were written when I was a fellow of the Civic Education Project based in Bratislava, Slovakia, and I would like to thank my colleagues in both the Czech and Slovak Republics for their helpful discussions with me and their companionship and inspiration. The final manuscript was prepared when I was lecturing in politics at Oxford Brookes University and I would like to thank my students and colleagues in the Department of Politics and the School of Social Sciences and Law for their support and encouragement. I would also like to thank the anonymous referees who offered me helpful comments. A special thanks goes to Philip Pettit, whose work has inspired and challenged much of my own thinking, for reading and generously commenting on an earlier draft (and subsequent revisions). Of course, any mistakes or shortcomings are mine to bear alone. The editorial team at Polity have been a joy to work with and I would like to thank all of them, especially Louise Knight and Rachel Kerr, for their belief in my work and in their friendly and professional attitude.

Parts of this book draw upon material published elsewhere. Although I have substantially revised chapters 2, 4, and 5, I would like to thank the publishers of the following articles for allowing me to use some of the material in this present work: Maynor, J. (2000), "Factions and Diversity: A Republican Dilemma" in C. Pierson and S. Tormey (2000); Maynor, J. (2002), "Without Regret: The Comprehensive Nature of Nondomination", *Politics*, 22: 51–8; and Maynor, J. (2002), "Another Instrumental Approach", *European Journal of Political Thought*, 1: 71–89.

Finally, I would like to thank the members of my family, both in the US and Norway. Regrettably, I have been absent from too many family gatherings and holidays and I hope that after reading this they will finally understand just what I have been up to these last few years. In particular I would like to thank my mother and father for being a constant source of inspiration and support and I would like to dedicate this book to them. I would also like to dedicate this work to my wife Cecilie who has endured with good humor my many ramblings on republicanism and has always been a great sounding board for ideas. She has taught me that while I have one of the best jobs in the world, much of what makes life worth living lies elsewhere. Thank you all, I am a very lucky man indeed.

Introduction:
Republicanism(s)

It is not surprising that the language and discourse of classical republicanism has been near or at the center of recent debates among political
philosophers. In response to the dominance of liberalism, some theorists have recently embraced the republican model as an alternative and
attractive way forward. The overriding appeal of these moves seems to
be the nature of the emphasis that forms of republicanism place on
citizenship and civic virtue in light of what many commentators see as a
decline in the social nature of modern politics (Sandel, 1996; Putnam,
1995 and 2000). Most notable among these is Michael Sandel, who in
Democracy's Discontent (1996) argues that classical republican ideals
are a needed prescription for the woes of today's modern polity. Others,
including such diverse theorists as Charles Taylor (1995: 193) and John
Rawls (1996: 205), have also touted republican values as a way to
reinvigorate liberal institutions by stressing the "civic" nature of the
ideals that accompany them. However, it is my belief that to an
alarming degree many of these discussions in contemporary political
discourse are inconsistent and fail to capture the essence of a classical
republican theory for today's complex and modern world.

What makes this point even more pressing is the degree to which the
ideas of some political philosophers have begun to cross into the policy-
making arena and have a measurable impact on politics and politicians.
There is a tendency for some politicians to use the language of civic
republicanism as citizen-friendly sound bites or ready-made "spin."
For example, in 1994 in response to the Democratic Party's massive
repudiation at the mid-term Congressional elections President Clinton
searched for a way to retake the political initiative he had lost in the first

two years of his administration and place his policy agenda on firmer ground. Another, more ominous, sign of the president's inability to press forward any of his policy objectives, such as the ill-fated health-care reform effort, was the growing undercurrent of mistrust and hostility many ordinary citizens had for government activity. State action was the problem, not the solution. To many, the 1995 State of the Union speech represented the last opportunity for the president to outline his vision for the country and revive his, and his party's, political fortunes in anticipation of the 1996 presidential election (*Time*, 1995: 38). In searching for answers to why his party lost so badly at the polls in November 1994, Clinton and his advisors believed that they had failed to connect with voters and put forth a policy agenda that addressed the concerns of ordinary citizens. The thought was that they had failed to convince the American people that the government could be a positive force for change.

In addressing this shortcoming, and to prepare for the State of the Union speech, the president summoned a wide-ranging group of academics to Camp David for a weekend retreat to solicit their views on repairing the ruptures in society and putting his policy agenda back on track (*Washington Post*, 1995: A8). Among these "big thinkers" was Robert Putnam, whose essay "Bowling Alone" focused on the breakdown of civic America and called for a renewed effort to encourage civic engagement to replace declining levels of social capital (Putnam, 1995 and 2000). Also in attendance was Benjamin Barber, whose work in *Strong Democracy* (1984) touches on the need for robust versions of citizenship to reinvigorate American political institutions. The president tried his new message out on Democratic lawmakers one week before the State of the Union speech, where he told them that they had to rise above partisan battles and instead focus on the deterioration of society and the worrying trends of voter anxiety and apathy. He implored the politicians to find new ways to get out and connect with voters and to "change the way we are conducting politics to make citizenship matter again" (President Clinton, as quoted in *International Herald Tribune*, 1995a: 3). The State of the Union speech itself was also a reflection of the president's new direction. The central themes of the speech revolved around building a "new social compact" between the federal government and civic responsible citizens to forge a cooperative effort to stem the erosion of community (*International Herald Tribune*, 1995b: 3). The task for the president was to convince the American people that a proactive federal government could make their lives better.

In soliciting the ideas of academics, the president highlighted the important role that political philosophy can play in the development of public policy. This role is perhaps best personified by William Galston's long career in mainstream American politics, including his tenure as a deputy assistant to the president for domestic policy during the first Clinton administration on the Domestic Policy Council, the linchpin of the White House's policy-making machine. There are other examples of political philosophers engaging with policymakers, such as Will Kymlicka's recent book, *Finding our Way*, which is a study in ethnocultural relations in Canada (Kymlicka, 1998a). The book is based on a series of papers Kymlicka wrote for the Department of Canadian Heritage, which was interested in knowing if debates among political philosophers could prove useful in the formulation of public policy (Kymlicka, 1998a: vii). In Great Britain, Bernard Crick has recently chaired a government commission charged with developing a set of guidelines to integrate citizenship classes into the national school curriculum (Qualifications and Curriculum Authority, 1999a). The new guidelines, due to take effect from the Fall 2002 school year, are a robust defense of citizenship designed to excite young people to help them reconnect with their government, and each other.

What concerns me is not that political philosophers are becoming involved in concrete policy matters. Indeed, I applaud this effort and believe that political philosophy can contribute positively to the direction of the modern polity by playing a prominent role in the everyday life of the people. Moreover, I believe that the better understanding we, both as practitioners of the discipline and as concerned citizens, have of the connection between philosophy and policy the more useful our work will be. What does concern me, however, are questions that relate to the operationalization of political philosophy and the degree to which important theoretical considerations may become ill considered as they become concrete policy remedies. In terms of my project, and in what follows in this book, I am alarmed by the degree to which the ideals and values of classical republicanism are spread around by both philosophers and politicians without a clear and consistent sense of their historical pedigree and their relevance to the modern world. A prime example of this lack of clear and consistent direction is evidenced by Michael Sandel's recent work. As mentioned above, in *Democracy's Discontent* Sandel argues that classical republican ideals are a needed prescription for the woes of today's modern polity (Sandel, 1996). The broad thesis of Sandel's book is that the republican civic tradition in American politics has been overwhelmed by "procedural liberalism," leaving the political landscape barren of important debates surrounding citizenship, civic virtue, self-government, and community. Instead, political debates have focused on neutrality and individual choice, causing widespread disenchantment with the political process. Sandel connects this growing disenchantment with the political agenda of the liberal procedural republic that lacks a substantive moral discourse leading to an overwhelming feeling of drift and disempowerment (Sandel, 1996: 323). What is needed, for Sandel, is a new commitment on behalf of public servants to initiate a national dialogue that moves beyond debates about the procedural republic, and instead focuses on the important moral questions facing the modern polity (Sandel, 1996). Not surprisingly, classical republican forms of citizenship and civic virtue help to inform this move and seek to fill the apparent gap between state, community, citizen, and individual.

Now my problem with Sandel is not that he invokes the ideas and language of classical republicanism to address what he sees as a major problem haunting the modern polity. Rather, my problem is the confusion and inconsistency not just in Sandel's work, but also in other theorists who take certain parts of republican theory without providing a clear and modern conceptualization of the whole theory in terms of a public philosophy for today. A common error in contemporary theory is to view classical republicanism as simply the opposite of monarchy. Another view of republicanism equates it with the principle of governments conducting the common business of the people in the name of the common good (Miller, 1987: 434). The term *res publica* is generally used to describe a set of "constitutional arrangements under which it might justifiably be claimed that the *res* (the government) genuinely reflects the will and promotes the good of the *publica* (the community as a whole)" (Skinner, 1991: 196). Republican thought can claim to have a lineage that dates back to Plato, Aristotle, and Polybius. This lineage also runs through the writers of Rome such as Livy, Sallust, and Plutarch, who developed its history and an account of its leaders, laws, and institutions that have come to symbolize the essence of republicanism. Thus, in terms of the diverse views on the republican approach, it is more accurate to speak of republicanisms, rather than one unitary theory. It is my contention that this is where much confusion about contemporary republicanism stems from, and that this undermines its relevance and usefulness in addressing important issues.

In response to this realization, I have two broad overriding aims in this book. The first is to develop a *modern* version of republicanism that is inspired by the classical models, but yet can serve as the basis for a public philosophy for today. In making this move, I hope to offer the reader a quick introduction to classical republican thought and demonstrate how the two broad strands, neo-Athenian and neo-Roman, relate to one another and how they inspire the modern version that

I advocate. The second overriding aim of this book is to take the modern republican approach and demonstrate not only its relevance to today's world, but also its attractiveness in coping with the many problems facing today's polity, including many of those that concern Sandel and the other theorists who are quick to invoke its principles, albeit in varying ways and with varying degrees of success. I also hope to "cash out" some of the theoretical aspects of modern republicanism and demonstrate how they can be used in today's world without having to abandon in wholesale measure many of the principles that currently inform contemporary liberal public philosophy.

In making my arguments, one thing that will become evident is my belief in the capacity of the state to be a positive force in the everyday lives of individuals. At first glance this admission may put some off reading further as they dismiss my ideas as being counter to life in the modern world where it is commonly accepted that the state should play a lesser rather than a greater role in our lives. However, I do not think that such criticism is entirely accurate with reference to the modern republican approach put forth in this book. So, to those readers who may be initially put off by the idea of a strong and active state I ask for patience and that they should read further, since the type of state activity envisioned by modern republicans is different to that of the liberal procedural state criticized by Sandel. Moreover, what follows in this book is not an effort to make policy. Rather, my aims are more modest. What follows is an effort to inform, influence, and change the way politicians, policy-makers, and everyday citizens relate to one another as they participate in the democratic process. I want the ideas presented in this book to serve as a sort of catalyst for important debates not only between political philosophers, but between other members of our society who care about the current condition and shape of the modern world and the state's position in it. Specifically, a central task of this work is to offer suggestions on how to reinvigorate politics in the modern democratic nation-state by embracing the energy created by its diverse population; encouraging active civic engagement through specific forms of citizenship and civic virtue; and, most importantly, showing how to utilize the modern republican conception of liberty as nondomination as the foundation of policy initiatives and institutional design. In making my argument, I will draw on the recent work of Philip Pettit and Quentin Skinner to develop and extend the theoretical implications of a distinct republican conception of liberty as nondomination. As a whole, I want to propose and explore a modern republican public philosophy that is held together by the complex interdependent relationship between nondomination, conflict, citizenship, and civic virtue.

The strategy of my argument centers on three important areas of inquiry. The first area seeks to explore the origins of modern republicanism by examining the development of classical republican ideas in both the neo-Athenian and neo-Roman versions. Chapter 1 takes a brief look at the development of classical republican thought and argues that the neo-Roman version is better suited to provide the philosophical foundations for modern republicanism. I argue that Machiavelli became the central character of neo-Roman republicanism and, following contemporary writers such as J. G. A. Pocock and Quentin Skinner, trace the impact that his work had on later writers and on the development of the republican alternative to liberalism. In addition to exploring the history of ideas, this chapter also attempts to locate neo-Roman republican liberty within Isaiah Berlin's famous distinction between positive and negative liberty. I argue that the conceptual landscape of freedom is not filled to capacity and that neo-Roman republican liberty represents an alternative way of understanding freedom that does not fit comfortably within Berlin's typology. As will become apparent, understanding the position of neo-Roman republican liberty will help to clarify the sense of liberty found in modern republicanism and provide the basis for a thorough exploration of it as it emerges as a relevant and attractive public philosophy.

Chapter 2 seeks to follow through on the theoretical points raised in the first chapter as I begin to explore the contemporary implications of neo-Roman republican thought. Utilizing the recent work of Philip Pettit (1997), this chapter examines the claim that neo-Roman republicans held an alternative conception of liberty to the traditional positive/negative dichotomy of freedom. The chief concern of this chapter will be to explore this alternative conception of liberty, which is characterized by the absence of arbitrary interference, or, in modern republican speak, nondomination. To this end, I examine what Pettit sees as republicanism's advantages over liberal approaches while highlighting a weakness found in his argument. In trying to move beyond Pettit's important work, this chapter considers how modern republicanism relates to positive and negative conceptions of liberty. I accept Pettit's contention that republican liberty as nondomination combines some aspects of both positive and negative freedom. However, I argue that Pettit does not go far enough in differentiating republican liberty from the type of negative liberty embedded in rival liberal approaches. In making my argument, I explore an alternative way of understanding nondomination and those elements of positive liberty that equate freedom with self-mastery. This chapter also explores the more personal and informal nature of modern republicanism by looking closely at two interdependent powers that accompany republican liberty: reciprocal and constitutional. I argue that contained within these two powers are attractive features that not only serve to deepen and enrich the lives of individuals, but also help to differentiate modern republicanism from liberalism – a theme taken up in the next part of the book.

The second area the strategy of my argument centers on is in distinguishing and defending modern republicanism from two contemporary liberal approaches: liberal neutrality and political liberalism. Specifically, chapter 3 explores the contemporary implications of modern republicanism in light of the argument for liberal neutrality put forth by Will Kymlicka (1998b). I seek to differentiate the modern republican project from liberal neutrality in two important respects. The first of these concerns Kymlicka's belief that the state should not appeal to the intrinsic value of some versions of the good in its ideals and institutions. I argue that modern republicanism is a non-neutral approach, but yet does not endorse a robust singular version of the good. The second part of my argument will focus on Kymlicka's belief that the state should not promote any perfectionist values. I argue that, while modern republicanism is not perfectionist in the way that neo-Athenian republicanism is or is often taken to be, nevertheless it does contain certain perfectionist elements that make it quasi-perfectionist in nature. In addressing these two important issues, I further develop and defend modern republicanism as an approach that can cope with the many problems facing today's states. Moreover, I argue that abandoning liberal neutrality allows modern republicanism to offer a richer and thus more robust account of freedom than liberalism without sacrificing key liberal aims.

Chapter 4 focuses on the recent *political* turn of John Rawls (1996). In this chapter, I maintain that despite Rawls's interpretation of the republican project, modern republicanism is not reducible to political liberalism. In making my argument, I focus on the first two of Rawls's "political" requirements of any public philosophy. I argue that modern republicanism does not satisfy these requirements and thus necessarily stands in fundamental opposition to the "political" project. In this chapter I also explore the key differences between Rawls's theory and that of modern republicanism and argue that my approach does presuppose certain comprehensive values that support republican liberty as nondomination without being classed as the sort of civic humanism that Rawls derides. The overriding argument in this chapter is that if modern republicanism restricted its approach in the way that Rawls advocates, nondomination could not be realized. In other words, modern republicanism would be fatally cut off from the necessary virtues and values that support nondomination if it is restricted in the same way as Rawls believes a "political" approach must be.

The final area my argument seeks to explore is how modern republicanism can cope when faced with the many problems confronting today's polities. I take the modern republican approach developed in earlier parts of the book on a "test drive" by first exploring a republican account of pluralism, and second identifying three important "pillars" that support the modern republican project. The upshot of this final part is to identify certain areas where a modern republican approach can manifest itself and affect the way in which today's polity addresses the problems facing it. In chapter 5, I argue that modern republicanism can cope with the difference and diversity found in today's modern polity without sacrificing several important liberal concerns. In this chapter, I explore how Machiavelli responded to the challenges raised by a population defined by difference and diversity in a progressive manner that sought to harness and channel its energy in a way that helped secure republican liberty. By stressing the interdependent relationship between liberty as nondomination, good laws and institutions, and civic virtue and citizenship, I argue that a modern republican state can cope with moral pluralism. By tolerating and institutionalizing the moral pluralism found within the modern polity, a modern republican state can channel the dynamic energy and activity generated by difference and diversity to secure and enhance liberty as nondomination. In the same manner, I argue that the citizenry as a whole have an important role to play in keeping the power of the state in check and ensuring that the state itself does not become a dominator. Furthermore, I argue that a contemporary republican approach can strengthen the institutions of the modern polity by stressing republican liberty as nondomination and the accompanying need for a politics based on strong forms of contestation and open and inclusive forums without negatively affecting cultural pluralism.

Chapter 6 examines how democratic contestatory institutions, the first of the three pillars, support modern republicanism and provide the citizenry with important checks on the power of the state and against the risk of domination from factions (including the majority). In particular, I argue that modern republican democratic contestatory institutions are the best way to ensure that domination is minimized. I then explore just what type of contribution these institutions can make to existing practices. I look at how these institutions can be constituted and examine how they relate to modern democratic theory. I also try to offer some real ideas that not only demonstrate the attractiveness of modern republicanism, but also represent achievable ends that can enhance the modern polity's ability to minimize arbitrary interference. Thus, in pursuing my argument, a secondary goal of this chapter is to "cash out" some of the ideas put forth earlier while addressing key areas of concern about modern republicanism.

In chapter 7 I discuss civic education and social norms, the two remaining pillars that support modern republicanism. I first argue that a modern republican approach to civic education can go further than the standard liberal account in cultivating certain forms of citizenship and civic virtue. In both a formal and an informal manner, I argue that modern republicanism teaches citizens distinctive skills that have far-reaching benefits in light of their final choices. Next I argue that modern republicanism can reinvigorate and mold the important social norms that characterize today's democratic polity by securing individuals and groups from domination. Taken together, all three of these pillars help to provide modern republicanism characterized by liberty as nondomination with a solid and compelling structure upon which to predicate a public philosophy for today's world. As a whole my argument centers around the contention that the modern republican approach developed here can reinvigorate social and political institutions in a manner that supports republican liberty as nondomination. I argue that, in many ways, modern republicanism fosters group-level commitments to certain distinctive ways of doing things so that republican liberty as nondomination can take root and become embedded in the prevailing public philosophy that characterizes today's democratic polity.

1

The Ideal of Polity

Introduction

Contemporary republicanism is steeped in a long tradition of thinking about politics that dates back to the ancient Greek writers and can be traced through the Romans and into writers such as Machiavelli, Montesquieu, Harrington, and Madison. Within this discourse republican thought roughly breaks down into two related, yet distinct, versions. On one side, some theorists invoke the type of republicanism inspired by Aristotle and civic humanism, which holds that individuals are social or political animals "whose essential nature is most fully realized in a democratic society in which there is widespread and vigorous participation in political life" (Rawls, 1996: 206). This "strong" or neo-Athenian version of republicanism maintains that political participation is an intrinsic good in a certain version of human flourishing or *eudaimonia*. This strand of thought is often associated with communitarianism, and ranges from the strong civic humanism of writers such as Hannah Arendt (1958) to the less robust versions put forward by others such as Alasdair MacIntyre (1985) and the aforementioned Michael Sandel (1984 and 1996). From an institutional perspective, Athens came to represent the ideal classical republic for those later writers who stressed the importance of civic virtue and self-government and their necessary connection to democracy. Democratic participation, fostered by a rich sense of civic virtue and strong versions of citizenship, came to be the hallmark of the Athenian version of republicanism. Central to this version is the emphasis placed on the formation of a certain ideal type of character that is highly skilled in the arts of democratic self-government. Such character traits are thought to be an essential part of the good life and are therefore justified as an explicit aim of the state (Pangle, 1988: 20).

Michael Sandel's recent work is typical of mainstream contemporary neo-Athenian republicanism. For Sandel, self-government is the only type of political system that can sustain the necessary resources for "the moral energies of a vital democratic life" (Sandel, 1996: 24). Sandel's neo-Athenian-inspired republicanism holds that rights should be defined in light of a particular conception of the good society – the self-governing republic – and not according to principles that are neutral among conceptions of the good (Sandel, 1996: 5–6). Sandel maintains that self-governing republics value the necessary link between self-government and the cultivation of civic virtue. Moreover, Sandel's republicanism regards moral character as a public, and not merely a private, concern (Sandel, 1996: 25). At the center of Sandel's thesis is the belief that, if individuals are to be free, self-government and the virtues and versions of citizenship that accompany it are essential elements that must be actively promoted by the state. To this end, these distinct and intrinsically valuable versions of civic virtue and citizenship are cultivated by the political communities and institutions that represent the people (Sandel, 1996: 117). Sandel believes that the United States has lost contact with this strand of republicanism, resulting in widespread discontent with the modern democratic project. The result is that the rise of the liberal procedural republic and its focus on rights and neutrality has disempowered the citizenry and caused a crisis in the American political system. In essence Sandel's version of republicanism can be said to be an effort to provide today's democratic state with strong versions of civic virtue and citizenship in the hope of reinvigorating public debates in light of what some see as a malaise afflicting the modern polity. For the most part, those who advocate neo-Athenian republicanism believe that it is only in a self-governing republic that individuals can find excellence and flourish (Sandel, 1996; Taylor, 1991). The overriding thought here is that sharing and participating in the "governance of a free political community" – one that controls its own fate – requires specialized and distinct virtues that help to facilitate the formative project. It follows that civic virtue and democratic participation are intrinsically valuable to the maintenance of liberty because they help individuals flourish as political beings, which is their true and essential nature. According to Sandel, "given our nature as political beings, we are free only insofar as we exercise our capacity to deliberate about the common good, and participate in the public life of a free city or republic" (Sandel, 1996: 26). Put simply, in neo-Athenian forms of republicanism, participating in the institutions of a self-governing democratic polity will not only provide individuals with a particular form of liberty, it will also help them realize a high degree of self-mastery because it contributes to a rich formative project.

On the other side of the republican divide are Roman-inspired versions of republicanism that have also become attractive to many theorists in contemporary debates. The neo-Roman republican argument has been put forth most eloquently in the work of Quentin Skinner and Philip Pettit. Both Skinner and Pettit argue that the approach put forth by Machiavelli and his contemporaries signaled a divisive shift away from the republicanism of the Athenians that featured the direct forms of democracy intrinsic to individual flourishing. Rather, according to Pettit, Roman republicanism was characterized by "a constitution in which government was built on a democratic foundation but was better devised to guard against problems of faction, demagoguery and tyranny." Certain Roman technologies were celebrated, such as the "dispersion of democratic power across different assemblies, adherence to a more or less strict rule of law, election to public office, limitation on the tenure of public office, rotation of offices among the citizenry, and the like" (Pettit, 1998: 83). In contrast to the strong version of republicanism put forth by neo-Athenians, the neo-Roman version is more moderate in its stance toward individual flourishing. Instead, its focus is on creating the institutional arrangements that preserve individual freedom. Another important feature of the neo-Roman approach is the extent to which these writers, especially Machiavelli, conceived the world as made up of competing *humors*, or dispositions, that individuals wish to pursue. At least conceptually, this feature makes the neo-Roman tradition more attractive to many contemporary liberal approaches since it does not stress conformity to a singular ideal of human excellence. Instead, as Chantal Mouffe has argued, it at least opens up the possibility that the neo-Roman model is more suited to modern democracy (Mouffe, 1993: 36).

When comparing these two forms of republicanism, two closely related differences emerge that have a direct bearing on the suitability of contemporary versions of republicanism as an attractive public philosophy for the modern polity. First, the neo-Athenian model stresses direct participation in the governing process as a way of realizing true freedom. The thought is that the act of participation itself helps to constitute certain ultimate goods that contribute to individual well-being and self-mastery. This populist and nostalgic approach involves citizens understanding their freedom as part of a certain type of community and belonging to that community as an active member (Taylor, 1991; also see Pettit, 1997: 19). The neo-

Athenian approach also seeks to unify the good and offer a system of politics and ethics that is indivisible (Mouffe, 1993: 36). Significantly, neo-Roman versions of republicanism also stress participation and civic goods. Furthermore, traditionally within this approach, the freedom of the individual is closely linked to the freedom of the city (Skinner, 1991: 193; Pettit, 1989: 141–68). However, unlike its neo-Athenian counterpart, this version stresses the need for strong laws and institutions that secure civic-minded individuals and leave them to pursue their chosen ends (*The Discourses*: Machiavelli, 1965: 332). In other words, although collective freedom and civic activity were important features of neo-Roman republicanism, individual freedom and security became paramount since each individual was driven by their own *humori*. The thought is that neo-Roman republicans like Machiavelli abandoned the narrow-mindedness and heavy commitment of earlier versions of republicanism because they not only failed to secure liberty and often led to servitude and oppression, but they also failed to countenance the realization that individuals sought different goods. Moreover, these ancient republics were seen as unworkable as the chaotic democratic institutions of city-states became susceptible to mob rule, factions, and tyrants. It is on this point that the second key distinction between the two forms of republicanism emerges, which concerns the conception of freedom inherent in each approach. Neo-Athenian models typically view participation and communally based freedom as being essential components of a specific form of flourishing or self-mastery. Put simply, being free means participating freely in the self-governing of the community. In return, individuals can come to know and identify their true self through this participation and achieve a high level of self-mastery. In contrast, neo-Roman models leave such final questions more open-ended while stressing the processes and constitutional arrangements that guarantee individuals a degree of personal freedom unavailable under their neo-Athenian counterpart.

Ancient liberty vs. modern liberty

The contrast inherent to these two versions of republicanism can be seen clearly in the nineteenth-century French writer Benjamin Constant's now famous lecture *The Liberty of the Ancients Compared with that of the Moderns* (Constant, 1988). Constant maintained that there was a clear distinction between the "liberty of the ancients," which is associated with living in a free state (or community), and the "liberty of the moderns," a conception of liberty that promotes the right of the individual to be free from unnecessary interferences (Constant, 1988: 309–28). Constant believed that the liberty of the ancients undermined the cause of individualism by promoting values and virtues that subjected the individual self to the will of the common good. For Constant, "among the ancients the individual, almost always sovereign in public affairs, was a slave in private relations" (Constant, 1988: 311). Ancient liberty, like that present in neo-Athenian republicanism, was characterized by a collective enterprise that consisted of individuals acting together to form a community. Within this community, an individual's freedom was secondary to the liberty and authority of the community. Rousseau's anti-Enlightenment republicanism is often taken as an example of this kind of liberty (Rousseau, 1978: 19). Rousseau favored a collective enterprise to establish the General Will, which would always be aimed at serving the common good over individual self-interests. Moreover, Rousseau believed that it was only in such a participatory community that individuals could free themselves from the tyranny of society and be able to achieve a moral freedom that would lead them to self-mastery (Williams, 1991: 91).[1]

It was the liberty of the moderns, for Constant, that freed the individual from the domination of the common good by securing "the enjoyment of security in private pleasures" and ensuring a protected space within which to act freely (Constant, 1988: 317). Thus, the liberty of the moderns was centered on individual freedom and independence from the community (Constant, 1988: 311–12). Put simply, modern liberty meant "being left to the rule of your own private will [whereas] ancient liberty is sharing in the rule of a public, democratically determined will" (Pettit, 1997: 18). Perhaps not surprisingly, Constant's distinction has become embedded within the discourse of contemporary political philosophy, mainly through the work of Isaiah Berlin. Berlin's taxonomy of positive and negative liberty borrows and conditions Constant's model so that positive liberty is associated with ancient liberty and negative liberty is equated with the liberty of moderns (Berlin, 1969). However, Berlin's efforts ignore an important aspect of Constant's treatment of liberty. Moreover, I believe that through the years Berlin's distinction has not served contemporary political philosophy well because of the tendency of some writers to use it as a template for what is acceptable and what is not in the modern polity. This is especially true to the extent that the no longer relevant shadow of the cold war casts its pallor over Berlin's concept of positive liberty, even though we are never fully told just what positive liberty actually is (Ivison, 1997: 5).

The almost religious adherence to Berlin's two-sided distinction has eclipsed an important, but yet mostly overlooked, aspect of Constant's original model. While Constant favored the liberty of the moderns over that of the ancients, he also believed that no just system could completely abandon the institutional priorities of ancient liberty. What was necessary, for Constant, was to "learn to combine the two together," a position that Berlin's strict delineation between negative and positive liberty would seem to preclude (Constant, 1988: 327). What Constant feared was that individuals would become "seduced by private enjoyments away from exercising their proper share of political power" (Miller, 1991: 7).

Along these lines, then, I will argue that Berlin's distinction between positive and negative liberty is too narrow because each concept is overly exclusive and ignores an attractive republican alternative. In making my argument, I will demonstrate that the relationship between positive and negative liberty does not have to be considered as an exclusive one, and thus should more closely resemble a construction that follows Constant's advice that we should endeavor to combine the two so that important elements of each support the overall system of liberty. In terms of the neo-Athenian versus neo-Roman republicanism debate outlined above, I want to suggest that the relationship between the two strands is closer than some contemporary theorists think. Too often many contemporary writers do not acknowledge, as Skinner and Pocock have done, that the two strands of republicanism coexisted for a time and that the relationship between them is a complicated and complex affair (Pocock, 1975; Skinner, 1978). However, while acknowledging the intimacy of the two approaches, I want to take my lead from Constant and assign priority to the sense of liberty found in neo-Roman versions while also acknowledging the role played by the substantive values of ancient liberty.

There are two overriding reasons for my position here. As I will argue below, first I believe that the sense of liberty found in neo-Roman republicanism is more suited to the demands of today's world. Second, I believe that Machiavelli's stress on conflict and contestation make his theory more suited to inspire modern forms of republicanism in light of the modern demands of democracy. However, in making these points I want to acknowledge the intimate relationship between the two strands of republicanism and the virtues and values that accompany them. With respect to contemporary debates, I want to argue that it is possible to combine Berlin's two concepts of liberty together in a meaningful manner.

Positive and negative liberty

In its most simplistic form, for Berlin positive liberty was said to describe a relationship where the subject acts as master: "[they] wish to be the instrument of [their] own, not of other men's, acts of will." Liberty as self-mastery suggests that agents who realize that they are free *are free* because they desire "to be a subject, not an object" (Berlin, 1969: 131). That is, agents wish to be the *source* of their freedom and to act consciously upon their will as opposed to reacting to the will of others (Berlin, 1969: 131–2). For Berlin, the agent who possesses self-mastery is fully conscious of what it is that she wants, and understands that, in addition to possessing the ability to act, she possesses the will to act. In other words, the agent is the source of her will.

> I wish to be somebody, not nobody; a doer – deciding, not being decided for, self-directed and not acted upon by external nature or by other men as if I were a thing, or an animal, or a slave incapable of playing a human role, that is, of conceiving goals and policies of my own and realizing them. (Berlin, 1969: 131)

However, as Berlin points out, this conceptualization of liberty in the positive sense has inherent difficulties because, if this formula is going to be successful, the agent must enjoy a high level of self-realization. That is, agents must not realize only that they are free; they must understand themselves and their freedom to take advantage of it. In other words, they must be conscious masters of themselves and their activity. For Berlin, positive liberty so conceived is problematic, however, because it is dependent inextricably on the agent having achieved some sort of self-realization, realizing the degree of their liberty, and finally acting upon it. Another fear for Berlin is that it also lends itself to control by agents who may "force" the subject to be free by manipulating them into acting in ways that they themselves have not chosen consciously. These agents can be other agents, classes, institutions, or even states and, for Berlin, this raises the haunting specter of cold war totalitarianism (Berlin, 1969: 134).

As I noted above, contemporary proponents of positive liberty, including many neo-Athenian republicans, argue that, despite Berlin's warnings, freedom conceived of positively captures the essence of freedom itself because it is an essential moral ideal. Broadly based upon Aristotelian claims, these positive theories of liberty often argue that it is only individuals' search for who they really are that allows them to be free. Thus, agents can only be truly at liberty if they engage in the very activities that are consistent with their *eudaimonia*, or the "human flourishing" that embodies their deepest meanings and purposes (Skinner, 1990b: 296).[2] That is, by overcoming internal obstacles, the self-realized agent is free to act in the sense that the agent not only understands what her actions are, but can also *be* who she understands herself to be. Thus, freedom consists in agents realizing their deepest meanings and then acting accordingly within these meanings. Freedom in this definition is a two-step process. The first step is an agent's self-mastery, whereas the second step is an agent using that self-mastery to flourish within a particular type of community, such as that of self-government. In the words of Charles Taylor, "doctrines of positive freedom are concerned with a view of freedom which involves essentially the exercising of control over one's life." To this end, agents can only be truly free if they have realized who they are and control their own life according to their self-realization. "The concept of freedom here is an exercise concept" (Taylor, 1991: 143). For Taylor, however, we must not take only this first step to discovering who we truly are, but we must also realize who we are within a "society of a certain canonical form incorporating true self-government" because it is only within such a society that we ourselves can be free. "It follows that we can only be free in such a society, and that being free *is* governing ourselves collectively according to this canonical form" (Taylor, 1991: 148; emphasis in original).

Alternatively, negative liberty for Berlin is best understood "in this sense [as] simply the area within which a man can act unobstructed by others" (Berlin, 1969: 122). Thus, agents are free negatively insofar as there are no interferences with, or external constraints on, their activity. Interference, in this sense, should be viewed as a deliberate attempt to influence or impede agents by coercion or other methods. Berlin attributes this conception of liberty to "classical English philosophers" such as Hobbes, Bentham, and Mill among others. For Hobbes, "liberty or freedom signifieth (properly) the absence of opposition" (Hobbes, 1968: 261). In this way, negative theories of liberty are often viewed as opportunity concepts because they consist of those things that agents can do, not what they actually do (Taylor, 1991: 143–4; also see Skinner, 1990b: 297). Liberty conceived in this fashion constructs a cordon around an agent within which she has the opportunity to act or not act according to her wishes (Berlin, 1969: 123). Any interference with agents' actions or any attempt to coerce them into acting in a certain way is viewed as intrusive, and thus limits their ability to act. To that end, many, like Hobbes, consider laws to be obstacles to being able to act freely and are thus thought to represent "interferences" to those who seek to be free. If freedom in the negative sense seeks to carve out a sphere within which agents can act unimpeded by others, we are led to inevitable questions concerning the scope of this area and how to achieve and maintain it. Proponents, then, of negative liberty have traditionally focused their concerns on the area insulating the agent from interference and how far it should extend to guarantee a just and basic set of liberties.

An influential critique of negative liberty has been offered by Gerald MacCallum, who argues that Berlin's scheme is flawed fundamentally and that it is impossible to divide liberty into two concepts (MacCallum, 1991: 100–22). MacCallum's contribution to this important debate serves two main purposes. First, it questions Berlin's original dichotomy and argues that freedom should not be understood as being necessarily negative or positive, but instead should be considered "as one and the same triadic relation" (MacCallum, 1991: 100). For MacCallum, freedom is "always *of* something (an agent or agents), *from* something, *to* do, not do, become, or not become something; it is a triadic relationship" (MacCallum, 1991: 102; emphasis in original). Different conceptions of liberty, then, are born not from distinctive concepts of liberty – such as positive or negative – but rather by the degree to which the *ranges* differ between agents, constraints, ends. This is based on his understanding of the dyadic characterization of positive freedom as "freedom to" and negative freedom as "freedom from." MacCallum argues that "this characterization, however, cannot distinguish two genuinely different kinds of freedom; it can serve only to emphasize one or the other of two features of *every* case of the freedom of agents" (MacCallum, 1991: 106; emphasis in original). If MacCallum is correct, the differences between the two conceptions of liberty can be found in the differing interpretations of just what the ranges are between the agents, constraints, and ends. Put another way, the differences between positive and negative notions of liberty are due to the various ways in which theorists construe or understand the relationships between the three variables. Furthermore, these differences are exacerbated by various interpretations of what constitutes an agent, a constraint, and an end.

Second, MacCallum's critique has led to other important reconsiderations of liberty that reject the claim that the positive/negative dichotomy is fundamentally flawed. Tom Baldwin, for example, has argued that MacCallum's critique of positive liberty is itself flawed (Baldwin, 1984: 125–42).[3] Using a theory of positive freedom developed by T. H. Green, Baldwin argues that MacCallum's formulation fails to secure itself against Green's conceptualization of moral freedom because it does not account for the importance of the *reasoning* behind an agent acting in a certain way. He bases this conclusion on an interpretation of Green's moral theory that holds that an agent must not only be at liberty to be free, but must actually realize herself to be free. Baldwin argues that within Green's moral theory – as is typical of most positive theories of liberty – the agent "who is free does not merely have an opportunity for virtue, he must be virtuous" (Baldwin, 1984: 134–5). Thus, moral freedom cannot just be an opportunity concept, like that of negative liberty, but rather the agent must realize their freedom and actually exercise it to be free.

Not surprisingly, these are not the only critiques of the different conceptions of liberty. It is not my purpose to offer a wholesale critique of the various manifestations of Berlin's famous essay. My goal is somewhat more modest. With these various conceptualizations of liberty outlined above, and the many others that I have not discussed, it would seem as if the conceptual landscape is filled to capacity. However, I believe that this is not so. It seems to me that there is indeed enough space for more than one or even two conceptions of liberty. Whether or not versions of positive or negative liberty survive the criticisms of MacCallum and others is less important for my purposes here than the fact that there are different conceptualizations of freedom which occupy some space within theories of liberty. I believe that Tom Baldwin is right to assert that there are different levels upon which liberty can be evaluated, each of them thoroughly worthy of investigation and debate (Baldwin, 1984: 141). Within the negative and positive debate, then, I believe that there is enough conceptual space to have an alternative conception that does not fit comfortably within Berlin's distinction while reflecting Constant's belief that a combination of the two is both possible and appealing. If it is possible that positive and negative liberty do indeed exist and operate at many different levels, it must also follow that liberty itself can be conceived of on many different levels. The point, then, is not which specific form – positive or negative, ancient or modern – liberty takes, but rather one of emphasis and whether or not once operationalized it forms the basis for a coherent and attractive public philosophy for the modern polity. In order to construct a modern system of liberty, we must first understand the complex relationship between the various levels upon which that liberty will operate and manifest itself in our lives. As far as my argument is concerned, a strict adherence to Berlin's typology is counterproductive and unrealistic in light of the complex problems facing the modern polity. To be sure, I am not arguing that the above conceptions of liberty are necessarily inherently impoverished or philosophically errant, but rather that as they have been advanced they are too narrow to accommodate modern republicanism and its conception of liberty as nondomination. In the next section, I will advance this argument by first taking a closer look at the neo-Roman republican conception of liberty.

Neo-Roman republican liberty

In the last section, I argued that there are different senses of liberty and enough conceptual landscape for an alternative republican account of liberty. With this claim in mind, this section explores neo-Roman republicanism in greater detail to not only take a closer look at the sense of liberty contained within it, but also to examine the substantive ideals that accompany it. Next, I want to consider an important critique of republican liberty put forth by Alan Patten, who argues that contemporary versions of neo-Roman republicanism are entirely consistent with normative liberal approaches because both are essentially instrumental in nature. Because the two approaches are entirely consistent, Patten charges that republicanism should not concern liberals. If Patten's overall critique of neo-Roman republicanism is accurate, then my modern republican alternative must be significantly different than contemporary liberal approaches or else it faces the charge that it offers little new as a public philosophy.

Instrumental republicanism

Arguably, Quentin Skinner has done more than any other contemporary writer to argue that neo-Roman republican liberty was inextricably tied to a view of freedom intertwined with virtue and public service (Skinner, 1984: 199). Skinner has argued that, historically, republican liberty has been ill considered by some, mostly due to its early critics, like Hobbes, fundamentally misunderstanding its essence. For Skinner, Hobbes's account of liberty in the *Leviathan* is purely negative in that liberty is signified by the absence of opposition (Hobbes, 1968: 261). Later in the eighteenth century, this line of thought became embedded in the discourse of contemporary debates on liberty and subsequently eclipsed republican thinking (Pettit, 1997: 42). Jeremy Bentham, for example, was known to have argued for liberty conceived of negatively when he stated that the idea of liberty "was merely a negative one ... and [is] accordingly defined [as] the absence of restraint" (Bentham, 1776, as cited in Pettit, 1997: 44). According to Skinner, contemporary contractarian theorists of liberty, like Hobbes before them, have failed to account for a conceptualization of liberty that argues that liberty be understood in the way that the Romans understood it. Using Machiavelli as his archetype and authority on civic republican liberty, Skinner believes that the "Roman stoic way of thinking about political liberty" provides an alternative and encouraging approach to the way we view liberty that fully exposes a distinct republican conception of liberty (Skinner, 1984: 204; also see Skinner, 1981). For many classical writers, it is important to note, any account of political liberty in the classical republican tradition "was generally embedded in an analysis of what it means to speak of living in a 'free state'. [Furthermore] . . . this approach was largely derived from Roman moral philosophy, and especially from those writers whose greatest admiration had been reserved for the doomed Roman republic: Livy, Sallust, and above all Cicero" (Skinner, 1991: 193; also see Cicero, 1991).

Subsequent writers, such as Machiavelli, adopted their language, and approached their subjects by illustrating the tension and conflicts over traditional liberties between the different classes of citizens comprising the emerging city-republics and their leaders. These writers were known to take very seriously the metaphorical represen-tation of the body politic. Just like a natural body, the body politic was said to be truly at liberty if, and only if, it was not subjected to internal or external constraints. Central to republican liberty, for Skinner, is that it guarantees "personal liberty, understood in the ordinary sense to mean that each citizen remains free from any elements of constraint (especially those which arise from personal dependence and servitude) and in consequence remains free to pursue his own chosen ends" (Skinner, 1990b: 302). Republican liberty, as explained by Machiavelli, is best understood in an account of the important relationship between two groups of citizens in ancient Rome, the *grandi* – the rich and powerful – and the *popolo* – the ordinary citizens (Skinner, 1984: 205). The *grandi*, driven by *ambizione*, aspire to be free to pursue power, glory, and honor for them-selves while the *popolo* simply wish to live a secure life, "without anxieties about the free enjoyment of their property, without any doubts about the honor of their womenfolk and children, without any fears for themselves" (Machiavelli, *The Discourses*, book 1.16, as cited in Skinner, 1984: 205). It follows that this *ambizione* must be tempered if a community is to be free or else it will be governed by uncontrollable freedom or *licenza* in which the narrow private inter-ests of the few are placed above those of the many.

To counter the threat of *ambizione* and *licenza* Machiavelli believed that political power needed to be dispersed throughout the body politic rather than lie with any narrow social group such as the *grandi*. The reason for this can be found in Machiavelli's belief that the nobility may use their political power for personal gain or to oppress the people, whereas the common people will use their political power to prevent themselves from losing their liberty. For Machiavelli, this is because "if one will look at the purpose of the nobles and of those who are not noble, there will be seen in the former great longing to rule, and in the latter merely longing not to be ruled, and as a consequence greater eagerness to live in freedom" (*The Discourses*: Machiavelli, 1965: 204). Echoing Cicero, Machiavelli believed that civic inequality created very dangerous conditions for republics because it resulted in unmanageable conflict (Viroli, 1990: 153). As for public offices, Machiavelli maintains that all citizens should be eligible to serve the republic regardless of class or social standing (*The Discourses*: Machiavelli, 1965: 242). Machiavelli reiterates many of these observations in the short *Discourse on Remodeling the Government of Florence*, where he stresses the need for inclusive public bodies comprised of representatives from the various classes and guilds found in Florence (Machiavelli, 1965: 101–15). Important in Machiavelli's belief in the rule of law is an understanding that no one is exempt from it and that all those who stand before it do so as equals.[4]

Central to an understanding of republican liberty is that social agents such as the *grandi* and *popolo* are not only concerned about being unfettered in pursuing their own ends, but they also desire the security to do so. Skinner argues that, so understood, republican liberty can be accommodated within ordinary theories of negative liberty. For republicans, then, the state must be maintained in such a way that guarantees its citizens the ability to act without interference by others, whether that interference is internal or external (Skinner, 1984: 213). Were a community to be enslaved, either externally or internally, the citizens would inevitably lose their individual liberty. Thus, it follows that citizens who wish to be secure in their liberty must live in a community that is itself free from either external or internal constraints. For these citizens, the cultivation of civic virtue and the ability to place the common good above an individual's own narrow interests was closely related to the maintenance of their liberty in the republican sense.

For these republicans, then, if individuals sought to undermine the ideals and institutions of the republic by ignoring the common good and placing their own interests above those of the community, corruption would increase and liberty would be lost. Therefore, if the community were to be overwhelmed by a loss of civic virtue and rising *ambizione*, it would inevitably fall into a state of corruption as individuals sought to place their narrow self-interests above those of the city, and liberty would be lost (Skinner, 1991: 198). If we are to believe that the *grandi* and *popolo* sought this type of freedom, then, for Skinner, it can be understood in terms of, and within, contemporary theories of negative liberty. The interference that these citizens experience, which comes in the form of civic virtue and republican institutions, is simply instrumental to the attainment of greater liberty. In other words, the demands placed on individuals by the republican state served to secure a more complete and equal system of liberty, not to instill them with any ultimate or intrinsic values. For liberal writers such as Alan Patten and John Rawls, republican liberty so conceived by Skinner is essentially a negative form of freedom that is not significantly different to the sense of negative freedom within liberal approaches (Patten, 1996: 25; Rawls, 1996: 205).

Patten maintains that, despite some differences, there is nothing significantly divergent between the two approaches since both contain instrumental accounts of certain ideals and virtues that have the effect of enhancing the overall system of freedom for individuals (Patten, 1996: 25). For Patten, political institutions, including forms of citizenship and civic virtue, are not intrinsically valuable themselves, but rather serve as a means to an end. Patten accepts Skinner's contention that the republican conception of liberty is essentially negative in nature, but he maintains that the republican commitment to civic virtue and active political participation is nevertheless instrumental, and thus republicanism does not deviate significantly from liberal approaches. According to Patten, it does not follow that "citizenship and public service are goods because they contribute to the realization of negative liberty" (Patten, 1996: 26). For Patten, republicans are wrong to maintain that individuals are motivated by a commitment to the common good and a high degree of civic virtue. Instead, Patten believes that republican citizens, like liberal citizens, are motivated by a sense of self-interest which sees them adopt certain distinctive virtues and ideals to maintain their liberty (Patten, 1996: 28). For Patten, then, republican virtues and ideals are instrumental to the maintenance of liberty. Thus, Patten asserts that the republican approach is essentially an instrumental approach that promotes civic virtue and versions of citizenship as preconditions for the realization of social justice.

In many ways, up to a point, Skinner seems to endorse this reading, although he does attempt to draw distinctions between the two approaches. Skinner argues that contemporary theorists place too much emphasis on rights and not enough on the type of liberty favored by republicans. For Skinner, critics of republican liberty should not view each citizen's rights as "trumps" over "interfering" social duties (Skinner, 1992: 215).[5] On this point, Skinner's argument centers on his belief that simply accepting that individuals are self-interested and then regulating their interests by instrumental values and ideals, is not enough to maintain republican liberty. Approaching rights and duties in this manner is undesirable for republicans because it allows some to opt out, or use their rights as trumps, from a broader commitment to the maintenance of liberty. Instead, Skinner maintains that republican liberty requires more than simply controlling narrow, self-interested individuals through instrumental values. Indeed, for republicans, when narrow self-interest is placed above the interests of the community, corruption will increase and liberty is at risk. The thought here for republicans is that narrow, self-interested individuals must be molded and conditioned in a manner that opens up the possibility that they can receive certain benefits and goods that are not necessarily attainable by liberal instrumental values and ideals. Thus, the main thrust of republican government for neo-Roman republican writers was to secure freedom for its people by promoting the common interest of the body politic while at the same time allowing individuals maximum liberty to pursue their own chosen ends. For Machiavelli and others, civic republicanism represented a dynamic and progressive outlook beyond that of mere maintenance, one offering forward-thinking principles aimed at securing and enhancing greater liberty for its people. To that end, neo-Roman republican governments were labor-intensive and required constant attention while demanding a high degree of involvement from the citizens that comprised them.

A closer look at Machiavelli's republicanism and his conception of liberty will highlight this point and illustrate the intimate connection between the maintenance of liberty and the necessary presence of strong forms of civic virtue and citizenship. According to Maurizio Viroli,

> To be a free people means for Machiavelli not to depend on the will of others and to be able to live under laws to which citizens have freely given their consent. Accordingly, an individual is free when he is not dependent on the will of another individual, but is dependent on the laws only. Hence, to be at liberty means to be in full agreement with the Roman republican tradition, the opposite of being enslaved or in servitude. (Viroli, 1998: 5)

Thus, for neo-Roman republicans like Machiavelli, to be free means not to depend upon the will of another. This type of freedom can be threatened in two important ways. In the first instance, a state that is under the control of an external force or another state is not considered by Machiavelli to be free. In other words, a state whose people are dependent on the will of outsiders is not free. In the second instance, tyranny and/or internal divisions that place narrow self-interests above the common good can undermine a state's freedom. Thus, a state that is at the mercy of a dictator or tyrant is not free just as a state that is governed by those who seek to place their own private self-interests above the common good is not free. For Machiavelli, the real challenge presented to republics was how to maintain and enhance liberty for their citizens. So that citizens can pursue their chosen ends within the scope of republican liberty, Machiavelli argues that they must be prepared to take an active part in political life and respect the laws and institutions of the republic (Viroli, 1998: 6). Importantly, it was the combination of these two elements that Machiavelli believed made republics superior to other forms of government.

Machiavelli maintained that only republican liberty could secure individuals from either domination and/or dependency on others. Moreover, in *The Discourses* Machiavelli states that paramount to this arrangement is that the people as a whole are best situated to place the common good above that of individuals' private interest because it is the "well-being of communities" that makes cities great (Machiavelli, 1965: 332). For example, early in *The Discourses* Machiavelli tells us that safeguarding liberty is one of the most essential services a government can provide its citizens (Machiavelli, 1965: 204). He reiterates this point later when he insists that a wise legislator is one who can anticipate laws required to maintain liberty. Rome's greatness, Machiavelli proclaims, was in part due to the innovative institutions that supported and enhanced liberty by legislating "new laws on behalf of free government" (Machiavelli, 1965: 295–7). People who had thrown off tyranny and expelled their despotic princes to institute representative government were said to have begun the process of acquiring and maintaining their liberty (Machiavelli, 1965: 235–6, 239). Because Machiavelli believed that citizens wanted different goals in their lives, he believed that republican laws and institutions would combine with the citizens' desire to be free of dependency, to enhance and secure their liberty (Machiavelli, 1965: 332). Importantly, he believed that properly constituted republican institutions and laws helped republics secure liberty for citizens of the republic, while at the same time the active participation of the citizenry was essential for these laws and institutions to be effective in safeguarding liberty.

By arguing that liberty was best created and maintained by the citizens themselves, Machiavelli and his contemporaries made the important connection between liberty and activity that is a recurring theme in republicanism. However, it is on this point that Machiavelli breaks with the traditional classical republican emphases on stability and internal concord. Contrary to the popular convention of his time, Machiavelli's revolutionary thoughts on the role of civil discord within a republic provide a marked departure that, I believe, has important implications for contemporary republican approaches. Machiavelli's controversial embrace of civic discord was a direct challenge to a historical–theoretical legacy dating back to Cicero and other Roman writers. Many Roman writers, and subsequently many of the civic humanists who were influenced by them, believed that one of the keys to maintaining a republic was to ensure that there was internal concord. Cicero's *concordia ordinum* was the basis of the belief that the common good took precedence over factional or selfish interest (Skinner, 1990a: 130). Machiavelli challenges this point of view and instead argues that one of the keys to maintaining republican institutions and laws was to be progressive in nature and to anticipate the inevitable clash of internal divisions that could potentially cause an increase in corruption and subsequently the loss of liberty. At the center of this departure is an issue that I believe goes to the heart of one of neo-Roman republicanism's most appealing and enduring assets: the stress on sculpting laws and creating institutions that accommodate a wide range of individuals and classes.

Early in *The Discourses* Machiavelli offers readers an account of how the early tumults of Rome characterized the laws and institutions that secured and maintained Roman liberty (Machiavelli, 1965: 202–4). It was Machiavelli's belief that Rome's liberty was enhanced by the clashes that resulted from the different dispositions of the upper classes and the populace. Machiavelli believed that this type of conflict was healthy for a republic and, unlike many of his contemporaries, did not think it was detrimental to it. Internal conflict and tumults may cause republics to be unstable at times, but they require citizens to maintain maximum vigilance and attention, which leads to the creation of good laws and institutions that can offer innovative solutions to the often complex problems brought about by an active citizenry. Machiavelli argued that republican institutions had to provide the citizenry with appropriate public forums where their competing interests could find meaningful expression. Although Machiavelli's thought here demonstrates that class and other types of internal discord and conflict require a great deal of attention and the creation of good laws and institutions to accommodate such diversity, a republic that addresses this issue up front is one that is likely to maintain a high degree of liberty for its citizens and prevent corruption.

The upshot of Machiavelli's theory here is that neo-Roman republicans accept that individuals will have different interests that may lead to internal conflicts and civil discord. The key was for republics to confront civil discord and the factionalization of society by promoting strong laws and institutions so that a government founded on shared meanings based on the common good would ensure security and liberty for its citizens by adopting mixed constitutions rooted in self-government. Thus, freedom was tied closely to the presence of certain necessary republican institutions and laws and high levels of civic virtue (Viroli, 1990: 152–61; 1998: 5). For these republicans, properly constituted republican liberty secured individuals from both external and internal threats to their freedom. It follows that this conception of liberty required a high level of commitment from its citizens and the presence of strong laws and institutions. Machiavelli maintained that citizens must be prepared to take part in an active civic life and respect the laws and institutions of the republic so that they could pursue those things that were important to them within the scope of republican liberty (Viroli, 1998: 6).

One of the keys to differentiating republican liberty from alternative approaches is in understanding the complex relationship between Fortuna, virtue, and corruption. Understanding this relationship is also crucial to understanding the close relationship between neo-Athenian and neo-Roman republican approaches. Fortuna represented the external force that tempted individuals to stray from a life of virtue and into a life of corruption. For Machiavelli, to realize virtue fully, the common good had to be placed above narrow private interests. The republic, and its public institutions and laws, became an essential vehicle that allowed citizens to attain the necessary virtue to combat Fortuna and stave off corruption. Significantly, Machiavelli argued that republican liberty was essential to the realization of virtue and, as I outlined above, that to ensure freedom, political power needed to be diffused throughout a mixed constitution and vested in the body politic. By arguing that a primitive system of checks and balances was the best way to ensure that liberty was maintained, these republicans firmly fused the future of the republic with the delicate equilibrium of competing interests and a need to create strong laws and institutions to ensure security. Responsibility lay with the citizenry to embrace a *vita activa* or public life that reflected the values and ideals consistent with virtue and kept narrow private interests secondary to the public good. Corruption was said to exist when narrow private interests eclipsed the common good. As Pocock informs us, a defining moment of this period was the realization that virtue, corruption, and Fortuna were interrelated and that a reciprocal relationship existed between virtue and corruption (Pocock, 1975: 38).

A central theme in both *The Discourses* and *The History of Florence* is the struggle between virtue and corruption, and the role that liberty and institutions play in countering Fortuna's subversive influence on the citizenry. Skinner maintains that corruption, for Machiavelli, "is a failure to devote one's energies to the common good, and a corresponding tendency to place one's own interests above those of the community" (Skinner, 1978: 164). In book 1 of *The Discourses*, Machiavelli recounts how corruption caused the Romans great strife because the powerful proposed laws for their own benefit and not the common good (Machiavelli, 1965: 235–43). For Machiavelli and his contemporaries, virtue and liberty, essential themes for republicans, cannot be known to corrupt people. In *The History of Florence*, Machiavelli argues that corruption plays a pivotal role in the erosion of virtue and the end of the Florentine republic. Throughout this work, Machiavelli informs us how the people began to place their own private interests over the common good, and did so more and more frequently as virtue fled and the republic began to crumble (Machiavelli, 1965: 1141). Machiavelli attributes the loss of virtue and the corresponding rise in corruption to the people being excluded from the political process. These alienated people began to lose sight of their collective liberty and became more concerned with their own narrow self-interest characterized by *licenza*, avarice, and graft. This sentiment is echoed again in *The Discourses* when Machiavelli attributes the rise of corruption to a corresponding decline in the equality found within a city where an oligarchy rules in its own narrow interests, and not in the interests of the body politic (Machiavelli, 1965: 240–1).

Citizenship and love of *patria* became key weapons of virtue and *vita activa* against Fortuna and corruption. Machiavelli equates citizenship and love of *patria* with the civil religion of Rome and argues that republics that wish to be free of corruption should maintain and venerate these institutions and ceremonies.[6] Moreover, these ideals can cultivate and encourage important republican values and keep the people united (*The Discourses*: Machiavelli, 1965: 226–7). Machiavelli's position on this issue is important for two main reasons. First, it allows us to gain an insight into how Machiavelli conceived virtue and the necessary skills that accompanied it. Machiavelli believed that certain character traits and skills were necessary for virtuous citizens,

and that the republic, through its laws and institutions, should cultivate these through distinctive republican versions of citizenship.
Second, it highlights another significant aspect of Machiavelli's
thought because it suggests that the citizen should revere and esteem
the republic with all of their heart. Therefore, when issues arise that
place the virtue of the citizen at odds with self-interest, Machiavelli
implores individuals to give priority to the maintenance of the republic. For Machiavelli, love of the *patria* is an essential component of a
properly constituted republic. According to Viroli, this love of country serves several important and necessary purposes for a republic:

> Machiavelli emphasizes that love of country is a moral force that
> makes the citizens capable of understanding what the common good
> of the republic consists of and pursuing it. It is a passion that makes
> them wise and virtuous; because they can see beyond the boundaries of
> their family or of their social group, they act in the way that is most apt
> to secure their own and the republic's interests. (Viroli, 1998: 157)

Thus, in both of these areas, republican citizens must practice and
understand the ideals and values associated with republican civic
virtue and citizenship because they help to secure the republic from
internal or external threats. Patriotism, or love of country, helps to
cultivate certain essential traits within the citizenry and underlies a
citizen's moral commitment to the common good and the maintenance of liberty by supporting the institutions and laws that constitute
the republic (Viroli, 1998: 163; also see Viroli, 1995).

We can also find the importance of this issue reiterated in a leading
theme of Machiavelli's *Art of War*. In this work, Machiavelli argues
that it is necessary that everyday citizens are involved in the protection of the city to protect and maintain the public good, and thus
preserve their individual liberty. Unlike the mercenary, the citizen-
warrior has a life of liberty to protect that requires a unique blend of
self-interest and military discipline that combines to create a committed protector of the republic and the common good (*The Art of War*:
Machiavelli, 1965). Citizen soldiers who protected their liberty by
defending their city themselves exemplified the proper ethic of
Machiavelli's military virtue because he believed that such citizens
would have more reason to fight in battle than those soldiers who
were hired mercenaries (Skinner, 1978: 164). In other words, citizens
who are part-time soldiers but full-time members of the body politic
with homes and occupations will wish to protect their freedom and
maintain the security to live their life according to their own desires.
Therefore, just as the citizen possesses virtue in the body politic, the

patriot will possess virtue in the protection of the republic. For Machiavelli, an interdependent and reciprocal relationship existed between private citizens and military patriots because military virtue transmits certain important moral and ethical dimensions of virtue that help to inculcate the citizenry with republican values and ideals (Pocock, 1975: 201–2). In the next chapter I will revisit this issue and further develop republican versions of civic virtue and citizenship and their intimate relationship to both the laws and institutions, and to liberty.

Conclusion

At the center of Machiavelli's approach was a distinctive conception of liberty that emphasized the necessity of strong laws and institutions to ensure that citizens were not dependent on others for their liberty. Paramount to Machiavelli was how to achieve and maintain this ideal of liberty. To that end, republican forms of mixed constitutions, and other technological devices such as checks and balances and open and inclusive institutions, were designed to secure republican liberty for the citizenry. However, institutions and laws alone could not secure liberty for these writers. Robust forms of civic virtue and citizenship had to be cultivated so that citizens could resist corruption and understand their role in creating the common good. Civic virtue and citizenship also had to cultivate and reflect the intimate interdependent relationship between citizens and the laws and institutions that governed them. For Machiavelli, conflict played a central role in the maintenance of liberty. Conflict that occurred within properly constituted republican institutions could be controlled and did not represent a fatal threat to liberty. By creating balanced laws and institutions that encouraged a life of virtue, the structural foundations of the republic promised individuals security and liberty so that they were left free to pursue their own ends.

A couple of points emerge here that have a direct bearing on the development of neo-Roman republicanism and its response to critiques such as Patten's. Earlier I outlined Constant's distinction between the liberty of the ancients and that of the moderns. Furthermore, we saw how that distinction was, for the most part, adopted by Isaiah Berlin in his positive and negative conceptions of liberty. There are, however, key differences between the two writers' theories of liberty. As we saw, for Constant these two forms of liberty do not exist independent of one another. Constant states that "far from renouncing either of the two sorts of freedom which I have described to you, it is necessary, as I have shown, to learn to combine the two together" (Constant, 1988: 327). The virtues and values associated with the liberty of the ancients played an important role in shaping the character of citizens exercising their "modern liberty" (Constant, 1988: 328). In other words, for Constant, the liberty of the moderns coexists with certain features of the liberty of the ancients to the extent that the latter plays an important role in the moral education of the citizenry. In neo-Roman versions of republicanism, we find a similar move being made by Machiavelli and his republican contemporaries. Pocock and Skinner have argued that, although the principles of civic republicanism were widespread throughout the classical world, it was not until the emergence of the civic humanists in Italy that it became a coherent and powerful ideology (Pocock, 1975; Skinner, 1978). According to Skinner, "there can be no doubt that the revival of Aristotelianism and the rise of Florentine humanism were both of vital importance in the evolution of republican thought" (Skinner, 1990a: 122). At its most basic, civic republicanism in Machiavelli's time consisted of several essential elements: *vita activa* or participation; civic virtue; security; civil discord; citizenship and patriotism; and an alternative conception of freedom. Importantly, though, it was with the rise of neo-Roman republicanism that the principles that inspired Constant's "liberty of the moderns" began to take shape and become a political priority, especially in those later writers who were influenced by the neo-Romans, such as James Harrington. On the one hand, the liberty advocated by the neo-Roman writers relied on strong forms of civic virtue and citizenship that seem to be more at home within the neo-Athenian model discussed above.[7] On the other hand, the firm focus on the liberty of the individual by these neo-Roman writers suggests that their conception of liberty is more closely associated with Constant's liberty of the moderns.

It is on this point that I believe Skinner does not do enough to make this distinction clear. The result is that, by arguing that neo-Roman republicanism can be accommodated within modern theories of negative liberty, critics like Patten are left asking what, then, are the real differences between republicanism and liberalism. The thought is that, if negative forms of liberty characterize both approaches, republicanism simply collapses into another form of liberalism. One way to counter this charge is to argue that republican ideals and values constitute or help to constitute republican freedom. It follows that, if these ideals and values were viewed constitutively, citizens would understand and relate to their freedom in a different and more significant way which would help them maintain their virtue and prevent them from falling into a life of self-interested corruption. Furthermore, if republican liberty is indeed an alternative conception of liberty from Berlin's dichotomy, it must diverge significantly from the sense of negative liberty within liberalism. My argument is that the failure to appreciate fully the close and intimate relationship between the liberty of the ancients and that of the moderns contributes to the lack of a clear *modern* republican approach that can be distinguished from liberalism, but yet remains compatible with many of its aims. In the next chapter I will attempt to fill out Skinner's argument along these lines. In doing so I will argue that Philip Pettit's recent work on republican liberty as nondomination is a promising start that signals the direction that modern republicanism must take. It is, however, a promise that Pettit fails to keep when developing his theory and differentiating it from rival liberal approaches. It is my goal in the next chapter to see through the early promise of Pettit's republicanism and lay the foundations for a defense of that theory against liberal critics.

2

Modern Republicanism: Liberty as Nondomination

Introduction

In my last chapter I argued that the distinction between the two broad versions of republicanism has become confused, which has led to widespread misuse and, in some cases, the general dismissal of republicanism as a compelling approach for the modern world. Along these lines, we saw that one of the most common liberal critiques of contemporary neo-Roman republicanism centers on the charge that, despite some differences, the two approaches do not significantly vary from one another. Arguments such as this one deliver a double blow to republicans. In the first case, these critics maintain that, since both approaches contain instrumental accounts of certain ideals and virtues that have the effect of enhancing the overall system of freedom for individuals, there is little of interest that separates liberalism from republicanism. In the second case, what little difference there is between the two approaches, according to these critics, is not significant enough to offer an improvement on the liberal standard (Patten, 1996: 25). One area these critiques have in common is sensitivity to the republican complaint that liberalism ignores the substantive values of citizenship and civic virtue and thus does not give sufficient attention to the promotion of these ideals. We saw how liberals like Alan Patten charged that political institutions, including forms of citizenship and civic virtue, are not intrinsically valuable themselves, but rather are instrumental and serve as a means to an end for republicans. The upshot of this critique is that, although there are some differences between liberal and republican approaches, the two do not vary significantly since both contain instrumental accounts of certain ideals and virtues that have the effect of enhancing the overall system of freedom for individuals (Patten, 1996: 25; also see Kahane, 1996). Other liberals, such as Don Herzog (1986), John Rawls (1996), Will Kymlicka (1998b), and Paul Kelly (2000), follow the thrust of Patten's argument that contemporary republicanism has yet to demonstrate that it is significantly different from normative liberal approaches and thus adds little value to existing debates. For the most part, these liberals contend that the republican approach is not something which should concern liberals since they believe that the two approaches are essentially compatible and not, in the words of Rawls, in "fundamental opposition" with one another (Rawls, 1996: 205). Other writers, such as Richard Dagger (1997), have made similar arguments along these lines. Dagger believes that it is possible to combine republicanism and liberalism to form what he calls "republican liberalism." He argues that republicanism and liberalism are not inherently incompatible, and believes that such a combination is a promising way forward.

In this chapter I will address critiques along these lines while further developing modern republicanism. In doing so I will explore the more personal and informal nature of modern republicanism by looking closely at two interdependent powers that accompany republican liberty: reciprocal and constitutional. I will argue that within these powers reside certain goods and character traits that do bear an instrumental relationship to republican liberty. However, I will argue that this instrumental relationship can be significantly distinguished from the type found in liberal accounts. It is my contention that these goods and character traits help to constitute the freedom that republican citizens experience. Furthermore, I will argue that both the constitutional and reciprocal powers contained within modern republicanism shape and mold certain character traits in a distinctively republican manner that is more robust than that found in rival liberal approaches. I have divided this chapter into three sections. The first section will look at the recent work of Philip Pettit who, building on Skinner's work, attempts to bring republicanism out of the history of ideas to cast it instead in a manner that is relevant to contemporary discourse. In the second section I will explore what Pettit sees as republican liberty as nondomination's advantages over liberal approaches. In this section I will also seek to drive modern republicanism forward by building on Pettit's arguments to distinguish modern republicanism from liberalism. Finally, in the third section I will develop and defend an account of the reciprocal power of nondomination, something not found in Pettit. This section will explore the types of virtues and values associated with nondomination and how they relate to the republican conception of liberty. I then tie the reciprocal power found in nondomination to its constitutional counterpart. The overall goal of this chapter is to offer an outline of modern republicanism that can be significantly differentiated from liberal accounts in a manner that is both compelling and attractive.

Instrumental republicanism revisited

As I pointed out in the last chapter, the roots of the contemporary republican/liberal debate lie in Isaiah Berlin's famous distinction between positive and negative liberty (Berlin, 1969). On one side, many theorists associated republicanism with the doctrine of positive liberty. These civic humanist or neo-Athenian republicans held that freedom was connected with a specific type of flourishing in a system of democratic self-government (Pettit, 1997: 27; also see Sandel, 1996; Taylor, 1991). For liberals like Rawls, this type of republicanism is often associated with forms of Aristotelianism which maintain that individuals are social or political beings whose essence is only fully realized in democratic societies that have widespread political participation (Rawls, 1996: 206). On the other side are theorists like Skinner, who argue that the republicanism of Machiavelli and other neo-Roman writers is best understood within the context of negative liberty as it relates to agents acting unimpeded by others (Skinner, 1984; also see Patten, 1996). I argued that this debate has become confused, resulting in an impoverished contemporary republican approach that holds little appeal as a relevant public philosophy.

With the arrival of Philip Pettit's recent work, some of this confusion has abated. Pettit's version of republicanism has gone farther than any other in seeking to offer a compelling contemporary republican theory of freedom that can be clearly distinguished from liberal approaches. Whereas Skinner's analysis of republican liberty is rooted in the history of ideas, Pettit relies on historical themes to establish the foundation of his contemporary conceptualization of republican liberty. A notable contribution of Pettit's work to current debates is in taking the neo-Roman republican approach out of the history of ideas and offering a contemporary, and thus relevant, account that can challenge liberalism's hegemony in current debates. Pettit, who uses Isaiah Berlin's equation of positive liberty with self-mastery and negative liberty as the absence of interference by others as his starting point, conjectures that republican liberty is an alternative conception of liberty (Pettit, 1997: 21–2). Pettit argues that because "mastery and interference do not amount to the same thing" it is possible to combine each of these important conceptual elements and understand freedom as the "absence of mastery by others," not an absence of interference as in the strictly negative conception (Pettit, 1997: 21). For Pettit, the republican conception of liberty as nondomination is a negatively based view that incorporates elements of positive conceptions because it focuses on mastery (Pettit, 1997: 21–2). It is, for Pettit, an alternative conception of liberty that cannot be accommodated within Berlin's strict positive/negative scheme.

Pettit, like Skinner, draws this distinction from neo-Roman republican writers like Machiavelli and those later theorists he influenced, especially the seventeenth-century English republicans. These writers, including James Harrington, Marchamont Nedham, and, to a lesser extent in his political works, John Milton, all became influential writers during this period and their works would later influence Henry Neville and Algernon Sidney, who would write after this tumultuous period in England's history (Burns and Goldie, 1991; Pettit, 1997; Pocock, 1975; Skinner, 1997; Tuck, 1993; Viroli, 1992; Wootton, 1994). English republicanism was heavily influenced by traditional republican sources through the works of Machiavelli, Livy, Sallust, and other ancient writers. The glories of Rome, Sparta, and Greece became an area of intense focus as the English republicans began to acknowledge a greater need for more effective political institutions and more meaningful liberty. Additionally, the Ciceronian values of political virtue and public service, combined with the ethical premises of Aristotle, became interwoven within a larger and more profound debate on humanity. Although not unchallenged at the time, English republicanism could be said to have centered on many of the issues associated with their ancient counterparts: good laws and institutions to create a healthy government; placing the public welfare above private interests; the promotion of the common citizen into the ranks of government; and, most importantly for the English, the establishment of a mixed or balanced constitution to ensure the liberty of the people and the ultimate survival of the republic (Worden, 1994: 53).

For Pettit, what is important here is that these republicans picked up on the liberty versus slavery theme first elicited by neo-Roman republicans like Machiavelli. For these writers, liberty was used frequently in the context of *liber* and *servus*, citizen and slave. Considered in this manner, "the condition of liberty is explicated as the status of someone who, unlike the slave, is not subject to the arbitrary power of another, that is, someone who is not dominated by anyone else" (Pettit, 1997: 31). For example, Harrington believes that living at the arbitrary will of another like a slave is representative of unfreedom (Harrington, 1992: 20; Pettit, 1997: 32–3). Another example can be found in the words of Sidney, who wrote a generation after Harrington that "liberty solely consists in an independency upon the will of another, and by the name of slave we understand a man, who can neither dispose of his person or goods, but enjoys all at the will of his master" (Sidney, 1990: 17). Moreover, this language became a feature of the arguments put forth by those concerned with independence for the American colonies such as Richard Price and Joseph Priestley, who used the master–slave metaphor to describe the plight of the colonies under British domination. The point to make here was that the American colonies were subject to the arbitrary will of the British (for example, "taxation without representation") without having their interests represented, no matter how "free" from British interference they might have actually been. As long as the British held the power to interfere arbitrarily with the American colonies, they would be unfree in the republican sense (Pettit, 1997: 32–5).

Central to an understanding of republican liberty is the relationship between interference and domination. Interference is thought to be when an agent's activities or choices are subject to some form of intentional intervention by another agent, whereas domination is understood to occur when an agent's activities or choices are subject to arbitrary interference by other agents (Pettit, 1997: 52–3). Under this conceptualization, an act can be said to be arbitrary if it is "chosen or not chosen at an agent's pleasure" and does not track their interests. Agents who have the power to choose, or not choose, to interfere with other agents without considering what the other's will or judgments are, interfere with those agents in an arbitrary manner. Put another way, agents who have the power to interfere arbitrarily with other agents can, or cannot, at their pleasure, act in a manner that does, or does not, consider or track the interests of other agents (Pettit, 1997: 55). These agents are dominators because they do not consider what others' interests or opinions are before acting. In other words, they subject them to interference that is arbitrary. They seek to maintain their position of power by subjugating the weak. In the extreme case, to dominators freedom is only about how *they* act, not about what consequences their actions might have on others because they retain the power. These agents may have no regard for their actions other than how they may affect themselves; they may not necessarily consider how their actions affect others, and they act without deference to others' interests. It follows that agents whose interests are not accounted for and tracked are said to be in a state of domination, even if the arbitrary interference the agent experiences is not something that is harmful. The key to determining what is considered to be arbitrary, then, is not whether or not the arbitrary interference is beneficial or harmful. Rather, the key to determining what is arbitrary centers on whether or not the interfering agent consulted and tracked the opinions or interests of the agent subjected to the interference. For an act to be non-arbitrary, the onus is on the interfering agent to seek actively the opinions or interests of others before acting, or at least to consider that their actions have consequences that may affect others. For republicans, such an obligation is one manifestation of civic virtue and civility. Moreover, it is not something that is driven by choice on a case-by-case basis. In order for me to treat others without domination they have to command my respect as nondominated equals, not have it by my grace or pity. As long as I remain in a position of superiority and have a choice to dominate them (or not), then my actions are still arbitrary and there is no republican freedom.

In Pettit's formulation, then, what is considered to be an agent's interest plays a central role in determining whether or not the agent is subject to domination.[1] Although Pettit does not elaborate fully on what he takes as an agent's interest, it is clear that he is concerned primarily with interests that are legitimate in nature in that they, for the most part, take account of the interests of others (Pettit, 1997: 56, and see also p. 198). An agent's interests are legitimate if they are ones that are shared in common with others and do not subject others to arbitrary interference. The test of an agent's legitimate interests boils down to whether or not they can be said to be of the kind that are common and avowable. They are avowable in that they exist at or near the level of consciousness and can be voiced "without great effort." In Pettit's words, "the definition of common interests ... holds that a certain good will represent a common interest of a population just so far as co-operatively admissible considerations support its collective provision" (Pettit, 2001: 156–7; also see Pettit 2000). Another way of looking at the type of interests that primarily concern republicans is to consider those which exist on the macro level and not necessarily those that exist on the micro level. For republicans, pure self-serving interests are not regarded necessarily as legitimate interests that individuals can demand are tracked, especially if those interests are not other-regarding or are inconsistent with their overriding commitments. For example, if my interests center on a dislike of driving on the left-hand side of the road, but yet I remain committed to a well-regulated and safe road system and have the opportunity to voice my opinions in a free and open manner, I cannot maintain that my interests are not being tracked when I am coerced by the state into driving on the left. My micro-level interest (driving on the right) is overridden by my macro-level interest (having a well-regulated and safe road system). An agent's legitimate interests cannot simply be their own self-serving preferences, especially if those preferences involve dominating others. I may dislike driving on the left-hand side of the road, but if I identify with and participate in the institutions and laws of the state which have determined that driving on the left is better (for whatever reason), then I have no legitimate grounds for believing that I am being dominated. If the rules and regulations make it illegal to drive on the right-hand side of the road thus forcing me to drive on the left, I am not subject to domination because my own self-serving preferences were not tracked. On a deeper and more fundamental level, my commitment and consent to the rules and regulations of road safety mean that my interests were in fact tracked. In other words, my *arbitrium* – my will or judgment – was accounted for and considered in a manner of which I approve by institutions with which I identify regardless of the outcome. Just because I do not like the outcome does not mean that I am being dominated. Because of the great importance of this issue, I will consider it in more detail in later chapters.

For republicans, interference and domination are two different things. It follows then, in terms of the master–slave relationship, that a slave may, or may not, be subjected to both domination and interference at the same time. If the slave has a kindly master there may be periods when the slave is not subjected to any interference. The slave may be allowed to pursue his own ends without any interference from the master. However, whether or not the slave experiences any interference is dependent solely on the whims of the master who may, or may not, choose to interfere with the slave. In this manner, a slave who does not experience any interference is still not free of domination in the republican sense because there is always the potential of arbitrary interference. For Pettit, "what constitutes domination is the fact that in some respect the power-bearer has the capacity to interfere arbitrarily, even if they are never going to do so" (Pettit, 1997: 63). It follows that agents who are subjected to the capacity of others to interfere arbitrarily with them are dependent on the will of others for their freedom and, therefore, are not free in the republican sense. Thus, for republicans, agents are free to the extent that they are not subjected to arbitrary interference.

To illustrate this point, Pettit highlights the case of the fearful spouse whose fear of her husband restricts her freedom. The thought is that the mere capacity to interfere arbitrarily with another is enough to cause an agent's un-freedom. Another example could be the neo-Nazi white supremacist who menaces his neighborhood without actually interfering with others, thus causing residents to feel threatened and limiting their activities. The point is that in both cases there is no actual interference taking place. Just the mere belief, however real or strong, is enough to cause fear and anxiety that ultimately leads to another's un-freedom. This point will be thoroughly discussed further later in this chapter, and indeed in later chapters. However, for the moment it is enough to highlight this key difference between liberty as non-interference and liberty as nondomination.[2] Returning to the master–slave analogy, a slave can only be free in the republican sense by not being a slave. A slave can only be free by being independent of the will of the master, interfering or not. In other words, under a system characterized by republican liberty as nondomination, agents can only be free to the extent that they are not subject to any interference which does not track their interests, whether that interference is actual, threatened, or even known.

Equally important for republicans is the inverse: an agent can be interfered with and not subjected to domination. An interfering power can account for and track other agents' interests without restricting their freedom. The interference that agents experience is not arbitrary if the interfering power considers what their interests and opinions are before acting, or not acting, with those interests in mind. Put another way, republican citizens do not consider any interference from other agents or agencies to be a restriction of their freedom if, and only if, the other agent or agency has consulted with them, gauged their opinions and interests, and then acted with those interests in mind. Such interference is not arbitrary because it considers just what their own *arbitrium* is before the action takes place. For Pettit, and thus for republicans, interference, or the absence of it, is not the primary measure of freedom. Instead, freedom is thought to be when an agent is free from any interference that does not consider and track her interests. In other words, for republicans, agents are thought to be free to the extent that they are free from domination (Pettit, 1997: 23). Thus, the republican conception of liberty allows the possibility that interference that is not arbitrary is not necessarily restrictive of an agent's freedom. From this alternative conception of liberty, republicans believe that certain interferences which track their interests and which are not imposed in an arbitrary fashion do not restrict their freedom. Individuals can be subjected to interference, but as long as that interference tracks their interests and is not arbitrary their freedom is intact and secure so that they can pursue their chosen ends under the conditions of nondomination. For republicans, these interferences help secure liberty through strong laws, properly constituted institutions, and distinctive ideals in a resilient manner (Pettit, 1997: 28). As Brennan and Hamlin have argued, the "idea of resilience is related to the idea of assurance – a resilient liberty is one that is assured in the sense that it is not contingent on circumstances, but rather is entrenched in the institutional structure" (Brennan and Hamlin, 2001: 47). Thus, in this way, republican liberty should be understood as a resilient core of protection that not only allows individuals to determine which ends they will pursue within the context of nondomination but, importantly, also frees them from the inevitable uncertainty, anxiety, and fear of subordination that they experience as they constantly act and react against those who seek to interfere arbitrarily with them (Pettit, 1997: 90).[3] Moreover, because this resilience is entrenched in the institutional structure it means that republican liberty can respond to the changing needs of the citizenry and, combined with properly constituted republican institutions, facilitates the active and contestatory nature of republican politics.

To sum up Pettit's argument thus far, within republican thought, agents are free to the extent that they are free to act without being exposed to any arbitrary interference from another. In the words of Pettit,

> [t]he antonym of freedom for the republican conception is not restraint as such but rather slavery and, more generally, any position of subjection. A person is free, and a person acts freely, just to the extent that she is not exposed, in the way a slave is exposed, to the arbitrary interference of another: to the sort of interference that only has to track the *arbitrium* – the will or judgment – of the interfering power. (Pettit, 1998: 84)

For republicans, then, agents are free to the extent that they are not subject to the mastery of another. That is, they are free to the extent that they are not subject to any interference that does not account for and track their own *arbitrium*. It follows that, for Pettit, nondomination consists primarily of two forms of power that secure agents against potential domination: a reciprocal form and a constitutional form. The reciprocal form of power comes with the realization that agents can defend themselves against forms of domination. They realize that they too can act to interfere arbitrarily with another, just as other agents have the same realization. "If each can defend themselves effectively against any interference that another can wield, then none of them is going to be dominated by another. None is going to be subject to the permanent possibility of interference on an arbitrary basis by another" (Pettit, 1997: 67). For Pettit, the reciprocal form of power is not ideal, nor is it completely effective in eliminating domination. It is my belief that Pettit overly discounts the reciprocal power of nondomination, which makes republican liberty as nondomination susceptible to the type of charges from liberals like Patten outlined above. In the third section I will take up this issue in more detail. Before pursuing that line though, I will outline the constitutional power of nondomination and examine Pettit's defense of it against the liberal critique.

For Pettit, the real strength of republican liberty is in its constitutional provisions that seek to promote the ideals of nondomination and to secure the agent against any arbitrary interference. It does this not by compelling or enabling dominated agents to defend themselves against dominators, but rather by denying those who seek to dominate the necessary power to interfere arbitrarily with others. That is, these constitutional provisions, whether they appear in the form of a judicial, executive, or other institution of the state, seek to prevent arbitrary interference before it can actually interfere with other agents. Furthermore, these constitutional provisions will be driven by the principles of nondomination and will therefore not dominate others in any way because they will be based upon the interests and ideals of those whom they seek to protect and "[are] suitably responsive to the common good" (Pettit, 1997: 68). State activity will be subjected to rigorous contestation in open and inclusive forums that seek to gauge the interests and opinions of individuals and groups in the republic so that they can be registered and tracked accordingly (Pettit, 1997: 195).

Another key feature of the republican approach is that republican citizens identify with and support the constitutional provisions of a republican state characterized by liberty as nondomination because they play a central role in their creation and maintenance. The laws and institutions of the republican state that seek to promote and maximize nondomination are created or amended by the citizens according to their interests in open and inclusive forums. If the constitutional provisions of nondomination are to maximize nondomination and not become dominators themselves, then the citizenry must play a central role in keeping them in check so that they track their interests and opinions, even as these change (Pettit, 1997: 207). In other words, it is essential that the citizens play an active and primary role in ensuring that the laws and institutions of the state do not interfere in their lives in an arbitrary manner. Without active contestation and oversight, the threat of state domination becomes greater and liberty is at risk. This point ties in to the resilience of republican liberty and the necessary promotion of contestatory forms of decision-making forums and processes I mentioned earlier. Because of the nature of republican liberty and the need to minimize arbitrary interference, republican institutions must be able to accommodate a diverse and vocal populace that engages constantly with the myriad interests found in the republic.[4] Vibrant and open constitutional structures are vital to the success of a republican state that puts liberty as nondomination at the fore of its public philosophy. As I mentioned above, Pettit believes that the real strength of the republican approach lies in the constitutional power of nondomination. I have no disagreement with Pettit on this point. As I will argue in later chapters, the constitutional features of modern republicanism represent some of the most attractive aspects of this approach as a relevant public philosophy. Where I do have a disagreement with Pettit is that, by ignoring the full range of features of the reciprocal power of nondomination, he denies republicanism a robust account of civic virtue and civility that helps to differentiate it from rival liberal approaches in a way which is compelling and attractive. Furthermore, by choosing to ignore the positive features of the reciprocal power of nondomination, he opens the door to those critics who believe that nondomination is just another instrumental approach that cannot be differentiated from liberalism.

Three advantages associated with freedom as nondomination

The first issue I want to tackle in this section is the liberal complaint that republicanism cannot be sufficiently differentiated from liberalism because nondomination is defended as an instrumental good. To these critics, Pettit's republican alternative seems to fall victim to the same kind of charges I outlined earlier that are leveled against Skinner. To be sure, Pettit himself maintains that nondomination can best be defended as an instrumental good that brings with it certain benefits. Although he allows that it may be defended as an intrinsic good, he chooses instead to argue that, even as an instrumental good, it has certain advantages over liberal approaches (Pettit, 1997: 82–90). In this section I intend to evaluate these charges against Pettit's alternative by exploring the instrumental nature of nondomination and whether or not it can be sufficiently differentiated from liberalism. I will argue that, despite liberalism and modern republicanism both containing certain instrumental goods, these goods have varying functions rendering the two approaches significantly different.

Despite Pettit's admission that republican liberty as nondomination can best be defended as an instrumental good, he maintains that there are some important advantages between pursuing freedom as the absence of arbitrary interference and pursuing freedom as the absence of any interference which make republican liberty more attractive (Pettit, 1997: 83–90). The first advantage that nondomination has over the ideal of freedom as non-interference is that, under nondomination, agents are secured from any anxiety or uncertainty they may experience from those who seek to interfere arbitrarily with them. Because some interference that agents might experience may be arbitrary, they do not know when, or from whom, it may come. This may lead to a high degree of uncertainty and anxiety as agents fret over being exposed to arbitrary interference. Maximizing freedom as nondomination will lower the degree to which agents are subject to arbitrary interference and, because the interference that they experience tracks their interests and opinions, uncertainty and anxiety are reduced (Pettit, 1997: 85). The opinions and interests of nondominated agents have been consulted and tracked, and any interference that they experience is not something that is unexpected. It follows, then, that nondominated agents do not experience a high degree of uncertainty or anxiety by being exposed to interference, since it tracks their interests. When nondomination is maximized, the uncertainty and anxiety that agents experience is minimized. The same does not hold under a system characterized by freedom as non-interference. If non-interference from the state were maximized, the interference that agents experience from others is likely to increase because they receive less protection from the state than from would-be offenders. As the level of interference that they experience rises, so too will their uncertainty and anxiety (Pettit, 1997: 86). The interference that they experience from others does not necessarily track their interests. It is not necessarily something that they were consulted about, which may cause them concern and may make them worry. In this case, the only way to reduce their uncertainty and anxiety would be to reduce the non-interference that they experience, but this fundamentally undermines the ideal of freedom as non-interference.

The second advantage republican liberty as nondomination has over the ideal of freedom as non-interference is that it reduces the degree to which agents have to be prepared to defend themselves against arbitrary interference. If nondomination reduces the uncertainty and anxiety that an agent might experience, it also reduces the degree to which agents must anticipate arbitrary interference and protect themselves from its effects (Pettit, 1997: 86). An agent who lives in a state characterized by republican liberty as nondomination will be freed from this responsibility. The degree to which agents have to plan strategically to cope with arbitrary interference is reduced the more nondomination is maximized. The interference that agents encounter is not unfamiliar to them because their opinions and interests have been tracked prior to its manifestation. Under a system characterized by the ideal of freedom as non-interference, agents will have to plan strategically to avoid arbitrary interference because they will not know from where it may come or in what form it may appear. This interference is unexpected because their interests were not consulted, nor were they asked to play an active role in its creation. In this manner, an agent's own choices will be curtailed and the range of options open to her reduced. Having to anticipate and plan to avoid interference will be a heavy burden on many agents, who will likely respond by limiting their exposure to situations where the potential for interference exists (Pettit, 1997: 87). These agents will have to rely on their own cunning and strategic planning to enjoy their liberty as they attempt to anticipate arbitrary interference. The result is that their overall liberty has been reduced. Once again, as the degree to which agents are exposed to interference is minimized, there is a corresponding drop in the freedom they enjoy. The same is not true under a system characterized by nondomination because, as arbitrary interference is minimized, agents are freed from having to anticipate arbitrary interference and strategically plan to avoid it if it does not track their interests. The range of options open to them increases as they feel more secure in their liberty and do not have to protect themselves from the arbitrary interference of other agents.

Finally, the third advantage that nondomination has over the ideal of freedom as non-interference is that agents who experience a decrease in their vulnerability to arbitrary interference from others will also experience subjective and intersubjective benefits. For Pettit, agents who live in a system characterized by nondomination will be more or less on an equal footing with one another when it comes to the amount of freedom they enjoy, and this will be common knowledge between them (Pettit, 1997: 87). This benefits both the way they view other agents and the way in which they view themselves. Put simply, they feel confident of their status and are thus able to extend a degree of trust and civility toward other nondominating agents who they know to be on an equal footing with them. As the amount of arbitrary interference that an agent experiences decreases, their self-image improves, as does the image that they project because it becomes common knowledge that they, along with others, stand on an equal footing, secure in their freedom. In the words of Pettit, "they can look the other person in the eye: they do not have to bow and scrape" (Pettit, 1997: 87). The same cannot be said of agents who live in a system of freedom characterized by non-interference. As non-interference rises, as the anxiety and uncertainty rise, as the need to anticipate and strategically prepare for arbitrary interference increases, the extent to which agents are subjected to interference from others affects how they view themselves. Put another way, in a state characterized by the ideal of freedom as non-interference, vulnerable agents who suffer uncertainty and anxiety worrying about potential arbitrary interference and who have to protect themselves from it will feel subordinate to others and, to a degree, dependent on the actions of others to enjoy their liberty.

If I am a vulnerable agent dependent on the good will of others not to interfere with me, I will feel subordinate to others. The freedom that I enjoy is limited by my own subjective and intersubjective status as a weak and vulnerable agent exposed to the whims of others. In a state characterized by the ideal of freedom as non-interference, agents will be engaged in a constant power struggle with one another, either interfering arbitrarily with others or defending themselves from arbitrary interference. It follows that this power struggle will eventually be won by the stronger, which exposes the weaker to an increased risk of arbitrary interference because they lack the capacity to defend themselves (Pettit, 1997: 88). Thus, as the state maximizes non-interference, the interference weaker agents experience from other agents may increase and affect their subjective and intersubjective status. The subjective and intersubjective benefits brought about by nondomination are not necessarily available to agents who live in a system characterized by the ideal of freedom as non-interference. For the weak, their social status is constantly in a perilous situation because they suffer anxiety and uncertainty and have to anticipate arbitrary interference. They are subordinate to others and cannot look them in the eye knowing that they are on an equal footing because they are all too aware of their limitations and are exploited because of them.

Adam Swift points out that some critics may charge that maximizing non-interference is not going to lead to the type of uncertainty or subordination described above in all cases (Swift, 2001: 67). Swift points to the example of a benign tyrant who is very liberal and grants his subjects a healthy degree of non-interference. These subjects may be on a more or less equal footing with others in that they all enjoy the non-interference granted by their leader. Nevertheless, in the modern republican way of thinking their position remains perilous because they, like the slave, are still in a position of domination and enjoy their non-interference only at the whim of their leader. To the extent that the tyrant does not interfere with them, they are in a disempowered position and suffer from living at his mercy. They may have to work hard to keep the tyrant sweet so that they can still enjoy a healthy slice of non-interference, but nothing they do brings them enough power to put them on common ground with the tyrant and look him in the eye from a position of equality. They remain subordinated to the tyrant and unable to enjoy fully their freedom as non-interference. They are like the slaves who are the property of a kindly master. They may enjoy a high degree of non-interference today, but their enjoyment hangs on the whims of the master, who not only holds arbitrary power over them, but places them in a subordinate position. The distinction becomes clear when we consider the difference between knowing that the other is not going to interfere arbitrarily with you and knowing that the other has the option of interfering arbitrarily with you (even if he chooses not to do so) (Pettit, 1997: 88). Knowing that another has the option of interfering arbitrarily with me (even if such actions are unlikely) is still going to place me in a subordinate position and damage my status and image of myself because while I might enjoy a high degree of non-interference I know that my status is that of a subordinate. I know that I have an unequal share of power in my relationship with the dominator, who retains the option of interfering arbitrarily with me.

In each of the three advantages outlined above, for Pettit, the benefits of pursuing nondomination improve upon the ideal of freedom as non-interference. From an overall standpoint, I think Pettit is right to argue that the advantages or benefits that accompany republican liberty as nondomination make pursuing this approach more attractive than those that rely on a conception of liberty as non-interference. To be fair, Patten does admit that the three advantages that Pettit claims republicanism has over the liberal approach may give liberals cause for further exploring republican liberty as nondomination (Patten, 1998: 808–10). However, Patten's central concern with instrumental republicanism remains intact because, as with Skinner, Pettit's account of citizenship and civic virtue appears to serve the same type of ends as these goods do in liberal approaches. However, I maintain that, while it certainly seems right that modern republican accounts of citizenship and civic virtue have an instrumental relationship to the overall enjoyment of liberty, I do not believe that it parallels the same type of relationship found in liberal approaches. This difference emerges when we consider whether or not the virtues and values that accompany nondomination and the ideals and institutions that support it are causally detachable from

republican liberty. The point to make here is that modern republicanism can be differentiated from liberalism because of the constitutive
relationship between nondomination and those virtues and values and
the accompanying institutions that help comprise the experience of
living in a society free from arbitrary interference. Thus, while
modern republicanism may be best defended as an instrumental approach (supported by instrumental goods such as civic virtue and
citizenship), it is not the same type of instrumental approach found
in liberal accounts. This is due to the constitutive nature of the ideals
and institutions that accompany nondomination. I turn to this issue
next.

Modern republican instrumental goods constitute liberty as nondomination

In a society characterized by the ideal of freedom as non-interference,
the ideals and institutions of the state are going to relate to the
freedom that they support in a causal fashion. As Pettit states,
"if freedom is non-interference, then freedom is causally brought
about by suitably protective and empowering institutions: it is a result
of the inhibiting effect of the protection and empowerment" (Pettit,
1998: 51; also see Pettit, 1997: 106–9). Put another way, the freedom
as non-interference that agents enjoy is causally related to the inhibiting nature of the institutions themselves. For example, instrumental
goods like citizenship are promoted by the liberal state because someone who is a good citizen is more likely to fulfill her obligations to
social justice. The interference that an agent experiences when
coerced by the liberal state into acquiring the habits of good citizenship is justified because this will help bring about a more secure and
complete system of freedom where citizens fulfill their obligations to
social justice. In other words, the liberal state interferes and coerces
agents to secure a more complete system of freedom. Instrumental
goods like citizenship are defended as a necessary means to an end.
We have already seen above how some liberals like Patten believe that
such goods are simply a means to an end and that their value is
derived solely from whatever they help bring about. The thought
is that being a good citizen helps individuals to fulfill their obligations
to social justice, which in turn brings about a more complete system
of liberty based on the ideal of non-interference. However, the paradox here is that the liberal state, in order to bring about a more
complete system of freedom, seeks to restrict or regulate certain
areas with the justification that doing so produces a more complete
system of basic liberties. In other words, the state purposely interferes

with agents (by coercing them to be good citizens or restricting their activities) so that a more complete system of non-interference can be put in place. Thus, even though I might treasure freedom as non-interference, I am content to allow the state to interfere with me in an instrumental manner because I in turn receive a more complete system of liberty. I rely on the causal nature of these instrumental goods to help bring about a state of affairs that has as its end-product my freedom as non-interference (even though they interfere with me to do this). For a theorist like Rawls, what matters here is how the basic liberties fit together to form a complete and just system of freedom that protects a core area of an individual's activity. The thought is that each of these basic liberties can be, when necessary, regulated or restricted in such a manner that, when they are combined with the other basic liberties, a more complete system of total liberty emerges. Importantly for these liberals, the basic liberties are regulated or restricted not for the public good nor for perfectionist goals, but only to ensure that a complete and total system of equal liberty can be secured for every individual (Rawls, 1996: 294–9; also see Rawls, 1971: 201–5 and 250). The justification for such moves lies in the fact that these interferences are viewed as regulations or restrictions that serve to enhance the total system of liberty.

The same justification for instrumental goods cannot be made in the modern republican approach. For republicans these interferences, which are not arbitrary, do not have a similar causal sequence where a restriction here may yield an enhancement there. Put simply, for modern republicans there is no one step back, two steps forward. Thus, under a system characterized by republican liberty as nondomination, interferences which are non-arbitrary are not viewed as being restrictions or regulations in the same way as they are in liberal approaches. Unlike some strict liberal negative conceptions of liberty, modern republican conceptions acknowledge that certain forms of interference are not necessarily wholly restrictive of an individual's freedom when a total system of liberty is in place. In many ways, for republicans, it is these very "interferences" that protect and enhance liberty. A modern republican state does not dominate me to bring about a more complete system of nondomination. The causal sequence outlined above is not necessary for me to realize my freedom in a modern republican state because I do not have to wait on my freedom after being interfered with by the state as it coerces me with instrumental goods. Provided the modern republican institutions that are in place are suitable, then any interference that I experience is not arbitrary because it tracks my interests. Thus, an instrumental good like citizenship is not seen by me as domination, nor do I view it as having caused my freedom. Instead I see such instrumental goods as constituting my freedom because they form a necessary part of it and are not causally detachable from it.

Where a liberal state characterized by the ideal of freedom as noninterference may in fact have to interfere with the citizenry to help bring about a more complete system of freedom, a modern republican state does not have to dominate its citizenry to bring about a more complete system of nondomination. Put another way, an agent does not have to wait for the properly constituted modern republican institutions to inhibit others from dominating him before he can enjoy his nondominated status. If he is in a position where he suffers no arbitrary interference, the nondomination he enjoys is not a result of a causal sequence brought about by any instrumental goods such as citizenship. There is no need for such causal sequences involving these types of instrumental goods in modern republicanism to bring about liberty as nondomination. It follows, then, that an instrumental good like modern republican citizenship does not have the exact same function as an instrumental good like liberal citizenship. Because the ideals and institutions that accompany modern republican liberty as nondomination constitute the liberty experienced by republican citizens, the modern republican approach I have been developing and defending can be differentiated from its liberal rivals. For modern republicans, properly constituted laws and institutions – laws and institutions which are made by and track the interests of those they govern – may be instrumental to the overall system of nondomination, but they are not synonymous with the kind of instrumental goods found in liberal approaches. Instead, the ideals and institutions that accompany republican liberty as nondomination are the essence of individuals' freedom and are a necessary part of it. The interference that these citizens experience due to the presence of these ideals and institutions is not viewed as a restriction or regulation of their freedom because this interference is not arbitrary. There is no need to restrict or regulate some liberty here to enhance liberty over there. Instrumental goods like civic virtue and citizenship, together with properly constituted laws and institutions, are component parts of republican citizens' freedom and represent the realization of nondomination in their lives. These citizens have a close and intimate relationship with these constituent parts because they are their freedom and, as mentioned above, bring with them certain substantive benefits or advantages. In this manner, nondomination is a status that agents achieve due to the constitutive nature of modern republican institutions. Once these institutions are in place, provided that they are properly constituted modern republican institutions, agents are free and enjoy nondominated status. The institutions do not cause their nondominated status; instead they are a necessary part of it and thus constitute it. Their nondominated status comes into existence at the same time as the institutions: there is no temporal gulf or causal sequence between being nondominated and enjoying one's nondominated status.

Pettit maintains that properly constituted modern republican institutions act in the same manner as the antibodies in our bodies: once we have sufficient antibodies in place we will be immune to certain diseases. These antibodies do not cause our immunity: they are our immunity (Pettit, 1997: 108). In other words, once the properly constituted modern republican institutions of the state are in place, members of the citizenry individually and collectively are immune to domination and can enjoy their freedom and their nondominated status without having to wait for the causal inhibiting effects of the state to kick in.[5] Suitable nondominating institutional arrangements help empower and protect individuals from arbitrary interference and can be seen by them as a means of realizing their nondominated status. The same is true when considering modern republican goods like citizenship and civic virtue. If I live in a state characterized by the ideals of modern republican citizenship and civic virtue that are embedded within the prevailing social norms, then I can enjoy my nondomination without having to rely on any causal sequences before realizing my freedom. If the social norms of my society are suitably nondominating, then I live a nondominated life and can enjoy my freedom and the benefits that accompany it. I am suitably secured and empowered as I pursue my chosen ends free from domination. In the next and final section I will argue that in pursuing these ends I can rely on the two powers that accompany nondomination to help deepen and enrich my life. In exploring these two powers, I will seek to further differentiate modern republicanism from its liberal rivals. I will also explore a key difference between my own republican account and that of Pettit.

The two powers of modern republicanism and personal self-development

In the section above I argued that, even though modern republicanism may be best defended as an instrumental good (just as liberalism is), there are significant differences between it and rival liberal accounts. The key difference between the two accounts emerges when we consider the type of relationship that exists between liberty and the instrumental goods that accompany and support it within each of the approaches. I argued that within modern republicanism certain instrumental goods like citizenship, civic virtue, and other institutional arrangements of the state constitute or help to constitute the nondomination enjoyed by the citizenry. Because these interferences track their interests they are not seen as a restriction of their freedom. Rather, they are seen as a means of realizing their freedom. On top of this important distinction, I also outlined three advantages of modern republican liberty as nondomination. In this final section I want to explore the type of possible effects these benefits might have on modern republican citizens' personal development and argue that modern republicanism does represent a significant improvement on the liberal standard. I then turn to my contention that Pettit fails to develop thoroughly the idea that nondomination contains some elements of positive liberty within it. To be sure, he equates those positive elements of Berlin's typology with the principle of mastery and derives the alternative republican conception of liberty as the absence of mastery. However, those theorists who promote a theory of liberty in the positive sense are not only concerned about mastery by others. One of their central concerns is self-mastery, and thus a degree of self-development and flourishing. Pettit does briefly argue for some type of self-mastery in the form of personal autonomy, but I believe that this line should be pursued further, especially in the sense of nondomination's reciprocal form of power and the relationship between nondomination and certain necessary republican ideals and institutions (Pettit, 1997: 81). It is not my contention that Pettit has this issue wrong. Instead, I maintain that Pettit has simply not gone far enough in defending his project.

To the extent that individuals are free from any uncertainty, anxiety, and anticipation that may accompany the ideal of freedom as non-interference, their opportunity for personal self-development increases in several important areas. Moreover, the security that they enjoy performs a double function. First, it secures them in a protective sense from arbitrary interference and, second, it promotes their social standing as full and equal citizens. They do not fear their fellow citizens because they can look them in the eye as equals; nor do they fear the consequences of arbitrary interference because any interference they experience tracks their interests. This interference is familiar to them because they were involved in its creation since, for it not to be arbitrary, it must consult or track their interests and opinions. In order for their interests to be tracked, they must have been registered and accounted for by the state and others. This idea connects to the republican emphasis on inclusive public forums and positive civic activity that are some of the defining features of the type of classical republicanism favored by Skinner and criticized by Patten. If the state is to track properly the interests of its citizens, then there must be a sufficient amount of virtue and participation in the forums of the state to register accurately just what those interests are (Pettit, 1998: 87). In this way, the necessary virtues that make up the republican version of citizenship help individuals explore and then articulate their own interests to the state and to others who must account for and track them if they are to live truly nondominated lives. By promoting substantive forms of civic virtue and access to a common language of citizenship, the republican state prepares citizens to play the necessary active role in their own nondomination.

As agents' need to defend themselves decreases and their ability to be secure in the enjoyment of their equal footing with others increases, the way in which they treat others will also be affected. Just as they know that they themselves are on an equal footing with other agents, so too must they realize that other agents are on an equal footing with them. Where Pettit draws the line of the reciprocal power of nondomination at defense (Pettit, 1997: 67), I maintain that it has progressive elements as well. If the essence of republican liberty is the realization that in order for agents not to be in a position of domination, their interests must be accounted for and tracked, then it must follow that the converse is also true. Individuals must take account of and track other individuals' interests before they can act without dominating them. To this end, individuals must consider how their actions will affect others and vice versa by treating others with the necessary civility and mutual respect that the reciprocal power of nondomination requires. In this manner, the reciprocal elements within republicanism contribute to individuals' mastery over themselves in a way that theorists who conceive of liberty in a positive fashion would approve. Agents who desire the resilient nature of republican liberty as nondomination and the benefits that accompany it are more secure in their own freedom if they cast their ends in a manner that does not subject others to arbitrary interference. By consulting or tracking other agents' interests and opinions, nondominating agents will not provoke or draw the rebuke of other nondominating agents. To not dominate others, agents must make an effort to discover what others' interests are, and then respond appropriately. In this manner, the equal footing that agents share is secure and common knowledge. So too is the identity to which each adheres and the standing of legitimacy and mutual recognition that will accompany this realization (Fullinwider, 1999: 133). In accounting for and tracking another's interests, I am exposed to another's non-dominating way of life as they promote it. I see that they are on an equal footing with me because they do not seek to interfere arbitrarily with my choices just as I do not seek to interfere arbitrarily in their choices. The same works in reverse: as I publicize my interests to others to ensure that they are being accounted for and tracked, I am secure in the knowledge that others will take my nondominating life and me as I am. The demands of reciprocity and the power that accompanies it mean that others will respect my nondominating life and they will treat my choices and me with civility (just as I treat theirs in the same manner).

Not surprisingly, communication plays a central role in the reciprocal power of nondomination. Those virtues that help to foster vibrant exchanges of information are favored by the republican approach. Some of these virtues are likely to involve such things as an ability to listen and articulate responses and the willingness and courage to accept decisions that are opposed to an individual's own view. These virtues, which have a long history in the republican approach, also support the constitutional power of nondomination that operates on a more formal and institutional level. According to Skinner, for republicans the "watchwords are *audi alteram partem*, always listen to the other side." Thus, the most suitable model to fit the republican emphasis on listening to the other side is that of a dialogue and "a willingness to negotiate over rival institutions concerning the applicability of evaluative terms. [Republicans] strive to reach understanding and resolve disputes in a conversational way" (Skinner, 1996: 15–16; also see Pettit, 1997: 189). Just as in the constitutional form of nondomination, the reciprocal form will be accompanied by a certain set of robust virtues that help to sustain nondomination and the benefits that accompany pursuing it. However, these virtues and values will have the effect of deepening and enriching individuals' lives while preparing them to play the necessary active role not only in their own nondomination, but in minimizing their domination of others. Having to articulate my interests to others will contribute to a deeper and richer understanding of just what my interests are. In light of my commitments to pursuing nondomination, I will have to reflect not only on how I publicize my interests, but also on how they will affect others.

Returning to the general liberal critique I outlined earlier will highlight yet more inherent differences between liberalism and modern republicanism. While liberals readily admit that some individuals' final life choices may be influenced by liberal virtues, this is not something that is (or can be) an explicit aim of the liberal state. The overriding goal of these virtues is to ensure that agents fulfill their obligations to social justice. Thus, liberals use these types of instrumental goods to help regulate individuals' behavior (and not their personal beliefs). To do otherwise would be to fundamentally undermine key liberal tenets such as state neutrality (Kymlicka, 1998b: 136; also see Rawls, 1996: 191–5).[6] While it is true that liberals allow that some individuals' final life choices may be influenced by the liberal virtues, this is not something that is an explicit aim of the liberal state. Indeed, Rawls specifically points out that the political virtues associated with his approach should not be presented or defended with reference to any comprehensive doctrine of the good nor with reference to state perfectionism (Rawls, 1996: 194).[7] The same cannot be true of the republican view of the necessary values and virtues that accompany nondomination. In each of the three advantages highlighted in the section above, republican virtue is going to have a definite effect on the personal life of individuals and cause "interference" in their choices. But as long as this interference is not arbitrary, it is not seen as a restriction of their life choices. In fact, as I have argued in this chapter, it is an enhancement of an individual's position to make their life choices since they do so in a nondominating environment safe in the knowledge that they are protected from arbitrary interference.

When we compare the republican version of reciprocity to that found in liberal accounts, meaningful differences emerge. For example, when Rawls uses the idea of reciprocity in political liberalism he intends it as an instrumental good to the idea of public reason. For Rawls, given that the justification of the use of public power must be in terms of public reason, each individual must engage in the public domain qua citizen prepared to give and take public reasons "according to what they consider the most reasonable conception of political justice" (Rawls, 1999: 136). In doing so qua citizen, reasonable individuals must uphold the criterion of reciprocity and the terms of fair cooperation by only proposing those policies that they sincerely believe it reasonable others can accept. For their part, they accept the reasons that others have offered under the understanding that the others have done the same. Following the legal enactment of the resolution of the issues, all parties agree to abide by the outcome whether or not it is in accordance with their respective beliefs (Rawls, 1999: 137). In this manner, reciprocity is an instrumental good; it serves as a means to an end and its value is derived solely from its consequences (Raz, 1986: 177), which in this case is upholding the idea of public reason. In other words, individuals qua citizens exercise reciprocity not because doing so is valuable in and of itself or puts them on the road to self-mastery. Instead, they exercise reciprocity because procedurally it is what they must do to uphold the idea of public reason and fulfill their obligations to social justice. Rawls certainly admits that some individuals may find benefits from exercising reciprocity (or any other "political" goods associated with his approach), but it is not something that should be promoted by the state on those grounds or else it would violate its neutral stance toward conceptions of the good (Rawls, 1999: 135–8; also see Rawls, 1996: xlvi–xlvii, 16–17, and 49–50).

For republicans, the reciprocal power of nondomination is something that must be promoted by the state through robust versions of citizenship and civic virtue. However, they must be promoted for what they are and the effects they are likely to have on the populace. The upshot here is that through the reciprocal power of nondomination an agent's character is shaped in a manner that is likely to deepen and enrich her life without being overly prescriptive. As we have seen, the republican tradition has a long history of robust forms of citizenship and educative institutions that inspire modern republicanism. Republicans seek to take self-interested individuals and, as Shelley Burtt argues, "educate their desires" so that they begin to identify their good with that of society (Burtt, 1990: 27–9). The modern republican state will seek to mold and condition individuals' ends so that they cast them in a manner that does not subject others to arbitrary interference. As I argued earlier, not to dominate others, individuals must learn to account for and track the interests of others so that they can respond properly to their demands without subjecting them to arbitrary interference. Certain substantive virtues will be cultivated in individuals by the republican state, such as the ability to reflect critically on their own actions and how the expression of these actions might interfere arbitrarily with others. For republicans like Machiavelli, the inculcation of certain virtues such as courage, temperance, and worldly knowledge or prudence was necessary for the successful maintenance of republican liberty (*The Discourses*: Machiavelli, 1965: 290–4).[8] These virtues have a modern role in helping individuals learn how to communicate with others so that they can not only discover and publicize their own interests, but also discover the interests of their fellow citizens. Once again, this ties in with the republican emphasis on civic virtue and civility discussed above. Without widespread participation in public forums, civic virtue, and civility on a personal level, arbitrary interference cannot be minimized (Pettit, 1997: 189; also see Skinner, 1996: 15–16). In this manner, civic virtue is understood as individuals' ability to cast their ends in a manner that does not interfere arbitrarily with others and an appreciation of how their actions impact the whole of society. To have civic virtue is to act with civility toward others by listening to the other side and reacting in a manner that tracks the other side's interests and treats those interests with respect.

A modern republican state will seek to mold and condition individuals' ends so that they cast them in a manner that does not subject others to arbitrary interference. This point ties in with my earlier discussion of the key differences between Skinner's and Patten's approaches. Where liberals take self-interested individuals and attempt to regulate their activity through certain instrumental processes and restraints, republicans take self-interested individuals and engage with them in the hope that they become individuals of a certain character type that can identify their good with that of the community and thus act in a nondominating manner. However, while shaping the ends that agents pursue into nondominating ones, another benefit of doing so is a likely increase in attractive nondominating life choices due to the improved subjective and intersubjective status enjoyed by the populace. As individuals track the interests of others (and have their own tracked), they are going to be in a better position to make certain choices as they seek fulfillment or self-mastery.

For some, the virtues and values that support nondomination, and in particular the ones associated with its reciprocal power, will have intrinsic value, and thus are not singularly of instrumental value to the ultimate good of self-mastery.[9] It is a mistake to assume that something that is of instrumental value cannot also have intrinsic value. As I have outlined and argued above, the benefits of nondomination and the virtues and values that support them do indeed have instrumental value.[10] However, as I have also argued, it is not the same type of instrumental value as is found in liberal accounts. It follows that the sum effects of republican liberty as nondomination will be far-reaching. Agents will be in an improved position to evaluate their life choices as they benefit from an improved subjective and intersubjective status. They will stand eye to eye with others knowing that they are secure in their freedom. They will be able to evaluate and explore their own interests from a newly found position of power and security. Republican forms of civic virtue and citizenship help them to articulate their interests to others and at the same time to take others' interests seriously and with respect. The republican emphasis on communication and accommodation also helps to foster civility and trust between myself and others as we collectively address our common problems. Others will recognize an agent's interests and they will be provided with open and inclusive forums in which to share them. Both the constitutional and reciprocal power of nondomination mix and combine together to improve an agent's position to enjoy their freedom. If my argument is correct then it is not hard to see that the modern republican institutional arrangements, and the virtues and values that accompany them, will contribute to an individual's improved position and help to cultivate certain ideal types of republican citizen. But these features do not cause the freedom enjoyed by republican citizens. Instead, as I have argued, they help to constitute that freedom and are seen as a necessary part of it.

As agents attain the virtues and come to realize fully the reciprocal power of nondomination, it is my belief that their lives will be deepened and enriched. This enrichment can be seen as a necessary but yet insufficient condition for self-mastery. Thus, it is my belief that nondomination ties in more closely than Pettit admits with Berlin's formulation of positive liberty. However, this is not to endorse those theorists like Taylor who maintain that such self-mastery can only be attained within a society of a certain canonical form incorporating self-government (Taylor, 1991: 148). Rather, my argument here is that if we accept that nondomination has the type of reciprocal and constitutional power outlined above, we must also accept that this realization is not purely defensive in that it singularly secures agents on a personal level from arbitrary interference through enforced equality (Pettit, 1997: 67). The improved status that agents experience in light of republican liberty as nondomination makes the task of looking inward less difficult because it is done from a position of security and empowerment. Moreover, if agents are freed from uncertainty, anxiety, and anticipation of arbitrary interference, and their social status of free and equal citizen is common knowledge, then it must follow that they realize the same about other citizens. In this way, the reciprocal power of nondomination is, in Taylor's words, an "exercise concept," but one with a difference. The exercise within the reciprocal power of nondomination is less robust than the type of self-mastery favored by those who subscribe to a civic humanist view of republicanism or communitarianism. It carries with it certain internal specifications on how an agent should act to realize their freedom fully along with others and the types of virtues that can help them enrich their lives. It does not specify in a singular fashion the "true" ends that they should pursue with their freedom such as a specific kind of human flourishing or *eudaimonia*, nor does it suggest that participation in democratic self-government is the end-all and be-all of the good life. In order to further protect and maintain their liberty, individuals must be able to cast their ends in a manner that does not subject others to arbitrary interference, which would undermine the equal footing they, and others, enjoy. If their equal footing is undermined, the pursuit of their ends will be also undermined because uncertainty, anxiety, and anticipation of arbitrary interference will return and their choices will diminish. If individuals lose their nondominated (and nondominating) status, they will find it more difficult to pursue their life choices. In other words, the security that individuals enjoy both protects their status and promotes their empowerment. For modern republicans, the question is not necessarily the quantity of liberty as non-interference they enjoy, although such considerations may be important in terms of enjoying nondomination (Brugger, 1999: 6). Rather, the question is about the quality of liberty and how the two interdependent powers of nondomination fit together to form a coherent and realizable complete system of freedom that allows them to pursue their chosen choices free from arbitrary interference.

Conclusion

Following the lead of Isaiah Berlin, many liberals favor a negative conception of liberty because it limits the amount of interference and coercion that the state has in individuals' lives. Such moves leave individuals to place value on their life choices or step back and revise them if desired. For many contemporary liberals, this option is made even more attractive by the realization that we live in a multicultural society limiting the ability of the state to endorse any one conception of the good due to the "fact of pluralism" (Rawls, 1996: 36). The fear is that some valuable ways of life may be lost as society is remade in the state's or the majority's image of the good. Civic humanists, or those that favor a positive conception of liberty, argue that any meaningful life must have a robust and rich sense of self-mastery and that comes with flourishing in a certain type of community that practices democratic self-government. If we are to believe Patten or Rawls, the neo-Roman version of republicanism put forth by Skinner and Pettit sides with liberals on these issues because, at the most fundamental level, they favor a negative sense of liberty. The thought is that the versions of citizenship and civic virtue of the neo-Roman republican approach are instrumental to the attainment and maintenance of negative liberty. However, I have argued that there is another way to understand the neo-Roman approach in terms of its alternative conception of liberty as nondomination.

In a modern republican approach liberty is neither solely the absence of interference nor the realization of self-mastery. Rather, liberty is the absence of mastery, which allows that certain interferences can have the effect of enhancing liberty and making it more resilient and secure. Contained within this conception of liberty are certain virtues and values and institutional arrangements that perform a dual role. On the one hand, through the constitutional power of nondomination they help to ensure that the ideas and institutions of the republic are properly constituted and that domination is minimized. On the other hand, through the reciprocal power of nondomination, modern republican virtues will interact on a personal and more intimate level to enrich and deepen individuals' lives while helping to constitute their freedom. Individuals who live in a state characterized by modern republicanism will receive certain benefits unavailable to them in a system characterized by freedom as non-interference. These individuals will have an increased capacity for choice and will be empowered and secure in making those choices. To sum up, modern republicanism is an approach that relies on the traditional value of liberty as nondomination and places it in a central role as an ideal for an inclusive population. Moreover, it emphasizes the need for properly constituted republican institutional arrangements and the necessity of certain robust virtues – such as citizenship and civic virtue – in the citizenry. So, despite Patten's claims otherwise, I believe, and have tried to demonstrate, that there are significant differences between the republican and liberal approaches even though they both contain accounts of instrumental goods. Furthermore, it is my belief that promoting this type of instrumental versions of citizenship and civic virtue (and the ideals and institutions that accompany them) impoverishes the liberal state and deprives it of important constitutive elements of freedom. By recognizing and promoting distinctive republican ideals, the modern polity can make the road that individuals must travel to self-mastery less treacherous and easier to traverse while protecting and enhancing their choices.

It is one thing, however, to argue that modern republicanism characterized by liberty as nondomination contains an alternative conception of liberty. It is quite another to demonstrate that it is an improvement on the liberal ideal of freedom as it appears in contemporary liberal approaches. Although I have laid the foundation for this argument in this chapter, it remains to be seen if the promise of modern republicanism's alternative conception of liberty can be fulfilled in a way that offers an attractive alternative to the liberal standard. Furthermore, it remains to be seen if my argument can demonstrate to liberals that while these differences are fundamental and meaningful, there are good reasons for adopting modern republicanism. In the next two chapters, I will explore these issues in greater detail by examining two prominent liberal approaches to define and distinguish further modern republicanism from its rivals. In particular, chapter 3 will consider Will Kymlicka's arguments for liberal neutrality and chapter 4 will examine the political liberalism of John Rawls.

3

The Challenge of the Cultural Marketplace: Modern Republicanism and the Neutral State

Introduction

Questions that surround the state's proper role in the lives of its citizens are some of the most important and enduring that confront contemporary political philosophy. Many liberal theorists maintain that the state's proper role in the lives of individuals should be restricted to establishing the just and fair conditions that enable them "to pursue their own conceptions of the good" (Jones, 1989: 9). In other words, the state should not promote or pursue any version of the good life itself, and instead should ensure that its citizens have the capacity to choose, question, and revise their life plans without any unnecessary state interference. In this manner, the principle of liberal neutrality holds that the state should only minimally regulate the choices available to its citizens. Moreover, when regulating the availability of life choices, these liberals maintain that the state should do so without appealing to any version of the good. In other words, when justifying state coercion and the use of public power, liberals believe that the state should not appeal to the good. Thus, the primary function of the state, for these liberals, is to ensure that individuals have the necessary conditions and context in which to choose those things that are important to them.[1] Critics of liberalism argue that state neutrality undermines citizens' commitment to the common good because it stresses their individual rights and not their common duties (Sandel, 1996: 25). By not acknowledging an overriding public philosophy that recognizes self-government, and the values and virtues that it requires and that help to contribute to the realization of the highest human ends, these critics argue that liberal neutrality is self-defeating.

Like republicanism, liberalism is not a monolithic doctrine and there are different approaches, each with its own distinctive features and ideals.[2] On one side, liberals such as Will Kymlicka advocate an approach that seeks to remain neutral among competing ideas of the good and does not publicly rank the intrinsic worth of life plans. For Kymlicka, "the role for the state is to protect the capacity for individuals to judge for themselves the worth of different conceptions of the good life, and to provide a fair distribution of rights and resources to enable people to pursue their conception of the good" (Kymlicka, 1998b: 133). In other words, Kymlicka believes that individuals should have the necessary freedom and capacity to choose, question, and revise their life choices rationally.

On the other side, inspired by the recent work of John Rawls, some liberals have proposed a freestanding conception of justice that asks individuals to bracket off their closely held comprehensive moral and philosophical claims and instead embrace a more limited *political* conception of justice. In doing so, the state's aims remain neutral among competing ideas of the good (Rawls, 1996: 191–4). In other words, like Kymlicka's approach above, these liberals believe that the state should not itself pursue a singular version of the good. Although distinct, both of these approaches hold that in order to maximize the liberty of citizens, given a myriad of competing moral traditions, the state should not publicly rank or endorse particular versions of the good. Instead, the state should concentrate on guaranteeing its citizens a just political system and equal rights under the law so that they can pursue and revise their chosen life plans without unnecessary state interference. By constructing institutions and procedures aimed at securing individual liberty and justice, the liberal polity avoids having to make any substantive moral claims other than those that are required to ensure its citizens the necessary rights that help form their capacity to pursue their chosen paths in life.

Even though both of these liberal approaches hold that the state should remain neutral toward competing conceptions of the good, within their respective strategies there are significant differences in their underlying principles that deserve a thorough review. Over this chapter and the next, I will explore how modern republicanism responds to these differences. In this chapter I will examine Will Kymlicka's defense of liberal neutrality while developing and defending a modern republican response to his concerns. To the extent possible, I will set aside questions related to the second of these approaches, John Rawls's political liberalism, so that they can be examined thoroughly in the next chapter.

Liberalism and republicanism: friends or enemies?

Responding to Michael Sandel's thoughtful work *Democracy's Discontent*, Will Kymlicka has argued that, despite the philosophical differences between liberalism and republicanism, the two approaches should be allies in addressing the problems confronting the modern polity (Kymlicka, 1998b; Sandel, 1996). As I mentioned in the last chapter, Richard Dagger (1997) makes a similar plea in advocating republican liberalism. Kymlicka maintains that, because both approaches share important philosophical principles, supporters of each approach should work together to combat the discontent that citizens feel towards today's polity (Kymlicka, 1998b: 131). Despite this convergence, however, Kymlicka maintains that Sandel's call to abandon liberal neutrality is misplaced, and that it is only within such a liberal system that citizens can be treated equally and fairly by the state. By focusing on the type of republicanism associated with the civic humanists, Kymlicka confuses the different versions of republicanism and thus ignores the alternative version of republicanism I have developed in earlier chapters.[3] As we saw, modern republicanism is distinct from Sandel's in that it does not endorse a singular version of human flourishing grounded in self-government. It is also distinct from the kind of liberalism favored by Kymlicka because it contains certain ideals and institutions that constitute and support its conception of liberty as nondomination. However, these two issues need to be further explored and developed in order to present modern republicanism as a viable and attractive public philosophy. To this end, I will argue that modern republicanism abandons liberal neutrality, but yet does not endorse a robust singular version of the good.

Despite these differences, I will argue that liberals like Kymlicka have good reasons to accept the modern republicanism I support. Ultimately, this chapter will argue that Kymlicka is right to assert that liberalism and republicanism should be allies in combating the many problems facing the modern polity. However, before these approaches can become fully compatible, I will argue that Kymlicka's principle of liberal neutrality must be abandoned in favor of a more substantive approach that countenances the values and institutional arrangements that accompany republican liberty as nondomination. My argument against Kymlicka's state neutrality will focus on two crucial areas. The first of these concerns Kymlicka's belief that the state should not appeal to the intrinsic value of some versions of the good in its ideals and institutions. The second part of my argument will focus on Kymlicka's belief that the state should not promote any perfectionist values. In addressing these two important issues, I will further develop and defend a modern republicanism as an approach that can cope with the many problems facing the modern polity. Moreover, I will argue that, by abandoning liberal neutrality, modern republicanism offers a richer and more robust account of freedom than liberalism without sacrificing key liberal aims.

Autonomy, individualism, and civic virtue

In the last chapter I argued that republican citizens have a unique relationship between their liberty and the ideals and institutions that support it. On both a theoretical and a concrete level, two interdependent forms of power, reciprocal and constitutional, accompany republican liberty as nondomination. These forms of power are constituent parts that comprise the essence of republican liberty and are recognized as such. The reciprocal form of power manifests itself in certain values and ideals such as civic virtue and citizenship. This form of power carries with it certain substantive benefits that mold and condition how individuals exercise their freedom and cast their final ends. The reciprocal form of power is supported in a legal and institutional manner by the constitutional form of power that may emerge in the form of strong laws or a legislative, executive, judicial, or other institution of the republican state. It follows that both the reciprocal and constitutional forms of power are constituent components and are necessarily interdependent. Without certain substantive goods that accompany the reciprocal power of nondomination that inform and track the common good, the ideals and institutions of the state will not be able to sustain republican liberty as nondomination. On the one hand, civic virtue and citizenship help transmit certain robust values to individuals that help them both realize and maintain their republican liberty as nondomination. On the other hand, properly constituted laws and institutions – ones that were made by and track the interests of the citizenry – are not seen as restrictions of citizens' freedom. Instead, taken together, they serve to make up and form their freedom. In other words, civic virtue and citizenship, together with properly constituted laws and institutions, are interdependent component parts of republican citizens' freedom and represent the realization of nondomination in their lives. It follows that republican citizens have a close and intimate relationship with these constituent parts because they are their freedom and bring with them certain substantive benefits. Assuming that they are suitable, once the ideals and institutions that accompany nondomination are in place the citizenry is free in the modern republican sense.

This is not the case in Kymlicka's view of liberal neutrality, where the virtues and values that support liberty are seen as instrumental goods in that they serve as preconditions for social justice and are causally related to the freedom as non-interference that individuals enjoy. For Kymlicka, it is individuals' capacity to choose those ends that they find valuable that is a primary concern of the liberal state. It follows, then, that an essential aspect of being free is individuals' capacity to choose, question, and revise rationally their conceptions of the good. In this section, I will argue that modern republicanism is not hostile to individuals' capacity to revise their life choices rationally. However, republicans believe that for individuals truly to be in a position to evaluate and question their life plans, they must be in a situation where they have a freedom meaningful and secure enough to make such judgments. The difference lies in the fact that republicans believe that it is only by viewing the ideals and institutions that accompany liberty as nondomination as constitutive goods that it is possible to ensure that individuals are in a meaningful position to question and revise rationally their life choices. If individuals lose the close and intimate relationship with the constituent values of their liberty and view them solely in causal instrumental terms, they may well create the conditions that undermine their liberty and this may negatively affect their capacity to revise rationally their life choices. Furthermore, the goods that are associated with republican liberty as nondomination do not only play an important role in the maintenance of freedom; they also interact with individuals in a substantive manner that affects the choices that they make. In this section, I will further develop this point and argue that the virtues and ideals of republican liberty as nondomination are not antagonistic to liberal aims such as autonomy and individuality. Furthermore, I will argue that the state must play a central role in the cultivation of these virtues and ideals associated with republican liberty.

Kymlicka's take on this issue is that liberal virtues and values should be justified in an instrumental manner because they help maintain the overall system of freedom so that individuals can pursue their own conception of the good without undue state interference (Kymlicka, 1998b: 135). In this sense, the liberty that individuals experience, and the virtues and values that support it, are causally instrumental to the projects that are important to them. These projects are ones that individuals choose with their freedom and it is this process that allows them to question and revise their choices as they make the necessary determinations as to how they want to live their lives. Individuals' liberty, then, is merely a conduit that they utilize as they evaluate the many different life plans available to them (Kymlicka, 1990: 209–10). What is valuable about freedom for many liberals is that it serves as a means to an end. In other words, the real value of freedom for liberals is that it allows individuals to pursue their own chosen ends and determine their own conception of the good. Beyond this, liberals generally make no value judgments on the ends being pursued. Thus, for Kymlicka, it is individuals' capacity to choose, question, and revise freely their final ends that is valuable and not the instrumental ideals and institutions that help them attain these ends. To support this effort, Kymlicka maintains that the state should remain neutral among these competing conceptions of the good so that individuals can choose and pursue those ends that are valuable to them without unnecessary state interference. In simple terms, Kymlicka's autonomy consists of two parts. First, individuals lead their lives from the inside, evaluating and making choices to satisfy their needs. Second, these choices are not fixed and individuals may wish to revise them. It follows, then, that the state's role in this is to remain neutral in terms of valuing the choices that individuals make.

Insofar as the state does play a role in individuals' lives, the values and ideals that help individuals to determine the value of their life choices are instrumental goods, and their promotion does not violate state neutrality. Kymlicka describes these goods as secondary values that may help individuals to achieve better life choices in certain circumstances, but that nevertheless remain instrumental to their final ends. For Kymlicka, the important factor is *why* the state promotes such values. It may be that the state has good reasons to promote some values, such as liberal citizenship and liberal virtues, because they make it more likely that individuals will fulfill their obligations to liberal justice. However, for the state not to violate its own neutrality, these ideals must be defended without recourse to any intrinsic goods or substantive ideals. In other words, for Kymlicka, while liberalism may have a commitment to certain "conception[s] of individual agency and social justice, it has no similar intrinsic or foundational commitment to a particular conception of communal identity or civic virtue" (Kymlicka, 1998b: 135). The motivation behind the state's promotion of these values is to enhance the overall system of liberal justice, and not to promote a version of the good life.

It all depends on *why* one is promoting a conception of civic virtue. If the state promotes certain virtues on the grounds that possessing these virtues will make someone's life more worthwhile or fulfilling, then clearly it is promoting a particular conception of the good. However, if the state is promoting these virtues on the grounds that possessing them will make someone more likely to fulfill her obligations of justice, then it is not promoting a particular conception of the good. It has made no claim whatsoever about what makes her life go better, or about what ends in life are rewarding or fulfilling. (Kymlicka, 1998b: 136; emphasis in original)

Importantly, then, for Kymlicka, the state can promote certain ideals without violating its neutral position. Thus, certain instrumental ideals are promoted by the liberal state because they enable individuals to "achieve liberal principles of individual agency and social justice" and not because they are intrinsically valuable final ends (Kymlicka, 1998b: 136). In this manner, then, the instrumental virtues and values promoted by a liberal state are purposely "thin" so that they allow individuals to identify with them in a sense that does not endorse a conception of the good or publicly rank the intrinsic worth of their choices. These "thin" identities are promoted only because they make it more likely that individuals will fulfill their obligations to liberal justice. Moreover, these virtues are not a reflection of a certain conception of the good, but rather are instrumental duties and serve as a "precondition of justice to others" (Kymlicka, 1998b: 136–7).

For Kymlicka, these "thin" goods, combined with the state's neutrality, allow individuals enough space to make meaningful choices free from coercion, which is important since individuals do not have fixed or unchangeable conceptions of the good (Kymlicka, 1990: 212). As individuals' lives change, so will the circumstances in which they find themselves change. Liberal neutrality enables them to go back and question their prior judgments. It follows that each individual should have the capacity to reflect rationally on her ends and change them if she deems them no longer valuable. For its part, the state acknowledges and maintains "a sphere of self-determination" that must be respected by others, including itself, so that individuals are free from unnecessary interferences that may distort both the context in which individuals make choices, and those choices themselves (Kymlicka, 1998b: 133; also see Kymlicka, 1990: 200). Kymlicka believes that, when left to their own devices, individuals will seek those things that are rewarding given their view of life. They will seek to investigate and compare different ways of life while constantly subjecting their choices to vigorous revision and questioning. Through this process, individuals are able to judge between competing versions of the good life and choose the one that suits them the best. Invasive state interference would be harmful to individuals and has the potential to take the value and meaning out of their self-determination as they seek to find the good life (Kymlicka, 1990: 203–4). Furthermore, intrusive state intervention has the potential to threaten the development of autonomy and individuality and to distort the context for meaningful choice that is necessary for individual agency (Kymlicka, 1998b: 139). For Kymlicka, no authority should be allowed such broad control over individuals' life choices. Ultimately, what is important is that individuals have the capacity and ability to make their own judgments, which in turn enables them to make and revise the necessary choices for their life plans free from state interference. Put simply, it is the choosing that is important, not necessarily what is chosen.

However, it is not clear that Kymlicka's neutral state can constrain the liberal virtues and values that specify the act of choosing, especially given the assumption that individuals live their lives from the inside. Bhikhu Parekh has argued that Kymlicka's assumptions are flawed on two basic levels. First, Kymlicka assumes that all lives can be led from the inside and thus ignores those individuals and groups whose identities cannot be divided in such a manner. Second, Kymlicka fails to acknowledge adequately the intimate connection between identifying with a set of principles and being governed by a completely different set of principles that may be inconsistent with that identity (Parekh, 2000: 107–8; also see Kymlicka, 1995: 153). The thought is that Kymlicka's approach undermines individuals' identity first by specifying that it should be solely lived from the inside and second in failing to acknowledge the effect on that identity of a coercive liberal state that judges individuals in liberal terms. What we are left with in the end, according to Parekh, is that the type of state neutrality favored by Kymlicka is violated through the back door. In making liberal assumptions about identity and trying to enforce neutrality on liberal terms, the state acts in a decidedly non-neutral way. It is my belief that modern republicanism is not subject to the type of objection put forth by Parekh and thus can cope with difference and diversity better than Kymlicka's approach. I now turn to this issue.

Modern republicanism and state neutrality

As we saw earlier, neo-Roman republicanism has a tradition of recognizing that individuals desire liberty to pursue their own chosen ends.

For example, Machiavelli maintained that different people would wish to pursue varying ends and that republican liberty provided them with the security to do so. In his account of republican liberty we learn that some people will wish to pursue honor and power, while others will wish to enjoy a life of security and pursue more modest ends (*The Discourses*: Machiavelli, 1965: 204; also see Skinner, 1991: 196). I believe that this sentiment is reflected in the version of modern republican liberty put forth in the last chapter. Thus, I have no quarrel with Kymlicka's position that individuals do not have fixed or unchanging conceptions of the good. My task, then, is to put forth an argument that demonstrates how modern republicanism reconciles this in light of Kymlicka's argument for liberal neutrality and the objections of theorists like Parekh.

For Kymlicka, as we saw above, the way to ensure that individual agency is respected is for the state to promote only instrumental versions of virtues and values and remain neutral towards competing ideas of the good. It follows that liberals, in answering Kymlicka's question of why the liberal state promotes certain ideals, argue that they do so for instrumental reasons. Because these instrumental ideals do not presuppose any conception of the good the liberal state is able to claim a neutral stance. However, I do not believe that in its present form this reply is available to modern republicans. As I argued in the last chapter, the type of instrumental goods found in the modern republican approach vary significantly from those found in liberalism. This is because the substantive goods associated with both the reciprocal and constitutional power of nondomination help to constitute republican liberty and secure individuals from external or internal threats to their freedom. This allows a modern republican state to put forth richer and more robust forms of republican values and virtues. In making this move, modern republicanism abandons liberal neutrality. Underlying my argument here is a point made by Christine Korsgaard when discussing the differences between old liberalism (which is in essence republicanism) and new liberalism (Korsgaard, 1993: 57–9). The thought here is that republicans seek to isolate and favor only one strand in individuals' conceptions of the good – the ideal that it is good not to have to look out and guard against arbitrary interference in one's life.[4] Thus, in pursuing this ideal, certain virtues and institutional arrangements become an essential element of the citizenry's freedom to be favored through the use of (nondominating) state coercion. In violating liberal neutrality a modern republican state acts in a non-arbitrary manner to secure and promote freedom so that citizens can realize and pursue their chosen nondominating ends.

So, in answering the question of why the state promotes these goods, modern republicans have two replies that violate liberal neutrality. First, republicans believe that the state should actively promote these goods because they help form a resilient and secure system of liberty that offers individuals certain benefits unavailable to them otherwise. This point ties in to the argument I made earlier regarding the benefits of living in a republican state characterized by liberty as nondomination. These benefits enhance individuals' ability to make choices and revise their life plans as they are freed from the uncertainty and anxiety of any actual or threatened interference that does not track their interests. They do not have to plan strategically to defend themselves against potential dominators and they experience certain subjective and intersubjective benefits that enhance their ability to make choices. What are restrictions to liberals turn out to be enhancements for republicans. The thought is that individuals will be in an enhanced position to choose, question, and revise their life choices within a wide range of nondominating choices. On a wider scale, as a political body, the community will pursue those ends that ensure that the conditions of liberty as nondomination are maintained and enhanced so individuals can make and question their own choices. Thus, in both republican and liberal approaches, individuals are free to choose, question, and revise their life choices. However, because a modern republican state abandons liberal neutrality, individuals are secure in their freedom, and thus secure in their ability to choose and revise their life plans in light of the nondomination that they enjoy. To this end, republicans believe that the institutions of government can be shaped in such a manner to provide the necessary security for individuals to pursue and revise their conceptions of the good while enhancing their liberty to do so. Seen in this way, I believe that this move does not represent a threat to the modern polity or to those who back a liberal neutralist approach. This is because individuals' identity is respected, whether they choose to live it from the inside or the outside. State activity aimed at them enhances their position to make such choices by securing them from interference that does not track their interests.

The second reply that republicans have as to why the state should actively promote republican virtues and values is that these ideals can and do aid in the development of the self by exposing individuals to different ways of life and alternative dimensions of personal identity (Pettit, 1997: 257). It is inevitable that as individuals interact with the ideals and institutions of the modern republic they will encounter ideas and values that are distinctively republican and may be alien to their way of life. Kymlicka maintains that liberal neutrality helps ensure a "free and fair context" for individuals to make the necessary judgments associated with rationally revising their life choices (Kymlicka, 1998b: 139). Modern republicanism, too, helps to ensure such a "context for choice," albeit a distinctive one. For modern republicans, the constant action and reaction to life in civil society helps to form an important context for choice for those citizens who know themselves to be free from domination. The republican context for choice will regulate the availability of some comprehensive moral traditions and may even challenge or distort some individuals' final ends. It does this because the wider, and more pervasive, role assigned to nondomination makes it impossible for ends that dominate to exist within the modern republican state without being challenged. This context for choice is not, as I will argue, overtly coercive or determinate, but rather is a guarantee to those citizens who know themselves to be free from arbitrary interference and have the necessary security to choose, question, and revise their life plans within a republican state characterized by liberty as nondomination. The republican context for choice serves to regulate and educate those citizens who understand their freedom as nondomination. For republicans, then, citizens, by understanding their liberty as the lack of arbitrary interference in their life choices, know themselves to be free to pursue their own ends according to whatever conception of the good they may have in light of the regulative nature of nondomination. Modern republicanism seeks to ensure that individuals are free from any actual or threatened arbitrary interference so that they can decide those things that are valuable, and those things that are not, as long as their choices are consistent with others enjoying liberty as nondomination.

In this manner, republicanism is not hostile to the autonomy and individuality supported by Kymlicka. Modern republicans can accept the importance of autonomous choice in the development of individuals' various life plans. For republicans, the key question is not whether or not autonomy and individuality are compatible with republican or liberal concepts, but rather what role the state should play in cultivating the ideals and values that accompany republican liberty as nondomination and why. Kymlicka's belief that the state should not publicly rank the intrinsic worth of the various conceptions of the good that are found in today's modern polity seems to suggest that the state should play no role in an individual's formulation of the good, but should play a role in the cultivation of autonomy. As mentioned above, Kymlicka maintains that, without violating liberal neutrality, the state plays a central role in the development of these capacities and abilities through certain basic civil rights:

For Mill and other liberals, a basic argument for civil rights is that they help ensure that individuals can make informed judgments about the inherited practices of the community. For example, mandatory educa- tion ensures that children acquire the capacity to envisage alternative ways of life and rationally assess them. Freedom of speech and associ- ation (including the freedom to proselytize or dissent from church orthodoxy) ensures that people can raise questions and seek answers about the worth of the different ways of life available to them. (Kym- licka, 1996: 87)

Thus, certain character traits and skills are promoted by the liberal state to ensure that individuals have the capacity and ability to revise their life choices. Because the liberal state does not publicly rank the choices available to its citizens, it does not violate liberal neutrality. Even though it seeks to instill certain skills and traits within the lives of its citizens, Kymlicka maintains that, because this effort does not publicly rank the various life choices available to its citizens, liberal neutrality remains intact. What Kymlicka fails to acknowledge, and thus what he fails to defend, is that the liberal state will have a thoroughly liberal impact on individuals and groups through liberal assumptions about identity and the promotion of liberal virtues. Put another way, because Kymlicka presupposes individuals' identities in the manner in which he does, the liberal virtues interact with this identity with an unacknowledged reference to state perfectionism by promoting a certain version of autonomy and individuality. Before addressing this topic in greater detail we first need to explore how modern republican virtues and values interact with individuals, and the consequences this is likely to have for the individual.

The republican "psychology" of civic virtue

Because modern republicanism favors a substantive version of civic virtue that places certain demands on individuals that are more robust than the account found within Kymlicka's liberalism, republicanism approaches autonomy in a different manner and thus violates the type of neutrality he favors. It is not my intention here to develop fully a republican conception of autonomy since, as mentioned above, there is no overt hostility to liberal versions of autonomy of the kind put forth by Kymlicka. I believe that the key difference between the two approaches lies in the role that each one believes the state must play in supporting autonomy since the republican state seeks to regulate the ends that individuals value and how they are expressed. This point ties in with Shelly Burtt's work on the different "psychologies" of civic virtue found in the republican tradition. Burtt maintains that there are three related, but yet distinct, republican conceptions of civic virtue: the education of desires; the accommodation of interests; and finally the compulsion to duty (Burtt, 1990: 23–38). Briefly, the education of desires approach is characterized by the attempt of the state to mold and condition the private desires of individuals for public aims. Similarly, the accommodation of interests approach finds republicans structuring the institutions of government in such a way that the private interests of its citizens are fused with the public good. Finally, the compulsion to duty approach finds virtuous citizens serving their country "because of a rational understanding that it is their duty to do so" (Burtt, 1990: 25–6).

I believe that the psychology of civic virtue found in modern republicanism is a combination of the first two of Burtt's character-izations. Exploring how Machiavelli and the English republican the-orists approached civic virtue can offer a way to update this historical theme.[5] According to Skinner, Machiavelli believed that republican citizens understood the law in such a way that their private interests were channeled in a manner that benefited the public good (Skinner, 1983: 10). By educating individuals' desires and by accommodating their private interests within the political institutions and constitu-tion, neo-Roman republicanism endeavored to regulate individuals' ends in such a way that the expression of those ends reflected a robust commitment to civic virtue. Burtt argues that Machiavelli believed that a properly constituted republican education would instill the necessary virtues in individuals so that they resisted corruption, and instead sought goods that supported liberty and the common good (Burtt, 1990: 28). Machiavelli maintained that, if education failed to instill any good in the citizenry, the republic risked falling into corruption (*The Discourses*: Machiavelli, 1965: 496). Machiavelli believed that individuals had to be taught certain substantive values, such as *prudenza* (prudence), *animo* (courage), and *temperantia* (tem-perance), which would help them secure and maintain republican liberty by informing and channeling their narrow self-interest (*The Discourses*: Machiavelli, 1965: 290–4). Thus, for Machiavelli, civic virtue had to be cultivated actively so that individuals would identify their own good with that of the republic. This would serve to keep corruption at bay by ensuring those individuals' narrow private and self-serving interests did not take priority.

Furthermore, as Burtt informs us, the writers of *Cato's Letters* believed that citizens were capable of fusing their interests with those of the public good because they saw the connection between the protection of their liberty and the promotion of a politics based on the common good. For these writers, personal liberty is secured and enhanced when citizens understand their common fate, and thus their private interests find expression in a way that promotes civic virtue (Burtt, 1990: 37). Moreover, a similar sentiment is expressed by Harrington in *Oceana*, where he argues that, if constitutions are constructed in an appropriate manner, individuals' common interests will have priority over narrowly tailored private interests (Harrington, 1992: 172). Harrington advocates a political structure that serves to channel the various private interests of those found within the community so that they play off one another and become "public" in nature once they are exposed to the political (Harrington, 1992: 416; also see Burtt, 1990: 26). The thought here is that the republican state must play an active role in channeling an individual's private, and sometimes narrow, interests into something that is more collective and aimed at a wider audience through its distinctive institutions.[6]

Thus, by combining these two "psychologies" of neo-Roman civic virtue, modern republicans must understand and accept that individuals have narrowly tailored private ends that are important and valuable to them. Moreover, as argued above, republicans must understand that individuals desire to pursue those ends that they decide are important and valuable. However, modern republicans must also understand that, without an active effort to shape these ends and properly constituted republican institutions for them to manifest themselves, individuals will pursue their own narrowly tailored self-serving ends without deference to what is best for the community, which may cause domination to rise. By creating public structures that allow individuals to express their own self-interest without subjecting others to arbitrary interference, modern republican ideals seek to regulate the way in which individuals' private interests manifest themselves by molding and conditioning those ends. Furthermore, modern republican forms of civic virtue and citizenship will help to cultivate and shape individuals' desires in a distinctive republican fashion so that they value and express their ends in a manner consistent with the enjoyment of nondomination. This point ties in with my discussion of modern republican civic virtue from the last chapter. It follows that modern republican forms of civic virtue and citizenship, when combined with properly constituted republican institutions, help individuals to acquire the necessary skills that must accompany republican liberty as nondomination.

Many liberals, including Kymlicka, will object to the regulation of individuals' life plans in this way because, as we observed above, it requires the public ranking of individuals' conceptions of the good by the state. The thought is that modern republicans seek to regulate the ends that people value whereas liberals seek to regulate simply how individuals behave in expressing their ends. Republicans seek to go farther than liberals on this point because leading a nondominating life will not only enhance individuals' overall ability to pursue their chosen goals, but also make certain goods available to them that will deepen and enrich their lives. Not surprisingly, some individuals' life plans will be more successful than others in upholding the principles of nondomination. Those life plans that subject others to arbitrary interference will be challenged by the republican state in two important ways. In the first way, dominators will be forced to account for their domination and may face the sanctions of the state if they do not cease to interfere arbitrarily with others. As in the liberal approach, the republican state will regulate how individuals act and insist that they abide by the principles that govern social justice. In the second way, and in contrast with liberalism, a modern republican state will seek to interact with and inform individuals' conceptions of the good so that they not only develop an ability to cast their ends in a non-dominating manner, but also have the opportunity to enrich their lives and attain certain goods that can make their lives better. Where liberals distinguish between an individual qua citizen and qua individual, modern republicans make no similar distinction.

Without a determined effort by the republican state to create suitable institutions and to instill a rich sense of civic virtue in the lives of the citizenry, individuals, when pursuing their own narrowly tailored self-interest, may not recognize the necessary wider commitment that they must have in order to cast their life choices into ones that do not dominate others. These institutions, when combined with a robust account of civic virtue and citizenship, help individuals find a way in which they can publicly express those things that they have chosen without interfering arbitrarily with others. Moreover, in doing so, their lives are enriched because they enjoy the benefits of republican liberty and are secure from domination in their pursuit of their goals. Thus, republican institutions cultivate specific forms of civic virtue and citizenship that seek to inform and shape the private interests of the citizenry. The republican state, through its institutions, seeks to accommodate the private interests that individuals express in a manner that channels them into the common good. In this manner, civic virtue, citizenship, and republican laws and institutions combine to help citizens formulate a politics of the common good that contains within it their own narrowly tailored needs and desires that can be revised in ways that are consistent with republican liberty as nondomination. Based on the principles of nondomination, modern republican ideals help to secure the necessary conditions of liberty for individuals so that they can successfully make their own life choices free from any arbitrary interference. When combined with republican liberty as nondomination, civic virtue becomes more than the ability to place the common good above that of individuals' own narrowly tailored self-interest, which is tied to classical republican models. Within modern republicanism civic virtue becomes the ability of individuals to cast their ends in a manner that does not subject others to arbitrary interference. In making this move, the common good is served, albeit in an individual manner. In direct confrontation with liberal neutrality, then, republicans believe that the state must necessarily play a distinctive regulative role in the lives of individuals as they develop and use their autonomy to revise their life choices. This regulation goes beyond how individuals act, and instead seeks to affect what they value. In later chapters, I will further explore how republican liberty as nondomination regulates the choices available to individuals without restricting their liberty, and the resulting distinctive version of civic virtue. For the moment, however, I will continue to examine the implications of modern republicanism's abandonment of liberal neutrality in light of state perfectionism.

Social or state perfectionism?

Thus far, I have argued that the modern republican project characterized by liberty as nondomination violates liberal neutrality because it regulates the life choices available to individuals by favoring nondominating ones. It does so through distinctive and substantive ideals and institutions that seek to instill modern republican versions of civic virtue and citizenship in the lives of individuals so that they can recast their final ends into ones that do not subject others to domination. In this manner, then, the state plays a more active and substantial role in the lives of its citizens than in Kymlicka's liberal approach. This type of state interference does not, however, curtail the liberty enjoyed by republican citizens because any interference they experience tracks their interests and is not arbitrary. Closely related to Kymlicka's objection to the public ranking of values is his belief that any approach that abandons state neutrality raises the specter of state perfectionism. This section will explore this objection and consider an account of modern republican state perfectionism that does not undermine the liberal approach.

Against state perfectionism

In addition to the liberal context for autonomous choice that keeps the state from unnecessarily interfering in individuals' capacity to revise their life choices, Kymlicka maintains that the liberal state must be free from any elements of state perfectionism. Although it is not clear that he can fully defend his approach from such charges, Kymlicka's sentiment is that any state perfectionism would be overly coercive. For Kymlicka, state perfectionism occurs when the state favors some life choices over others by publicly ranking their intrinsic value. In other words, state perfectionism promotes certain choices available to liberal citizens over others that potentially may threaten the development of autonomy and individuality and restrict liberty. According to Kymlicka, the "state should be neutral amongst conceptions of the good, in the sense that it should not justify its legislation by appeal to some ranking of the intrinsic worth of particular conceptions of the good. The role of the state is to protect the capacity for individuals to judge for themselves the worth of different conceptions of the good life" (Kymlicka, 1998b: 133). Thus, in being neutral, Kymlicka claims the liberal state does not publicly rank the intrinsic value of the choices that individuals make. Instead, he believes such moves lead to a vibrant cultural marketplace where individuals can choose, question, and revise the choices that they have made. This ensures that a liberal society has a rich and diverse culture that provides the necessary options for meaningful and rewarding self-determination for its citizens. For Kymlicka, any state that actively intervenes in the cultural marketplace to encourage or discourage any particular conception of the good irreparably damages the capacity for true self-determination (Kymlicka, 1990: 217).

However, this is not to say that notions of perfectionism do not have an important role in a cultural marketplace free from state interference. Kymlicka argues that the choice is not between perfectionism and neutrality, but rather between social or state perfectionism. The cultural marketplace, which for Kymlicka should be free from state perfectionism, will be saturated with social perfectionism. Individuals will be able to determine for themselves how they rank the intrinsic value of each of the conceptions of the good in the cultural marketplace as they choose, question, or revise their choices. Kymlicka places his faith in the cultural marketplace's ability to create and maintain the social conditions necessary for individuals to judge, choose, and revise their life plans according to their own preferences (Kymlicka, 1990: 219). In this manner the survival of different ways of life will depend on their relative merits or failures as judged by rational and autonomous individuals, rather than by the state. It is only within such a system of liberal state neutrality that individuals can evaluate fairly, and without undue state coercion, the various life plans available to them. For Kymlicka, perfectionist ideals are important, but are better situated in the realm of civil society free from any state coercion (Kymlicka, 1990: 219). In other words, a public marketplace dominated by the state is an inappropriate forum for the sort of genuinely shared deliberation and commitments necessary for the reflective capacities of individuals to flourish. This is because it represents a coercive apparatus with immense authority and the capacity to force the public ranking of values of different ways of life on unwilling or unsuspecting individuals. For Kymlicka, state perfectionism "serve[s] to distort the free evaluation of ways of life, to rigidify the dominant ways of life, whatever their intrinsic merits, and to unfairly exclude the values and aspirations of marginalized and disadvantaged groups within the community" (Kymlicka, 1992: 178–9).

In the presence of state perfectionism and the public ranking of values, individuals may be forced against their will to defend publicly the various choices that they make as they seek to formulate their life plans. Kymlicka's objection centers on his belief that state perfectionism may require individuals to acquire the skills and rhetoric necessary to articulate positions which are often deeply personal and sometimes controversial given prevailing public sentiments. If people fail to account for their choices publicly, they may be subject to state action that could force them to abandon their chosen ends against their will. In other words, to be compelled to defend certain ways of life may force unwilling individuals out of their chosen paths and into ones they do not value (Kymlicka, 1992: 179). The upshot is that many valuable ways of life may be severely limited, which has the potential to lead to a tyranny of the majority as some lifestyles are eliminated because individuals either cannot or will not defend them publicly. This "dictatorship of the articulate," as Kymlicka calls it, inherently discriminates against those who are inarticulate or come from backgrounds that do not value the publication of their own conceptions of the good. This could be true especially in today's pluralistic society, where many different social groups are either not understood by the majority or are denied appropriate forums in which to articulate fully their positions. This would stifle open and free evaluation of various life choices and reinforce the position of dominant ways of conceiving the good (Kymlicka, 1992: 179).

Another problem brought about by the public ranking of the value of different forms of life is that disadvantaged groups may have to change fundamentally their way of life as they seek to explain certain cultural understandings that may be in conflict with some views held by the state. They would have to explain themselves using a language and discourse that may be alien to them, and any adjustment that they make to be intelligible may force them to shift their way of life in a manner to which they object (Kymlicka, 1992: 180). This type of state hegemony would make it difficult for many of today's diverse groups to survive if they did not adopt some, or all, of the conceptions of the good put forth by state perfectionism and the public ranking of values forced on them by the coercive apparatus of the state. However, Kymlicka admits that these threats may also take place in a cultural marketplace free from state interference. "Insensitivity and prejudice will be problems no matter which model we choose, since both models reward those groups who can make their way of life attractive to the mainstream" (Kymlicka, 1992: 180). Kymlicka maintains that the state's power will likely complicate interactions in the marketplace because it will be in a dominant position to choose the forums and timing for any minority view to be aired.

In his view, the neutral liberal state gives culturally diverse groups more latitude when it comes to promoting or defending their life plans in the cultural marketplace. A cultural marketplace free from state coercion will allow minority groups to select the forum and time that suits their way of life best when they seek to engage others. Importantly, Kymlicka's position on state perfectionism in the cultural marketplace does not mean that the state should be absent completely from the cultural marketplace. For Kymlicka, the state has a responsibility to interfere in the cultural marketplace to counteract any biases against minority views, especially when doing so redresses any historical or social biases (Kymlicka, 1992: 181). Furthermore, the state has a positive duty "to protect the cultural conditions which allow for autonomous choice" among diverse groups. This positive duty does not mean that the state abandons liberal neutrality, in fact quite the opposite. In seeking to protect culturally diverse groups, the state is enforcing its neutrality by not forcing them to accept dominant viewpoints. It does so because the overriding goal of the state is to ensure that the conditions exist for meaningful, autonomous choices that occur within a marketplace that is free from any state coercion through perfectionism or the public ranking of values (Kymlicka, 1992: 183).

As mentioned above, in many ways modern republicanism has perfectionist qualities that would seem to violate liberal neutrality. At its most basic, perfectionism begins with a prior ideal of human excellence. It follows that it is the responsibility of a perfectionist state to promote that ideal so its citizens are assisted in their endeavors as they seek this excellence. For some, as we saw earlier, autonomy or *eudaimonia* are forms of excellence that are representative of perfectionists' views. Indeed, some liberals, such as Joseph Raz, believe that it is the responsibility of the state to "create morally valuable opportunities, and to eliminate repugnant ones" as it promotes autonomous choice (Raz, 1986: 417). The state, then, abandons any claim to neutrality and promotes those ideals and values that reflect a certain belief in what is valuable and what is not. However, for other liberals, such as Rawls, human perfection should be pursued by individuals using their basic liberties to their own ends without any undue coercion from the state (Rawls, 1971: 328–9). Even for some republicans, such as Pettit, perfectionism is not something that should be promoted by the state. In making his argument Pettit asserts that the republican state reflects a "shared-value" neutrality (Pettit, 1998: 91; also see Pettit, 1999: 291). The implication of his position seems to support Kymlicka's contention that republicanism and liberalism are compatible. In the next section I pick up on these points and expand on the type of perfectionism found in modern republicanism.

Modern republican state perfectionism

As for modern republicanism's perfectionism, throughout my argument I have explored how republican liberty as nondomination manifests itself in the lives of individuals in two interdependent forms of power, reciprocal and constitutional. Inherent within these forms, which serve to protect and secure individuals from any actual or threatened arbitrary interference, are ideals and values that may challenge or distort some individuals' final ends. On the one hand, the reciprocal form of power is not solely defensive but rather carries with it progressive responsibilities. Within the reciprocal form of power, individuals can exercise their capacity for autonomous choice and choose those ends with which they identify while realizing that others have the right and capacity to do the same. They understand that their commitment to republican liberty as nondomination means that those ends that they choose must not be cast in a manner that interferes arbitrarily with others.

On the other hand, from a legal and institutional standpoint, the constitutional power of republican liberty seeks to promote the ideals of nondomination and secure the agent against any arbitrary interference. Once again, the state plays an active role in interfering in the lives of individuals by promoting certain perfectionist values that regulate individuals' ends. In many ways, however, these elements are not wholly perfectionist in that, while they do require individuals to attain certain substantive values and virtues like the ones discussed above, they also secure them from any actual or threatened arbitrary interference and thus enhance the choices available to them. Therefore, it is my belief that at most they can be said to be quasi-perfectionist because they secure a vast range of final ends which are consistent with republican liberty, which individuals can pursue while securing them from any interference that does not track their interests. Within republicanism, being a nondominator, that is, being an individual who casts her ends in a manner that does not interfere arbitrarily with others, is valuable and individuals have good reasons to pursue it.

For republicans, individuals do not solely pursue nondominating ends in order to fulfill their obligations to social justice. Rather, they pursue these ends because their lives will be enriched and the full range of benefits that accompany republican liberty as nondomination will be available to them to utilize. Upholding the values and virtues associated with republican liberty as nondomination and abiding by the state's legal and institutional framework will free individuals from any actual or threatened arbitrary interference that will enhance their position to make their own informed decisions. Each of these benefits increases the range of options open to republican citizens because their liberty is more secure and they have an improved subjective and intersubjective status. Moreover, as Machiavelli argued, the successful cultivation of republican versions of civic virtue and citizenship not only made the citizenry more secure in its freedom; it also made republics increase in wealth and opportunity (*The Discourses*: Machiavelli, 1965: 329). For modern republicans, the thought is that if individuals can exercise their freedom from a more secure and empowered position, their ability to make informed and meaningful choices among a range of nondominating options is enhanced. In other words, within a modern republican approach individuals not only have an increased opportunity to make meaningful choices from a range of options, they have both the power and security to do so. However, I believe that those elements that appear perfectionist within modern republicanism are not as strict as some perfectionist accounts in that a wide range of final ends is available to individuals as long as those final ends cannot be said to dominate others. Modern republicanism secures a vast range of permissible final ends for individuals to pursue while maintaining the necessary commitment to nondomination.

Where Kymlicka's approach limits the state's role in the cultural marketplace to one of maintenance and promotion of certain minimalist liberal values, the republican approach requires the state to interfere in the available life choices within the cultural marketplace in a distinctive, yet non-arbitrary, manner. Thus, a key difference between the liberal and republican approach is not over whether or not the state will play some type of regulative role in the lives of individuals, because both approaches share this feature. What separates the two approaches are the reasons behind and the scope of that role. The liberal state regulates the cultural marketplace in two main ways to ensure that individuals and groups are treated fairly and that justice prevails. In the first way, the liberal state relies on social perfectionism between individuals and groups. Within the liberal cultural marketplace, the relative success of life choices will in large part depend on whether or not they are rewarding and attractive to individuals and can attract and sustain adherents. In the second way, liberals believe that the state should play a limited role in regulating the cultural marketplace by not actively endorsing any conception of the good nor coercing individuals' choice of what to value. Instead, the state regulates the behavior and actions of individuals to ensure that they fulfill their obligations to social justice.

By contrast, the republican state seeks to interfere, albeit in a non-arbitrary manner, with individuals' choices in both of these areas by, first, promoting certain substantive ideals and values that constitute individuals' understanding of the reciprocal power of nondomination, and, second, regulating the available life choices through the constitutional power of nondomination in the cultural marketplace and challenging dominating values and ways of life. At the heart of these differences is republicanism's alternative conception of liberty as nondomination that holds that interference that tracks individuals' interests does not restrict their freedom. Therefore, through its quasi-perfectionism and the public ranking of values, modern republicanism abandons liberal neutrality without restricting the freedom enjoyed by its citizens. In non-arbitrarily interfering with individuals' life choices, the republican state enhances their position to pursue their own choices while maximizing nondomination.

Republican quasi-perfectionism: threat or enhancement?

But what of Kymlicka's objection that this type of state interference may negatively affect some individuals and groups? The first of his objections centers around his belief that state perfectionism may force some individuals to defend the various choices that they make publicly as they seek to formulate their life plans. This may force these individuals to acquire the skills and rhetoric necessary to articulate deeply held, and sometimes controversial, positions. Kymlicka's fear is that being forced to account publicly for their life choices may subject people to state action which may force them to abandon their chosen ends against their will (Kymlicka, 1992: 179). Thus, some valuable lifestyles may be eliminated because individuals either cannot or will not defend them publicly. The fear is that modern republicanism may dominate those individuals and groups by forcing them to acquire republican values and ideals in registering their interests to others and the state. Kymlicka is especially concerned about the effects this type of state perfectionism may have on today's multicultural and pluralistic society where many different social groups are either not understood by the majority or are denied appropriate forums in which to articulate fully their positions (Kymlicka, 1992: 179). The second of Kymlicka's objections centers around his belief that state perfectionism and the public ranking of the value of different forms of life may force disadvantaged groups to change fundamentally their way of life as they seek to explain and account for certain cultural understandings that may be in conflict with some views held by the state or other dominant forces within the cultural marketplace. Kymlicka fears that, to do this, these individuals and groups may have to explain themselves using a language and discourse that may be alien to them, and any adjustment that they make to be intelligible may force them to shift their way of life in a manner to which they object. For Kymlicka, "there would be an inevitable tendency for minorities to describe and debate conceptions of the good in terms of dominant values, which then reinforces the cultural conservatism of the dominant group itself" (Kymlicka, 1992: 180). Such interference by the state, for Kymlicka, would make it difficult for many of today's diverse groups to survive if they did not adopt some, or all, of the conceptions of the good put forth by state perfectionism and the public ranking of values forced on them by the coercive apparatus of the state.

I think that Kymlicka's concerns are well placed, and modern republicanism must address these issues. However, it is my view that Kymlicka's solutions are undesirable because they would fundamentally undermine republican liberty as nondomination. Kymlicka believes that minority and other traditionally disadvantaged groups should not be forced to account for their way of life to the state or others. Instead, they should be armed with the principles of social justice, protected from would-be interferers, and then allowed to pursue their conception of the good free from state coercion. As mentioned earlier, cultivating and instilling certain instrumental values such as autonomy and individuality, that make it more likely that they will fulfill their obligations to social justice, may fundamentally undermine some ways of life and, thus, some conceptions of the good. For some, the principles of autonomy and individuality are incompatible with their chosen way of life and practicing them qua citizen is undesirable, if not impossible. Asking these individuals and groups to fulfill their obligations to social justice will inevitably affect their conception of the good, especially if their conception of the good is incompatible with liberal principles. As they fulfill their obligations to social justice, they are asked by the liberal state to attain, and abide by, certain values and ideals. The upshot is that the effects on minorities or the traditionally disadvantaged individuals or groups that prompted Kymlicka's concerns remain in a system characterized by liberal neutrality. When fulfilling their obligations to social justice, these individuals and groups will nevertheless have to embrace values and ideals that may be incompatible with their chosen conception of the good and their way of life. They may be forced to adopt an identity qua citizen that fundamentally undermines their identity qua individual. If they suspect that they have been treated unfairly in the cultural marketplace they may have to embrace alien values when representing their demands or grievances to the state. Modern republicans must accept that Kymlicka's concerns are genuine and that every care must be taken to minimize any potential negative effects on minorities and other traditionally disadvantaged individuals and groups. However, the state must be able to communicate on some level with these individuals and groups through its ideals and institutions so that their interests can be accounted for and tracked. Because this issue is of paramount concern to the modern polity, I have devoted the whole of chapter 5 to exploring how modern republicanism copes with this and related issues.

For the moment, it is enough to say that the republican state must take seriously claims by minority and other traditionally disadvantaged groups and must seek to find a common ground upon which to communicate. In modern republicanism, communication is essential to the success of liberty as nondomination. Thus, if these groups or individuals are to reap the benefits of modern republicanism and be secure to pursue their chosen way of life, they must make an effort to be heard in a way that allows the state and others to track their interests. But this effort must work both ways. A modern republican state must listen and register these demands in a manner that respects an individual's or a group's method of communication. Every care must be taken to ensure that this requirement does not subject individuals and groups to domination. However, for republican liberty to secure individuals and groups from domination, each party must be willing to articulate and register just what their interests are so that the state and others can track them. If individuals and groups do not let others and the state know what their interests are, how can their interests be tracked and responded to appropriately without their being subjected to domination? To this end, fair and open access to republican institutions and a common language of citizenship and civic virtue help to ensure that individuals and groups are not subjected to arbitrary interference, whether it comes from other individuals or the state itself. For the state and others to track the interests of all citizens, there must be a sufficient amount of virtue and participation in the forums of the state to register accurately just what those interests are (Pettit, 1998: 87). In other words, without a rich sense of republican civic virtue and properly constituted republican institutions, the maintenance of republican liberty as nondomination is imperiled. The necessary virtues that make up the republican version of citizenship help individuals articulate their own interests to the state and to others who must account for and track them if they are to live truly nondominated lives. Republican citizenship helps to provide a common discourse for individuals to voice clearly and accurately their concerns and demands so that the state and others can register their interests and respond appropriately.

By promoting civic virtue and access to a common language of citizenship, the republican state prepares citizens to play the necessary active role in their own nondomination. To ensure that all individuals and groups have a fair and just opportunity to register accurately their interests to others, the state will seek aggressively to ensure that minorities and other traditionally disadvantaged individuals and groups are secured from the arbitrary interference of others and itself. Modern republicans understand that today's multicultural and diverse society will contain individuals and groups who hold minority or controversial conceptions of the good, and it will seek actively to secure these citizens from arbitrary interference. However, republicans also believe that these conflicting conceptions of the good exist within a marketplace that must resolve disputes and conflict in a conversational manner (Skinner, 1996: 15–16; also see Pettit, 1997: 189). To this end, as I argued in the last chapter, republican versions of citizenship promote the necessary substantive virtues that help individuals not to dominate others, which means that they must learn to account for and track the interests of their fellow citizens so that they can respond appropriately to their demands without dominating them. Moreover, this requirement is placed on all citizens, while the state too must be subjected to rigorous contestation.

In subsequent chapters I will defend this position more thoroughly, but for our present purposes my argument is that the republican state will seek aggressively to end the domination of all of its citizens, especially when certain citizens have been traditionally discriminated against. Furthermore, if my argument is correct, because modern republicanism has mechanisms that are not available to those liberal approaches characterized by neutrality, the republican state will be in a better position to secure and protect these individuals and groups from arbitrary interference. It follows that disadvantaged and minority groups will be more secure in their status and it is more likely that their ways of life will flourish under republicanism. The benefits that accompany republican liberty as nondomination will enhance their position so that they can live their lives free from any interference that does not track their interests. They will be freed from any uncertainty or anxiety that they may experience from any actual or threatened interference that does not track their interests. Likewise, they will not have to plan strategically to defend themselves from arbitrary interference and they will also have an improved subjective and intersubjective status. Their identities will be legitimized by the recognition of their nondominating way of life by others and on their own terms as they seek to register their interests so they can be accounted for and tracked. They will know that it is common knowledge that they are on an equal footing with others, which will enhance their confidence, and they will feel secured and empowered in their position. They not only have the reciprocal power of nondomination on their side, they also have an aggressive and strong constitutional power that protects their liberty from an institutional and legal standpoint to ensure that any interference they encounter tracks their interests.

To be sure, a modern republican state will confront those individuals or groups whose expression of their life choices or conceptions of the good causes the domination of others. The state's constitutional provisions will ask these individuals and groups to account for their domination, and may force sanctions on them if they do not recast their ends in a nondominating manner. To avoid the sanctions of the state, or possible retaliation from those they seek to dominate, individuals and groups must learn to account for and track the interests of others so that they can respond appropriately without dominating them. Once again, the substantive elements of republican citizenship and the virtues that accompany it help individuals and groups to do this. Not surprisingly, like the liberal approach, some conceptions of the good will fare better than others in a state characterized by republican liberty as nondomination. However, it is only those moral doctrines that seek to dominate others which will be confronted by the state. Certain conceptions of the good that fundamentally seek to deny justice and liberty to others must be challenged aggressively by the republican state. By subjecting all life choices to evaluation and exploration, the republican state seeks to ensure that domination is minimized and that individuals and groups are free from any interference that does not track their interests.

It is my belief that modern republicanism will not subject minority or other traditionally disadvantaged individuals or groups to unfair scrutiny by the state, but rather will serve to secure and protect them from more dominant viewpoints that do not track their interests. Those groups who hold more mainstream or prevailing conceptions of the good will also find their practices subject to scrutiny to ensure that they do not interfere arbitrarily in the lives of others, especially minority viewpoints. If they cast their ends in a manner that interferes arbitrarily with others, these individuals and groups will be challenged by the republican state as it protects those who are vulnerable to domination. Kymlicka is right to argue that this type of state perfectionism may eliminate or distort severely some individuals' and groups' final ends. But if the republican state eliminates certain viewpoints that are so rooted in the domination of others that to change how they are cast would fundamentally undermine their viability, then so be it. The republican state must protect its citizens, especially the most vulnerable, from any arbitrary interference. If such lifestyles were allowed to flourish in the cultural marketplace and cause the domination of others, the multiculturalism and diversity found in today's modern polity would be at great risk. Modern republicanism seeks to challenge and root out dominating conceptions of the good in a more robust manner than liberalism. This is not to say that liberals will ignore certain individuals and groups who do not abide by the principles of justice. Kymlicka argues that without violating liberal neutrality, the state must intervene in the cultural marketplace to eliminate bias and other forms of discrimination (Kymlicka, 1992: 181). However, where state intervention in a system characterized by liberal neutrality stops at regulating how individuals and groups behave, the republican state continues by challenging how individuals or groups cast their ends. If they cast their ends in a manner that subjects others to any real or threatened domination, they will be aggressively confronted.

Conclusion

While Kymlicka argues that the intervention by a state characterized by liberal neutrality is necessary to ensure that the cultural marketplace is free from bias and discrimination, he argues that any other regulation must take place below the level of the state. In other words, the state must play a minimal, albeit important, role in maintaining the viability of the cultural marketplace. The state makes no value judgments on the beliefs held in the cultural marketplace. Kymlicka maintains that individual autonomy is best promoted when judgments about different life plans are removed from any political influence from the state. According to Kymlicka, these "opportunities for collective inquiry simply occur within and between groups and associations below the level of the state – friends and family, churches, cultural associations, professional groups and trade unions, universities, and the mass media" (Kymlicka, 1990: 220–1). Ultimately, for Kymlicka, liberal "neutrality requires a certain faith in the operation of non-state forums and processes for individual judgments and cultural developments and a distrust of the operation of state forums for evaluating the good." Although he admits that nothing he has said "shows that this optimism and distrust are warranted," he still maintains that the cultural marketplace must remain free from unnecessary state intervention because the state itself may suppress freedom, which in turn may deny individuals and groups the opportunity to choose, question, and revise their life plans (Kymlicka, 1990: 222). Kymlicka believes that, before the state is brought into the cultural marketplace, the forums of civil society for nonpolitical debate should be improved to ensure that all groups have real equality and free access to the marketplace. According to Kymlicka, "culture which supports self-determination requires a mix of both exposure and connection to existing practices, and also distance and dissent from them. Liberal neutrality may provide that mix but it is not obviously true" (Kymlicka, 1990: 223). My contention is that Kymlicka's faith in the operation of non-state forums and processes and his skepticism about state interference are misplaced because they weaken the ability of the state to intervene meaningfully in the cultural marketplace. I believe that the modern republican approach that I have defended in this chapter provides the necessary mix he desires in a more vigorous and robust manner than an approach that remains neutral. Without sacrificing key liberal aims, modern republicanism secures individuals and groups from arbitrary interference through its distinctive and substantive ideals and institutions. Individuals are free to revise their conceptions of the good rationally while being protected from any actual or threatened arbitrary interference from others.

Kymlicka is right to suggest that liberals and republicans should be allies in confronting the many problems facing the modern polity. However, if these approaches are indeed to be allied, Kymlicka must embrace a more substantive account that abandons liberal neutrality.

Moreover, I believe that I have demonstrated good reasons for Kymlicka to embrace the republican approach that I have presented because it is not hostile to autonomy and individuality, nor does it prevent or deny individuals the ability rationally to revise their life choices. Instead, modern republican institutions, and the civic virtue and citizenship that support them, regulate and channel the private desires of citizens in a manner that secures society as a whole from arbitrary interference, and on another level secures the individual from domination. It does so through distinctive and substantive ideals that regulate individuals' final ends in a manner that is consistent with the maximization of liberty as nondomination. My argument is that the republican approach outlined above is more successful than the liberal approach characterized by neutrality in confronting the difficult issues experienced by the modern polity. In the next chapter, I will further explore modern republicanism to see if the same can be said when compared with the *political* approach of John Rawls.

4

Without Regret: The Comprehensive Nature of Nondomination

Introduction

A striking feature of John Rawls's political liberalism is his contention that his theory of "justice as fairness as a form of political liberalism" is compatible with classical republicanism (Rawls, 1996: 205). Rawls is careful, however, to draw a firm line between republicanism and what he calls civic humanism. For Rawls, civic humanism is that strain of thought often associated with forms of Aristotelianism which maintains that individuals are social or political beings whose essence is only fully realized in democratic societies that have widespread political participation. This participation in the democratic process is seen by Rawls as a form of the good life itself and is thus a comprehensive moral doctrine (Rawls, 1996: 206). This is not true of his view of classical republicanism, which he takes "to be the view that if the citizens of a democratic society are to preserve their liberties which secure the freedoms of private life, they must also have to a sufficient degree the 'political virtues' (as I have called them) and be willing to take part in public life" (Rawls, 1996: 205). Acknowledging the role played by Machiavelli in influencing republican thought, Rawls also names Alexis de Tocqueville as another republican exemplar (Rawls, 1996: 205, esp. n. 37; de Tocqueville, 1969).[1] Rawls maintains that a central feature of republicanism is the claim that a society that wishes to be free needs a widespread commitment to participate in democratic processes by an active and informed populace. Rawls's conception of republicanism ties the maintenance of liberty to the existence of certain virtues and ideals exhibited by an informed and active citizenry which willingly takes part in public life, which in turn prevents those who wish "to dominate and impose their will on others" from doing so (Rawls, 1996: 205). Although Rawls invokes Tocqueville as a more appropriate representative of republican thought than Machiavelli, implicit in his reading of republicanism are ideals and values that read very much like modern republicanism, especially in his adoption of the language of domination.

Notwithstanding Rawls's use of the language of nondomination, he maintains that, because republicanism does not presuppose any partially or wholly comprehensive philosophical, religious, or moral doctrine, it is not in "fundamental opposition" to political liberalism. Moreover, Rawls's claims are even more interesting in light of his recent efforts to clarify political liberalism (Rawls, 1999). Rawls maintains that a "family of liberal political conceptions of justice" informs the content of public reason, which is then presented independently of any wider comprehensive doctrine (Rawls, 1999: 143). For Rawls, the determining factor in whether or not an approach is consistent with the political nature of public reason is the extent to which it satisfies the three conditions of a political conception of justice: that it only applies to the basic structure of society; that it is independent of any wider comprehensive doctrines; and "that it is articulated in ideas consistent with the political culture of a constitutional democratic society" (Rawls, 1996: 223; also see Rawls, 1999: 143). Since Rawls is clear that there is no one fixed conception of justice that satisfies the requirements of public reason, his belief in republicanism's compatibility with his project is a possibility. All Rawls needs to demonstrate to make his claim accurate is that republicanism is consistent with each of the three conditions of a political conception.

Rawls's belief in the compatibility of the two approaches is strengthened by certain similarities that make his claims plausible. Both republicanism and Rawls adopt a similar political sociology as their starting point.[2] Rawls assumes that the modern democratic polity is characterized by a fact of pluralism that brings equally legitimate, but yet incompatible, life choices into conflict with one another (Rawls, 1996: xviii–xix). Machiavelli's neo-Roman republicanism (or, in Rawls's language, classical republicanism) also accepted that there was a plurality of interests within the state. For neo-Roman republicans, the key was to accept this as the starting point and work to constitute the institutions of the state to cope with the many legitimate differences found in the republic (Garver, 1996: 206–8). There is also an overlap in the language utilized by the two approaches. For example, both Rawls and republicans often invoke the ideals of citizenship, civility, virtue, and reciprocity in their respective discourses. Other similarities in methodology and outlook will be important to consider as well, and I will take these up in due course.

Despite these similarities, in this chapter I will argue that modern republicanism does not collapse into just another political approach compatible with Rawls's. Moreover, I will also explore the claim that even Rawls's political liberalism fails to establish firmly that it qualifies as a strictly political approach in the way that he intends it to do. In pursuing these issues I will challenge Rawls's assumptions about republicanism while further developing my overall argument. I will demonstrate that modern republicanism does not meet the first two of Rawls's political requirements and thus that my approach necessarily stands in fundamental opposition to his political project. This is because the values and ideals that support modern republicanism cannot be confined to the political domain as Rawls defines it (Rawls, 1999: 134). Furthermore, by exploring the differences between the two approaches, I will argue that modern republicanism does presuppose certain comprehensive values that support republican liberty as nondomination without being classed as the sort of civic humanism that Rawls derides.

The essence of my argument is this: if modern republicans were to restrict their approach in the way Rawls advocates, republican liberty as nondomination could not be realized. Put another way, as a strictly political approach, modern republicanism is fatally cut off from the necessary ideals and values that constitute and support republican liberty as nondomination. It follows, then, that the central argument of this chapter is that if Rawls maintains that justice as fairness is a purely political conception, he cannot hold that there is no fundamental opposition between his approach and modern republicanism. My argument here is that, despite the similarities between the two projects, modern republicanism cannot be reduced to political liberalism without undermining its alternative conception of liberty. In seeking to support my claim that modern republicanism is not reducible to political liberalism, I will first concentrate on one crucial point which illustrates the incompatibility of the two approaches: Rawls's regret that the "political virtues" of political liberalism may have the same effect on individuals as the comprehensive doctrines of Kant and Mill (Rawls, 1996: 200, 1999: 135). I want to ask whether Rawls's admission, and his subsequent "regret," render the two projects incompatible in light of the demands of republican liberty as nondomination.

There is another reason why I argue that the modern republican approach I have presented is not reducible to political liberalism. Earlier I mentioned that it was my belief that modern republicanism does not satisfy two of Rawls's three conditions for a political approach. I believe that the modern republican approach presented here is consistent with Rawls's third condition of a political conception – "that it is articulated in ideas consistent with the political culture of a constitutional democratic society" (Rawls, 1999: 143). As we have seen, constitutional democratic principles have traditionally played a role in classical republican thought, often developing within a republican context and being seen by many as inextricably linked (Sunstein, 1993). To this end, then, I make no claims about the third of Rawls's conditions, which specifies a political conception. However, this issue is an important one to the extent that Rawls believes that political liberalism is a form of deliberative democracy. This point will certainly be of interest to modern republicans since their approach contains certain elements of deliberation. For Joshua Cohen, in its most simple formulation, a deliberative democracy is a state "whose affairs are governed by the public deliberation of its members" (Cohen, 1989: 17). In a more general sense, deliberative democracy is often taken to mean one whose citizens limit those reasons that they give to ones which others can accept when participating in the forums of the state.[3] What makes this issue relevant is the extent to which Rawls utilizes political liberalism to inform his model of deliberative democracy. If we follow his argument, modern republicanism too would be able to inform deliberative democracy in the same manner as political liberalism. While this point is certainly relevant to my overall argument, I will not directly take up this question here. At the moment it is enough to say that, if I am right that modern republicanism does not satisfy the first two of Rawls's conditions for a political conception, it follows that it will not inform deliberative democratic models in the same manner as political liberalism. This realization becomes important to my argument not just in this chapter, but also in later chapters when I take up a modern republican account of pluralism and speculate on what forms modern republican institutions, civic education, and social norms will take. As for this chapter, the first section broadly overviews Rawls's project while highlighting what I see as a considerable weakness. In the following section I will examine two main reasons why modern republicanism is incompatible with Rawls's political project.

Political liberalism and the "Idea of Public Reason"

As mentioned earlier, Rawls's recent work represents an effort to move away from a conception of justice that relies on any wholly or partially comprehensive moral or philosophical doctrine. Instead he argues for a theory of justice that is more limited in scope, is free-standing, and presupposes no particular wider doctrine (Rawls, 1996: 40). Rawls's attempt to recast his earlier work is based on some important assumptions about the political culture of modern demo-cratic society. Firstly, Rawls maintains the "diversity of reasonable comprehensive religious, philosophical, and moral doctrines" is a permanent feature of today's democratic culture (Rawls, 1996: 36). This "fact of reasonable pluralism" leads us to Rawls's second assumption, that "a continuing shared understanding on one compre-hensive religious, philosophical, or moral doctrine can be maintained only by the oppressive use of state power" (Rawls, 1996: 37). Finally, since no one reasonable comprehensive doctrine can be affirmed by all citizens, the theory of justice affirmed by today's democratic society must be limited to what Rawls calls "the domain of the political" and the values that support it (Rawls, 1996: 38). In proposing political liberalism, Rawls is attempting to strengthen the stability of his theory of justice in the face of many incompatible conceptions of the good (Mulhall and Swift, 1996: 175). Of paramount concern to Rawls is that, in a society characterized by pluralism, any theory of justice that is comprehensive in nature can only be enforced by the coercive use of state power (Rawls, 1996: 36–8). The overriding goal of Rawls's project is to construct a theory of justice that is free from any reliance on reasonable comprehensive doctrines so that today's democratic society, which is characterized by a "fact of reasonable pluralism," can be stable and secure justice. The benefit of this move, according to Rawls, is that by recognizing that there are many reasonable, but yet incompatible, comprehensive doctrines present in today's democratic society, and by constructing a theory of justice that is free from any reliance on any one comprehensive doctrine, individuals will be able to affirm a more limited and freestanding conception of justice that, as outlined above, only applies to the basic structure of society.

In unpacking Rawls's approach, several key points emerge that have a crucial bearing on my argument in this chapter. The first point concerns what Rawls means when he speaks of a comprehensive doctrine. As I discussed earlier, for Rawls, "a doctrine is fully com-prehensive when it covers all recognized values and virtues within one rather precisely articulated scheme of thought; whereas a doctrine is only partially comprehensive when it comprises certain (but not all) nonpolitical values and virtues and is rather loosely articulated" (Rawls, 1996: 175). Thus, religious, moral, and philosophical doctrines are comprehensive when they inform and permeate the ideas and values of either the whole or part of an individual's life. Alternatively, as mentioned above, a political conception has three main features: it is meant to apply "solely to the basic structure of society" (the main political, social, and economic institutions); it "is presented independently of any wider comprehensive religious or philosophical doctrine;" and it "is elaborated in terms of fundamental ideas viewed as implicit in the public political culture of a democratic society" (Rawls, 1996: 223; also see Rawls, 1999: 143). The next important point Rawls makes is in qualifying the type of individual that he is interested in as one that is "reasonable." For Rawls, persons can be said to be reasonable "when, among equals, they are ready to propose principles and standards as fair terms of cooperation and to abide by them willingly, given the assurance that others will likewise do so" (Rawls, 1996: 49). Furthermore, for Rawls, "the reasonable is an element of the idea of society as a system of fair cooperation and that its fair terms be reasonable for all to accept is part of its idea of reciprocity" (Rawls, 1996: 49–50). It follows, for Rawls, that reasonable individuals must also be prepared "to recognize the burdens of judgment and to accept their consequences for the use of public reason in directing the legitimate exercise of political power in a constitutional regime" (Rawls, 1996: 54). Thus, reasonable individuals will have a political identity that embraces the political principles of justice, and a nonpolitical identity that affirms some religious, moral, or philosophical comprehensive doctrine. These identities may, of course, overlap, but there is no requirement that they do so. The key is that, in accepting the burdens of judgment and the ideals that govern the idea of public reason, these individuals will interact in the political sphere qua citizens. These individuals recognize the "fact of reasonable pluralism" and accept that others may hold different, but equally legitimate, comprehensive doctrines.

Broadly speaking, Rawls's argument thus far is that, given the fact of reasonable pluralism, in fundamental issues concerning justice and in matters affecting the basic structure of society, reasonable individuals who have accepted the idea of public reason and embraced the burdens of judgment will affirm a political theory of justice which is embedded within the public political culture of democratic society. This "overlapping consensus," as Rawls calls it, helps to ensure that the polity remains stable because the political conception of justice does not affirm any comprehensive religious, philosophical, or moral doctrine. It follows, then, that reasonable individuals will bracket off their nonpolitical comprehensive doctrines when engaging in political issues because any reliance on those doctrines would be tantamount to giving them priority over other reasonable comprehensive doctrines. Thus, an individual embraces one set of values qua citizen and may embrace another set of values qua individual. On the one hand, individuals in their nonpolitical lives are free to follow their own religious, philosophical, or moral comprehensive doctrines and these inform and guide this part of their lives (Rawls, 1996: 215). On the other hand, because these individuals are reasonable and accept the requirements of public reason and the burdens of judgment, they can embrace a set of "political virtues" which are for the most part instrumental in nature and aimed at supporting only "a political conception of justice for the main institutions of political and social life, [and] not for the whole of life" (Rawls, 1996: 175). In other words, for Rawls, the justification of the use of political power must be in terms that uphold the idea of public reason. It follows that individuals must engage in the political domain as citizens who have bracketed off their comprehensive identities.

At the center of Rawls's project is the idea of public reason which specifies at the most fundamental level the "basic moral and political values that are to determine a constitutional democratic government's relation to its citizens and their relation to one another" (Rawls, 1999: 132). The upshot of Rawls's project is this: given that the justification of the use of public power must be in terms of public reason, each individual must engage in the public domain qua citizen prepared to give and take public reasons "according to what they consider the most reasonable conception of political justice" (Rawls, 1999: 136). In this way, individuals uphold the criterion of reciprocity and the terms of fair cooperation and, by doing so, are deemed to be "reasonable" in Rawls's scheme. Put another way, qua citizen, reasonable individuals only propose those policies that they sincerely believe reasonable others can accept. For their part, they accept the reasons that others have offered under the understanding that the others have done the same. Following the legal enactment of the resolution of the issues, all parties agree to abide by the outcome whether or not it is in accordance with their respective beliefs (Rawls, 1999: 137). Of course qua individuals they are also moved by non-public reasons connected to their non-public conceptions of the good. However, according to Rawls, they have a moral duty to uphold the political principles and treat others with the necessary degree of civility and reciprocity that supports the idea of public reason (Rawls, 1999: 136). There may be a problem of stability because of the possible conflict between public reason and reasons of the good. However, for Rawls the political principles of justice are such that individuals can accept them from within their own reasonable conception of the good.

To support his project, Rawls asserts that his approach will need a meaningful set of values and virtues that support the political theory of justice and the institutions that accompany it (Rawls, 1996: 195). These virtues help to form the civic qualities that government officials and citizens need to uphold the demands of public reason in their associations with one another when engaging in constitutional issues and matters of public justice. These "political virtues," as he calls them, are not said to be based on any wholly or partially comprehensive doctrine, and thus do not violate the political project. Moreover, he contends that these virtues are general in nature and restricted in scope. In making this move, Rawls assigns the right priority over the good. However, this does not mean for Rawls that the good itself is completely abandoned. He explicitly states that the "right and the good are complementary," and what is needed is a combination or mix of the two that will support a political conception of justice that places the right prior to the good (Rawls, 1996: 173).

A curious aspect of Rawls's argument in this regard is his reference to Benjamin Constant's famous distinction, briefly discussed earlier, between the liberty of the moderns and that of the ancients (Constant, 1988: 309–28). As we saw, Constant believed that, even though the liberty of the moderns was paramount over the liberty of the ancients, no just system could completely abandon the institutional priorities of ancient liberty. Constant states that the "institutions must achieve the moral education of the citizens" (Constant, 1988: 328). Furthermore, he states that the teaching of ancient virtues to citizens "enlarges their spirit, ennobles their thoughts, and establishes among them a kind of intellectual equality which forms the glory and power of a people" (Constant, 1988: 327). It is clear that Constant believed that, although modern liberty was paramount, the institutional priorities and the nonpolitical moral development of the liberty of the ancients had important roles to play. In other words, without nonpolitical moral development, Constant believed that modern liberty alone was insufficient to maintain meaningful freedom. It is my belief that, on this point, Rawls does not follow Constant closely enough (Constant, 1988: 327; Rawls, 1996: 173). It may be that Rawls simply chooses to overlook Constant's thoughts on the subject since, as mentioned above, within Rawls's scheme the political virtues must be general in nature and narrow in scope. However, I believe that Rawls's project fails to constrain completely the political virtues.

Furthermore, as I will argue, I think that Rawls too recognizes this shortcoming despite his belief that neither the idea of public reason, nor the political virtues that support it, violates his project.

Constraint, regret, and overspill

As we have seen, for Rawls, the political virtues are general in nature, restricted in scope, and are not based on any wholly or partially comprehensive values. For example, education, for Rawls, will have to include certain virtues, such as toleration and an appreciation of the constitutional and civil rights that support political institutions. Furthermore, Rawls's definition of "reasonable" seems to suggest that individuals must have the ability to stand back and reflect rationally on not only their own life choices, but also those of others if they are to act with the necessary civility and good faith in upholding the idea of public reason. When engaging with others in the political sphere of society, Rawls believes that citizens should "think of themselves ideally as if they were legislators following public reasons" and should be able to explain their reasons to others in a manner which they will understand (Rawls, 1999: 135–7). However, it is difficult to see how individuals whose final ends are not committed to this type of reflection will be able to do so without acquiring a high degree of moral autonomy, something that Rawls explicitly believes violates the political project (Rawls, 1999: 146). Even some of Rawls's supporters, like Eamon Callan (1997), believe that Rawls's approach fails to completely restrict itself to the domain of the political. Callan suggests that the political virtues that support the fair terms of cooperation in the idea of public reason have the effect of bringing "autonomy through the back door of political liberalism" (Callan, 1997: 40).[4] Callan's objection notwithstanding, Rawls admits that "certainly there is some resemblance between the values of political liberalism and the values of the comprehensive liberalisms of Kant and Mill." But for Rawls this is unavoidable and the consequences must be accepted with "regret." Even if these virtues are general in nature and narrow in scope, as Rawls claims, he implicitly admits that they will affect an individual's nonpolitical moral development (Rawls, 1996: 199–200; see also Rawls 1999: 135, esp. n. 16). The political virtues, by Rawls's own admission, cannot be completely constrained in the manner that his theory requires. Put simply, Rawls believes that these political goods will spill over into the nonpolitical, albeit this is a matter of regret.

For modern republicans, however, such an overspill would not be viewed as something that has to be regretted: it is something that is sought actively and has positive benefits. These values and virtues help to constitute the liberty experienced by individuals in the republican state. They help mold and condition individuals' life choices and instill in citizens a rich sense of civic virtue and citizenship so that they uphold the civility required by nondomination. In other words, I believe that the virtues and values associated with modern republicanism substantively contribute to individuals' nonpolitical moral development, and all without Rawls's "regret." In the next section I will take up this argument and outline two main reasons why modern republicans cannot accept Rawls's position.

Modern republicanism: comprehensive or political?

In the last section I suggested that Rawls fails to live up to his promise to constrain the political virtues so that they do not negatively affect the comprehensive nonpolitical doctrines of some members of society. Furthermore, I argued that Rawls implicitly recognizes this point by "regretting" the impact that certain features of political liberalism will have on the lives of some in society. In this section I want to take a closer look at the implications of Rawls's admission and highlight two important features of modern republicanism that demonstrate the incompatibility of the two approaches. Building on my argument in the last chapter, I want to explore how modern republicanism violates Rawls's claim that any political approach will be neutral in its aim. Next, I want to explore the implications for modern republicanism of Rawls's belief that individuals and groups should bracket off their comprehensive identities when entering the political sphere. On this point I want to suggest that modern republicanism does not countenance Rawls's distinction between the political and nonpolitical and thus is more sensitive to claims from feminist and difference theorists who complain that this split reinforces barriers to equality and liberty for certain individuals and groups (Young, 2000).

In both of these areas, if modern republicans restrict nondomination and the ideals and institutions that support it in the way Rawls's project requires, the benefits to citizens who know themselves to be free from the uncertainty and anxiety caused by domination will be fundamentally undermined. For nondomination to be maximized, the virtues and values associated with it must take root in the whole of society, which includes both the political and nonpolitical domains. In other words, the virtues and values associated with modern republicanism must be such that they affect the whole of an individual's life, not just the political part of it. This point ties into one I made in chapter 2 about Rawls's theory of reciprocity. That point focused on how Rawls intends the idea of reciprocity to be one whose reach does not extend beyond the political and is utilized to support the idea of public reason. In political liberalism reciprocity cannot be promoted on the grounds that treating others with it will make individuals better people in terms of their final ends. Instead, promoting reciprocity as a political good is something Rawls believes will make it more likely that citizens will uphold the idea of public reason and fulfill their obligations to social justice. Thus, the state does not promote the political idea of reciprocity on the grounds that adhering to it will make citizens better individuals or else it risks violating its neutral stance toward conceptions of the good (Rawls, 1999: 135–8; also see Rawls, 1996: xlvi–xlvii, 16–17, and 49–50). This point obviously ties into my discussion of liberal neutrality in the last chapter, where I argued that modern republicanism has certain quasi-perfectionist qualities and thus cannot be said to be strictly neutral.[5]

Modern republicanism and neutrality of aim

Rawls maintains that political liberalism upholds the ideal of liberal neutrality because the political virtues are distinguishable "from the virtues that characterize ways of life belonging to comprehensive religious and philosophical doctrines" (Rawls, 1996: 195). Even though these virtues are political, they may be regarded by some as goods themselves, but this still does not violate their neutrality because they do not affirm any religious, philosophical, or moral comprehensive doctrine (Rawls, 1996: 202–4). Rawls is careful to qualify the type of neutrality he is defending. To be sure, because the political virtues and justice as fairness as a political doctrine are goods they are not neutral in a procedural sense. The institutions of the state and the political virtues do presuppose some forms of public political goods, but since they are goods nonetheless there is no neutrality of procedure (Rawls, 1996: 202). Another sense in which political liberalism is not neutral for Rawls is in its effect. Rawls maintains that some forms of the good life will fare better than others, while some may come into conflict with the structures and principles of the state. Because of this, the state is likely to favor some forms of moral character over others, while encouraging certain moral political virtues (Rawls, 1996: 194). Rawls does defend political liberalism as a doctrine that displays a neutrality of aim. In other words, the aims of justice as fairness are neutral because it is a non-comprehensive doctrine that seeks a common ground to provide citizens with equal opportunities to pursue permissible conceptions of the good life (Rawls, 1996: 190–5). Among these permissible conceptions of the good life, political liberalism makes no judgments about the relative worth of the decisions made by reasonable individuals. Central to this assertion is Rawls's belief that a political conception of justice is compatible with reasonable comprehensive moral and philosophical doctrines.

In this respect, an important question for my purposes in this chapter is whether or not modern republicanism displays this same neutrality of aim. It is my belief that modern republicanism fails Rawls's "neutrality of aim" test because its aims are not neutral in the sense that nondomination and the reciprocal and constitutional forms of power that support it actively challenge some individuals' final ends and seek to eliminate or change those ends that lead their adherents to interfere arbitrarily with others. Furthermore, the republican state recognizes and promotes certain nonpolitical goods that support the principles of nondomination as a central ideal. However, these goods are not restricted to purely political goods in the same way as in Rawls's project. In the last chapter I argued that the republican state must abandon any claims to neutrality by advocating and supporting certain substantive ideals, institutions, and versions of civic virtue and citizenship that support and maintain the principles of nondomination. The ideals and institutions of nondomination can be said to be quasi-perfectionist in nature and are relevant to the whole of an individual's life. To this end, the republican state will set up certain procedures and forums in a distinctively republican manner. It will interact and adjudicate between the many moral traditions that comprise the republic in a distinctive and substantive manner guided by the principles that support republican liberty as nondomination. In doing so, the quasi-perfectionist elements of republican citizenship and civic virtue educate individuals in the distinctive and substantive ideals of nondomination which stress some goods over others. Individuals will realize the reciprocal and constitutional power of republican liberty because it regulates or shapes the ways in which they evaluate their needs. By recognizing these essentially common goods as legitimate ends for the state to promote, modern republicanism abandons neutrality of aim and stands in contrast to Rawls's political liberalism.

Within modern republicanism, by understanding their liberty as the lack of arbitrary interference in their life choices, citizens believe themselves to be free to pursue their own ends according to whatever conception of the good they may have in light of the regulative nature of nondomination. Nondomination as a political principle, as I argued above, will inevitably affect certain nonpolitical beliefs and character traits. But the only fixed ideal of human excellence that it promotes is that of an individual's ability to express her ends in a manner that does not subject others to arbitrary interference. The state, through its ideals and institutions, will promote actively those activities aimed at securing the republican context for choice. That is, the state will seek to ensure that individuals are free from any arbitrary interference so that they themselves can decide those things that are valuable and those things that are not as long as their choices are consistent with liberty as nondomination. Living such a nondominating life enriches individuals' lives and helps them to "do well" on their own behalf (Skinner, 1984: 219).

If republicans were to accept the thrust of Rawls's neutrality, the maximization of nondomination would be hampered. The aim of a state characterized by the ideal of freedom as nondomination is to promote those ideals and values that support republican liberty in both the basic structure and the whole of society. It follows, then, that a modern republican state advocates certain character traits such as civility and civic virtue through strong forms of citizenship that combine with particular republican ways of doing things to enhance the position of its citizens and secure the republican context for choice. A modern republican state seeks to provide open and inclusive forums where relevant matters can be adjudicated and resolved. When certain comprehensive doctrines challenge the principles of nondomination by subjecting individuals to arbitrary interference, the state will act with the bias of republican liberty as nondomination to secure liberty and maintain the republic. Rawls argues that, because the types of goods supported and promoted by political liberalism are not comprehensive in nature and have neutral aims, justice as fairness is a political doctrine. In contrast, as I argued above, modern republicans maintain that nondomination and the comprehensive values that support it are not value-neutral.[6] In other words, the substantive principles of nondomination are biased in a distinctive republican manner that favors life choices that do not interfere arbitrarily with others. Thus, the modern republic promotes the values and ideals that support such lifestyles and seeks to deny dominators the power to interfere arbitrarily with others. Moreover, the institutions of the state and the processes and procedures it follows will also be influenced by the bias of nondomination and this will inevitably affect individuals. On this point, there is nothing in modern republicanism that would suggest that the state should "regret" such an act. Throughout I have argued that there are certain benefits attached to nondomination that enhance an individual's capacity to make meaningful choices in light of their final ends.

As I argued above, the type of republicanism that I defend is not the same as the republicanism associated with civic humanism. In that account, human flourishing is tied specifically to the development of the self into an ideal type within a certain type of community characterized by democratic self-government. However, there is less specificity in the republicanism outlined in my argument. The particular ends that individuals pursue are not tied to their flourishing in a singular specific fashion or to their realizing their true nature as political animals. The regulation of these ends is not about a specific activity; it is about a range of activities that can be said not to dominate others. It is about securing individuals from any interference that does not track their interests. This, in turn, brings them certain benefits that are not available under a system characterized by the ideal of freedom as non-interference. These benefits increase the range of activities available to individuals who are secure in their liberty and free from the uncertainty and anxiety that may accompany the ideal of freedom as non-interference. These citizens know that they are on an equal footing with others and can look them in the eye. Each of these benefits increases the range of options open to republican citizens because they are more secure in their liberty. This thought is also mirrored in Machiavelli's belief that the republican commitment to the cultivation of civic virtue, citizenship, and the common good allowed republics to increase in wealth and opportunity, and, more importantly, to be more secure in their liberty (*The Discourses*: Machiavelli, 1965: 329). Thus, those elements that appear perfectionist within republican thought are not as strict as some perfectionist accounts. Within a state characterized by modern republican quasi-perfectionism, a wide range of final ends is available to individuals as long as those final ends cannot be said to involve the domination of others. Furthermore, citizens who attain the character traits and skills associated with republican perfectionism will be better able to "do well" by themselves.

These elements are, as I argued in chapter 3, at most quasi-perfectionist in nature because, while republicans have a firm idea of what types of ends are acceptable – those that do not involve the domination of others – they also believe that the character traits associated with modern republican quasi-perfectionism secure a wide range of final ends available to individuals to pursue unhindered by the state or others. Within modern republicanism, being a nondominator, that is, being an individual who casts her ends in a manner that does not interfere arbitrarily with others, is an ideal of human excellence. However, there is nothing metaphysical or mysterious about republican liberty, nor does it appeal to some rigid *a priori* idea of what individuals specifically should do to flourish or "find themselves" (Skinner, 1984: 217). Thus, the quasi-perfectionism inherent in the republican approach is about securing those conditions that allow individuals to determine what is valuable and what is not within a vast range of final ends that cannot be said to dominate others. Moreover, in promoting these quasi-perfectionist elements without regret, modern republicanism recognizes that certain life choices support nondomination better than others, and thus acts to secure republican liberty so that all citizens can pursue their own chosen ends free from arbitrary interference. Because the substantive values and virtues that support nondomination do affect the nonpolitical lives of individuals in the republican state, modern republicanism can be said to be, according to Rawls's definition, at least a partially comprehensive doctrine.

This is not to say that a modern republican state has recourse to unlimited state activity in the lives of its citizens. Nor does it mean that the state will not tolerate competing conceptions of the good. A modern republican state must not itself be a dominator and must be constituted with this in mind. Pettit has rightly argued that significant limits must be placed on a republican state since there is always the risk that it may become a dominator itself (Pettit, 1998: 95; also see Pettit, 1997: 76–7). Here again, civic virtue and participation play a positive role in checking the power of the state and ensuring that it does not dominate. Modern republican values and ideals must be subjected to constant and rigorous efforts of contestation which not only ensure that they respond to the various demands placed on them, but also help to educate those citizens who place these demands on the state in the ways of government and of a varied and pluralistic society (Pettit, 1997: 230–4). However, just as individuals can become corrupt and seek to dominate others, the state too can become corrupt and seek to dominate those it is supposed to protect. The state must track the interests of its citizens and ensure that they are free to choose, question, and revise their life choices without arbitrary interference either from others or the state. Without certain institutional arrangements and substantive forms of modern republican virtues and values, there is always the risk that the state will increase its power over the citizenry. I will pick up on this idea further in chapters 6 and 7. Now, I turn to the second of my key objections to Rawls's project.

Tracking values and the wide view of public culture

The second problem associated with constraining modern republican-ism in the manner that Rawls's theory requires is that republican liberty as nondomination not only needs to permeate the whole of society if it is to be successful, it also needs substantive inputs from the whole of society without individuals being forced to bracket off their comprehensive ideals (Miller, 1995: 447; also see Burtt, 1992: 162–3). If the republican state is to maximize liberty as nondomination, individuals cannot be asked to bracket off their comprehensive ideals. Another related problem is that, if some individuals are unable (or unwilling) to bracket off their comprehensive ideals, Rawls leaves us to ponder how they will fulfill their moral obligation to the idea of public reason and attain the necessary skills and virtue it requires without fundamentally altering their beliefs or being labeled "unrea-sonable" (Rawls, 1999: 172–3).

Rawls's liberal state asks individuals to bracket off their compre-hensive beliefs when interacting with the state over issues of basic justice, and instead embrace a political identity. However, insisting that individuals bracket off these ideals fundamentally undermines the republican effort to track their interests. Even though republicans fully understand the importance of individual decisions, they also recognize and appreciate the inability to bracket completely private preferences from public exposition (Burtt, 1992: 162–3). Rawls's reply to this type of charge is to introduce the "wide view of public political culture" which contains a proviso stating that individuals may bring their own reasonable comprehensive doctrines into the public sphere "provided that in due course public reasons, given by a reasonable political conception, are presented sufficient to support whatever the compre-hensive doctrines are introduced to support" (Rawls, 1999: 152–6; also see Rawls, 1996: li–lii). In other words, Rawls believes that reasonable individuals should make every effort to embrace public reasoning based on political ideals. However, comprehensive ideals may be introduced insofar as they are backed up by political ideals and, at some point, these ideals begin to merge with political values.

While the proviso has deepened many critics' view of Rawls's project, there seem to be two main thoughts behind this move. First, Rawls is pointing out that sometimes there may be an overlap between political and comprehensive values and that, when such a situation occurs, there is nothing in the wide view of public reason to prevent comprehensive values being introduced. He points out that such an overlap existed when civil rights leaders campaigned for basic constitutional values with reference to their religious (comprehensive) doctrines (Rawls, 1999: 155). What allows such comprehensive reasons to be given is the fact that they can also be justified by appealing only to certain political values such as justice and equality. It just so happened that justice and equality were values that were also found in the civil rights leaders' comprehensive doctrines. Thus, in Rawls's view, justification for such values need not rely on religious grounds and thus, in this example, there is no violation of public reason – there is simply overlap between political and comprehensive values.

Closely related to the first point, the second reason for Rawls's introduction of the proviso seems to be in legitimizing certain motivations behind public reasons. By allowing that certain comprehensive ideals may enter public reason as long as they are replaced by political arguments at some point, Rawls admits that some individuals and/or groups will be motivated by ideals and values that fall outside of the political. For example, an agent may be motivated on religious grounds to oppose the right to an abortion and may enter public debates with such comprehensive ideals driving their passion for the issue. To the extent that they are able to give their reasons in terms of political values, their participation is legitimate and thus they have fulfilled their obligations to social justice. In taking these two points together, Rawls suggests that the wide view of public political culture will actually be beneficial to a state as people are brought out of their comprehensive identities and asked to participate in the common project of public reason. There will be certain educative effects of the wide view of public political culture on public reason as individuals and groups are exposed to other reasonable comprehensive identities (Rawls, 1999: 154).

There are, however, some problems with Rawls's proviso that suggest that individuals or groups will still have to bracket off parts of their identities when engaging in public reason. One problem is that it is unclear the extent to which the proviso will allow *unreasonable* comprehensive doctrines into public reason. If Rawls intends to not extend the proviso to unreasonable comprehensive doctrines, the admission ticket seems to turn on whether or not a doctrine is thought to be reasonable. However, as pointed out above, the line between what is considered reasonable or unreasonable is not always clearly defined in political liberalism. As long as there is confusion over who is and who is not reasonable, whether or not Rawls introduces the proviso, public reason will remain off limits to some. There will still be a considerable number of individuals or groups who, despite the proviso, are going to be asked to bracket off some part of their identity when engaging in public reason. A further problem with such moves is highlighted by Seyla Benhabib. When criticizing the liberal model of the public space, Benhabib maintains that there is a tendency within liberalism to take some controversial issues off the discussion agenda because they may be deemed unreasonable by some (Benhabib, 1998: 74). Another problem is that Rawls gives no time frame for when the transformation from a comprehensive doctrine into a political one is to take place. He believes that such specific time frames are impossible and only adds that such matters should be solved "in good faith" (Rawls, 1999: 153). He does imply, however, that the time frame is going to be longer rather than shorter to the extent that he extols the educational benefits of the wide view of public political culture. We are left to ask, then, if there are certain benefits to allowing comprehensive doctrines into public reason, why we should not make this a permanent feature. In my view, it does seem that the introduction of the proviso has not relieved the pressure on individuals' need to bracket off their comprehensive doctrines (Rawls, 1999: 153). Thus, despite Rawls's concessions, it is not clear to me that anything has really changed regarding the need for individuals to bracket off their comprehensive beliefs. Thus, proviso or not, there is still a sense within Rawls's approach that some individuals will need to bracket off parts of their identity when engaging in the processes related to public reason and that some issues will be ineligible for discussion.

On this point, David Miller has argued that it is essential to the republican project that the state not limit "what sort of demand may be put forward in the political forum" (Miller, 1995: 447). For Miller, a strong version of republican citizenship is the key to engaging in a common debate that addresses the important public questions. The specifics of the republican version of citizenship help to provide the necessary common skills and technologies that are available to all and serve as essential components in effective dialogue. These questions, it is argued, should be settled through open and inclusive discussions utilizing the necessary skills and forums of the republic that hold out the promise of a substantial degree of consensus (Miller, 1995: 444). Groups and individuals that hold competing versions of the good are given the necessary skills and forums to legitimate their claims in the public sphere and to pursue them. However, unlike Rawls, Miller believes that republicanism does not ask individuals or groups to bracket off their nonpolitical identities when debating public matters. Realizing that it is not possible for some individuals to bracket off their nonpolitical identity, Miller maintains that republicans legitimate difference and diversity by encouraging those whose attributes are an essential part of their identity to engage with others in dialogue as themselves, unencumbered or encumbered. According to Miller,

> [t]he republican conception of citizenship, then, places no limits on what sort of demand may be put forward in the political forum. It does not discriminate between demands stemming from personal convictions...and demands stemming from group identity.... In all cases the success of any particular demand will depend upon how far it can be expressed in terms that are close to, or distant from, the general political ethos of the community. It requires of citizens a willingness to give reasons for what they are claiming, but not that they should divest themselves of everything that is particular to them before setting foot in the arena of politics. (Miller, 1995: 447)

Furthermore, Miller states that it is not necessary for citizens to "regard political activity as the *summum bonum* in order to adopt the republican view." Instead, they can embrace a more modest standpoint that holds that "different people can be expected to give [politics] different weight according to their own personal values" (Miller, 1995: 448).

I think Miller's instincts are right on this issue and that a modern republican state would have to follow his lead when it comes to whether or not permissible demands are comprehensive or political in origin. There are, however, two points that need to be made to round off Miller's formulation in light of the modern republican project. The first focuses on the types of interests that are permissible in these forums and the second concerns why a modern republican state needs open and inclusive forums free of the type of bracketing required by political liberalism. The first point ties into one I made earlier with respect to the types of interests that are legitimately promoted in a modern republican state. The permissible ends allowed in modern republican forums must be consistent with republican liberty as nondomination. In other words, where Rawls excludes arguments that are comprehensive in nature, modern republicanism would exclude arguments that seek to cause the domination of others. Arguments or reasons that seek to cause the domination of others will be confronted by the modern republican state and the full range of constitutional measures aimed at eliminating domination will be brought to bear in such cases.

On the second point, whether or not individuals' or groups' points of view have their origins in political or comprehensive identities, the processes and forums of a modern republican state must be prepared to allow such demands to be heard. To this end, if a modern republican state and others are to track an individual's or a group's interests, they must be asked to register their interests as they are, comprehensive or not. In this manner, I believe that modern republicanism is better equipped than Rawls's approach to give individuals and groups the recognition that they deserve and the public legitimacy necessary to register their interests to the state and to others. A citizenry that only registers what its political interests are, especially if these political interests vary greatly from citizens' comprehensive beliefs, cannot sustain nondomination. The key here is the realization that modern republicanism employs nondomination as a tracking value and the understanding that this value must apply to both the form and the content of deliberations. In doing so, individuals are not required to bracket off their comprehensive identities as long as those identities do not subject others to domination. When difficult issues come before a modern republic, all claims must be evaluated in light of the greater republican commitment to nondomination. If the participants in the issue all reach agreement that ensures that no domination can occur through the outcome, then the issue is not about labeling one group or the other unreasonable as political liberalism requires. Modern republican efforts are instead about arriving at conclusions that do not dominate individual or community beliefs. Unlike Rawls, then, republicans have the tracking value of nondomination. In other words, the type of public justification that republicans prefer moves beyond whether or not a belief can be said to be reasonable to whether or not a belief can be said to be dominating. Thus, despite the claims of some liberals, there is a substantive difference between liberty as nondomination and other normative liberal claims (Christman, 1998: 205). The distinction emerges when we consider the differences in using nondomination as a tracking value and not limiting participation to those who are "reasonable."

So far I have pointed out two key differences between political liberalism and modern republicanism. In the first case, modern republicanism cannot be said to be neutral because it stands for the supreme value of nondomination and acts with a particular bias to cultivate certain valuable ideals and virtues that enable individuals to do well. In the second case, where political liberalism seeks to arrive at procedures that all reasonable comprehensive doctrines can agree upon, the modern republican goal is to arrive at procedures that do not dominate any of the comprehensive doctrines present in society, whether or not they are considered to be reasonable. In other words, where Rawls draws the frontier at what is reasonable, modern republicans draw it at what is nondominating. However, my argument in both of these cases highlights another point: the difficulty in delineating between the various spheres necessary in Rawls's project. I turn to this issue in the next section.

Splitting the spheres

Earlier I mentioned that some critics of Rawls's work have argued that his division between the political and nonpolitical has the effect of denying some groups and individuals, especially the traditionally disadvantaged, social justice.[7] Also, it is not clear that Rawls's division between the political and nonpolitical does not place some individuals and groups in a position of domination, something that would trouble modern republicans. I do not want to take up this discussion in its totality here since I address it and other related issues more fully in the next chapter. However, there is one point I want to make on this topic that relates directly to my argument in this chapter and further demonstrates a key difference between the two approaches. The point is this: modern republicanism does not countenance the division between the political and nonpolitical in the same manner as does Rawls. And to the extent that the division is different, it is my belief that modern republicanism is more compatible than political liberalism with the aims of feminists and difference theorists, which in turn makes it more attractive as a public philosophy in the modern world.[8] Many theorists prefer to characterize this split as one between the public and private spheres, and thus the line of demarcation between the state and civil society. As Judith Squires notes

> Politics is equated with the public power of the state. Freedom is equated with the absence of constraint imposed by the state – freedom from political power. Civil society is therefore cast as that sphere of life in which individuals are allowed to pursue their own conception of the good in free association with others. Civil society is "private" in the sense that it is not governed by the public power of the state. (Squires, 1999: 25)

A main complaint from feminists or difference theorists is that such a binary split fails to acknowledge the complex nature of modern life, especially when it comes to certain features, such as family life, which may spill across the frontier into both spheres. Furthermore, such a split also fails to answer some critics who question the "maleness" of what is now thought of as the public sphere.[9] Rawls too acknowledges the difficulties surrounding his position on this matter and defends political liberalism as a doctrine that can cope with these difficult issues (Rawls, 1999: 156–7, esp. n. 58). Rawls characterizes the public/private split as one between the basic structure and the whole of society. As we saw above, the object of political liberalism is the basic structure of society, which comprises the basic political and social structures. Thus, political ideals and values apply only to the basic structure of society, whereas comprehensive ideals and values apply to the whole of society.

Rawls maintains that political liberalism is respectful of the complexities of modern family life and the difficulty of delineating a clear line of demarcation between the political and the nonpolitical, especially in terms of the reach of the coercive power of the state (Rawls, 1999: 156–64). In response to criticism of his initial position in this area, Rawls has recently asserted that the political virtues would extend into the realm of the family when issues of basic justice such as equality are involved (Okin, 1989). Moreover, he maintains that "the family is part of the basic structure, since one of its main roles is to be the basis of the orderly production and reproduction of society and its culture from one generation to the next" (Rawls, 1999: 157). The thought is that the family plays a key role in ensuring the survival of society by its unique role nurturing and developing citizens to fulfill their obligations to social justice. Moreover, the coercive power of the state can be brought to bear to ensure the basic liberties and rights of each family member without violating the political project since their status is guaranteed by the principles of justice that govern the basic structure of society.

This is not to say for Rawls that the state can coercively organize the internal structure of family life, but rather to indicate that there are parts of that structure that are of legitimate concern to the state (Rawls, 1999: 159). For example, as we saw above, Rawls believes that the state can legitimately exercise coercive force when that force is general in nature and narrow in scope and is aimed at the basic structure of society. Thus, the inculcation of the political virtues through civic education becomes a legitimate concern of the state's and it can require that certain restraints are placed on families with respect to their demands to exempt their children from citizenship courses (Macedo, 1995). Such a move, for Rawls, does not mean that the coercive power of the state can enforce a certain structure on the family or govern its internal affairs that do not affect the basic structure of society. Notwithstanding Rawls's response to the feminist critique, the real problem with Rawls's approach is in identifying the areas that the state must abstain from entering. This is made even more complicated in Rawls's scheme since he (rightly) maintains that each individual is entitled to the full protection of the basic liberties and is a citizen first (Rawls, 1999: 160–1). The complications stem from identifying the line of demarcation between, in Rawls's words, the basic structure and the whole of society. In some instances there is no clear indication in political liberalism that there even *is* a line of demarcation since, as Rawls admits, political liberalism penetrates far into family life. In doing so, again it is hard to see how the "narrow scope and generality" of the political virtues can be constrained in the way that Rawls maintains. Moreover, there are good reasons to advocate the permeation of certain virtues and values into family life, especially given what Rawls refers to as the "long and historic injustice to women... [who] have borne, and continue to bear, an unjust share of the task of raising, nurturing, and caring for their children" (Rawls, 1999: 160).

What concerns me is not that Rawls's instincts on this issue are necessarily wrong. Indeed, the problem Rawls is addressing must be of central concern to the modern polity and demands attention. Rather, what this point demonstrates is that his political project cannot be sustained because a clear line of demarcation between the political and the nonpolitical is not possible, nor is it something that should necessarily be reinforced through a polity's public philosophy. If we instead focus on domination and the coercive use of state power to minimize arbitrary interference we avoid the types of problems encountered by Rawls's political project. My position on this issue is influenced in part by the thought of Jürgen Habermas, who traces the development of the public sphere from the time of the high Middle Ages into what he calls the modern social-welfare state. Within this history, the dominance of liberal ideals began to take hold in light of the development of the market economy which extended the reproduction of life "beyond the confines of private domestic power" (Habermas, 1997: 108). Habermas suggests that

> [i]n the first modern constitutions the sections listing basic rights provide an image of the liberal model of the public sphere: they guarantee society as a sphere of private autonomy; opposite it stands a public power limited to a few functions; between the two spheres, as it were, stands the domain of private persons who have come together to form a public and who, as citizens of the state, mediate the state with the needs of bourgeois society, in order, as the idea goes, to thus convert political authority to "rational" authority in the medium of this public sphere. (Habermas, 1997: 107)

We can see how the original idea of basic rights embodied in liberal constitutions began to cleave off an area within the public sphere that was not subjected to political regulation. It follows that within this model there were three separate levels, the first two of which, the private and the public, were thought of as areas protected from state coercion by basic constitutional liberties heavily influenced by liberal political ideas. The third area, that of the political, was a tightly defined area that was the only sphere subject to legitimate state coercion. Like the feminist approach mentioned above, Habermas believes that this model is no longer consistent with the realities of modern life because of the complex way in which individuals and groups communicate in the public sphere. This is even more compounded by the extent to which dominant interests or certain technological resources that favor some individuals and groups over others often distort communication or "publicity" within the public sphere. For Habermas, insofar as such realities have the knock-on effect of distorting the public use of reason, what was formerly the sole domain of nonpolitical public debate is not legitimately the domain of political public debate. The result is that there is an "interlocking of the public and private domains" that brings about a legitimate and considerable overlap between what is considered to be the political public sphere and the nonpolitical public sphere (Habermas, 1997: 108). Modern republicanism ties into Habermas's theory to the extent that both approaches countenance the interdependent and intra-dependent nature of modern public and political life.[10]

What must be important for modern republicans on this issue is that the state can legitimately interfere in certain areas of what was once considered to be the sole domain of the private or nonpolitical public life to the extent that domination becomes an issue in those areas. Put another way, there is a sense within modern republicanism that extends the area of legitimate state interference into what was once the sole preserve of the private and nonpolitical public spheres. Where there is domination present in either (or both) of these spheres it is legitimate for the state to become involved as it seeks to eliminate arbitrary interference. Thus, through constitutional and reciprocal power modern republicans hope that nondomination will permeate the whole of society and be a positive influence on the personal interactions between individuals. Wherever domination exists, whether it appears in the family or far outside of what Rawls refers to as the basic structure of society, a modern republican state will seek to end it. This is not to say that the state can enforce its own will on the private or nonpolitical public sphere. Indeed, such a situation would seem to constitute a case of state domination and something that must be actively opposed. However, as an agency charged by the people with preventing domination and with its constitutional power at its disposal, the state must play an active role in the resolution of any arbitrary interference in these two spheres.

In these types of situations, the benefits of modern republicanism and nondomination can be seen in considering the scope of non-arbitrary state activity in securing and empowering vulnerable agents against domination. In other words, as Pettit states, "those individuals who live at the mercy of others . . . are dominated by those others in the sense that even if the others don't interfere in his or her life, they have an arbitrary power of doing so: there are few restraints or costs to inhibit them" (Pettit, 2001: 137). Thus, the wife who finds instances when the burdens of family life dominate her because her husband (for whatever reason) has a hold over her is not freed from her predicament under Rawls's scheme since not all cases as such will necessarily involve a violation of the basic liberties. For example, think of the woman whose husband has a menacing presence in the family and dominates internal decisions. It may be that he does not physically interfere with his wife, nor does his treatment of her run afoul of any legal restriction. There is nothing in Rawls's approach that would suggest that the state should interfere in this situation in whatever manner. However, within modern republicanism, the ideas and values of nondomination and the benefits that accompany them are likely to interact with such a situation with the goal of minimizing the wife's exposure to domination. Thus, not only will the state's constitutional power be involved; the reciprocal power of the wife is likely to be brought to bear on the non-interfering, but dominant, husband. She will benefit from her improved position of power and increasing confidence knowing that she deals with her husband as an equal and can look him in the eye. Moreover, she has the constitutional power of the modern republican state to back her up. The constitutional power of the state and the wife's reciprocal power work in concert to minimize the level of domination she is exposed to while both forms positively interact with the husband to educate him in the ways of nondomination so that he ceases to be a dominator. The same two forms of republican power will also support a wife who is dependent on her loving husband (Phillips, 2000: 288). It may be that the husband in this case provides his wife with ample freedom in the non-interference model so that she lives a seemingly "free" life. However, to the extent that he holds the power in the relationship and does not track her interests she is in a position of domination and is thus not free in the republican sense. Only by becoming independent of her husband's will does she become free in the modern republican model. Again, there is nothing in political liberalism that would offer any relief to the non-interfered-with, but yet dominated, wife since the line of demarcation between the basic structure and the whole of society is unclear and confusing. By instead utilizing the constitutional and reciprocal power of nondomination, a modern republic avoids such confusion and can seek to minimize the amount of domination in the whole of society without restricting the liberty of its citizens.

Conclusion

In this chapter I have argued that, despite Rawls's claims otherwise and his use of the language of nondomination, modern republicanism cannot be reduced to political liberalism since it fails the first two (of three) conditions of such an approach. This conclusion is despite other similarities between the two approaches such as the evocation of a rich language of virtue and citizenship and a similar political sociology that accepts the difference and diversity of today's society. To the extent that Rawls believes that a number of liberal political conceptions of justice inform the idea of public reason, modern republicanism is not one of them since it does not exist independent of any wider comprehensive ideals nor is it aimed only at the basic structure of society. Thus, despite the introduction of Rawls's proviso, and despite the similarities between the two approaches, it is my belief that modern republicanism fails to satisfy the criteria of political liberalism.

In my view modern republican laws and institutions can only be fully effective if they have a sufficient degree of legitimacy and allegiance among the people and are recognized as the norms of society, not just as the norms of politics. To this end, if the republican state and others are to track individuals' interests, individuals must be asked to register their interests as they are, comprehensive or not. A citizenry that only registers what its political interests are, especially if these political interests vary greatly from its members' comprehensive beliefs, cannot sustain nondomination. Where Rawls is asking individuals to be reasonable, republicans are asking them to be nondominating. The republican state will promote certain character traits and virtues through distinctive versions of citizenship and, in doing so, will educate individuals in the substantive ideals of nondomination. The necessary virtues that make up the republican version of citizenship help individuals articulate their own interests so that the state, and their fellow citizens, can account for and track their interests before responding appropriately. Furthermore, and without Rawls's "regret," these virtues seek to ensure that all individuals act in a nondominating manner and treat others with the necessary civility to sustain the republic.

Using Rawls's own definition of what makes a doctrine comprehensive (or not), the modern republican approach defended here seems to qualify as a comprehensive doctrine and thus stands in "fundamental opposition" to political liberalism. I have argued that the virtues and values that support the republican project necessarily must affect individuals in the whole of their lives, not just the political part of them. If not, the modern republican project cannot be sustained. Moreover, modern republicans believe that the ideals and values that support republican liberty as nondomination must be actively embedded within the whole of society, not just its basic structure. They must permeate the whole of society and not be bound by traditional divisions such as the one between the public and private or that between the political and the nonpolitical. It is my belief that if modern republicanism were to restrain its virtues and ideals in the way that Rawls's project requires, nondomination would be fundamentally undermined.

5

Factions and Diversity: A Modern Republican Dilemma

Introduction

Thus far I have argued that republicanism is a non-neutral doctrine that promotes the values and ideals of liberty as nondomination. For republicans, citizenship, civic virtue, and other forms of participation are goods that have quasi-perfectionist elements that provide stability and are able to command allegiance without actual or threatened domination. To this end, republican citizens are provided with a distinctive republican context for choice that secures the necessary conditions for individuals to choose, question, and revise their life choices. However, at the forefront of the important issues facing republicans is how they will cope with what John Rawls calls "the fact of pluralism" that characterizes the modern world. Modern republicanism will have to demonstrate that nondomination is a fluid doctrine and that the ideals and institutions of the republic can respond to the changing needs and demands placed on it by today's multicultural and pluralistic society. In this chapter, and indeed in the remaining chapters, I will explore these issues and, in so doing, will further distinguish the modern republican approach I have presented from its rival liberal accounts. For if modern republicanism is to be taken seriously, then I must demonstrate that its approach can not only cope with the difficulties confronting today's diverse citizenry, but that it adds something of substantive value to the modern world and offers an improvement upon the liberal standard. Republicans need to bring their theory out of the history of ideas and offer compelling arguments that challenge liberalism's hegemony in contemporary discourse.

In the last two chapters we have seen that, in responding to the "fact of pluralism," liberal theorists have broadly reacted in two related, but yet distinct, manners. On one side, some liberals like Will Kymlicka and Ronald Dworkin have argued that Kantian autonomy and Millian individualism guided by liberal neutrality is the most appropriate way to cope with the many incompatible moral and philosophical doctrines found in today's diverse and multicultural societies (Dworkin, 1977; Kymlicka, 1989). These theorists argue that the values of autonomy and individuality are essential ideals for the development of the self, and that liberal neutrality is imperative to the modern polity if it is to ensure justice and equal respect among the many competing ideas of the good. Furthermore, these liberals believe that the capacity of individuals to form, question, and revise their ideas of the good must be an essential feature of the modern state. On the other side, others, led by John Rawls, have proposed an alternative liberal theory that they believe is more successful in coping with today's pluralism, while at the same time respecting the impossibility or undesirability of autonomy for some people (Rawls, 1996). These theorists argue that, by abandoning comprehensive moral and philosophical claims, a more limited, but yet still liberal, political theory of justice is possible.

However, as I have been arguing, there is another alternative, which, although distinct from liberalism, is compatible with many of its aims. In this chapter I will argue that, although they have largely remained silent, republicans have a distinctive and compelling account of liberty that can cope with the pluralism found in today's modern polity. Such an account is made possible by building on the central assertion that individuals desire freedom from arbitrary interference. By exploring historical republican remedies to the diversity of interests found within ancient republics, I will argue that today's modern polity can seek to secure the necessary conditions of liberty as nondomination and provide the members of its diverse citizenry with the conditions to live their lives according to their own chosen ends. To explore this issue thoroughly, this chapter is divided into two sections. In the first section I will briefly summarize my argument thus far and discuss how a distinctive neo-Roman-inspired modern republican approach to pluralism is possible using nondomination as its central ideal. I will also discuss how nondomination relates to distinct republican technologies that were first proposed by Machiavelli in response to the internal tumults caused by the different and diverse interests found in Rome and later in Florence. In the second section I will seek to bring these republican ideals out of the history of ideas to construct a compelling modern republican response to pluralism.

I will argue that, by securing liberty as the absence of arbitrary interference, a modern republican state can move the liberal project forward by abandoning state neutrality and offering a richer and more robust account of citizenship and civic virtue. In making my argument I will explore what a modern republican approach to pluralism would look like by comparing it with rival approaches and addressing important complaints from its critics. To be sure, my claim is not a historical one, but rather one that seeks to bring republicanism out of the history of ideas to provide a firm foundation for the contemporary claims of modern republican liberty as nondomination. Taken as a whole, this chapter will demonstrate that liberty as nondomination is a resilient and fluid doctrine that can respond to the many changing needs and demands placed on it by a multicultural and pluralistic society.

Discord and diversity: the life and death of the republic

There is a widespread belief that the republican tradition is hostile to difference and diversity as a result of the stress placed on strong forms of civic virtue and citizenship in the hope of reinvigorating public debate in light of the moral pluralism found in the modern polity (Miller, 1995; Sandel, 1996; also see Galston, 1991; Macedo, 1990; Phillips, 2000). The thought is that classical republicanism does not give diversity its due by denying the value of difference and forcing overly robust forms of civic virtue and citizenship onto its citizens. While I think that much of this criticism may be valid in terms of the classical pre-modern version of republicanism, I do not think the same can be said about the account that I have been developing throughout this book. I believe that modern republicanism, with its stress on nondomination and the ideals and values that accompany it, can overcome this type of criticism and offer an account of pluralism that is not only relevant to the modern world, but also attractive, since it focuses on both the intersubjective relationship between individuals and groups and the recognition of agents' identities.

The main thrust of my argument is that, in order to secure and maintain liberty, modern republicans believe that we must be prepared to explore our differences guided by the ideals and values of republican citizenship and civic virtue. In doing so, a modern republican state will promote certain character traits and virtues through distinctive versions of citizenship and will educate individuals in the substantive ideals of nondomination. Importantly, as individuals come to realize the reciprocal and constitutional power of nondomination, the ways in which they evaluate their needs will be shaped in two areas. First, if the state is to track properly the interests of its citizens, then there must be a sufficient amount of virtue and participation in the forums of the state to register accurately just what those interests are (Pettit, 1998: 87). The necessary virtues that make up the modern republican version of citizenship help individuals articulate their own interests to the state and to others who must account for and track them if they are to live truly nondominated lives. Modern republican citizenship helps to provide a common discourse for individuals to voice clearly and accurately their concerns and demands so that the state and others can register their interests and respond appropriately. If individuals are not prepared to let the state or others know what their interests are, how can others or the state not dominate them? By promoting civic virtue and access to a common language of citizenship, the republican state prepares citizens to play the necessary active role in their own nondomination.

In the second area, modern republican citizenship not only educates future citizens in the ways of politics and government, but also teaches them the necessary virtues that help individuals not to dominate others. Not to dominate others, citizens must learn to account for and track the interests of their fellow citizens so that they can properly respond to their demands. They must learn to listen and to attempt to understand why these individuals and/or groups have different values from themselves. In other words, a modern republican state must prepare its citizens to settle their differences in a conversational manner. Furthermore, it must provide them with appropriate forums and procedures for doing so. To be sure, nothing in republican theory suggests that individuals have to agree with or accept alternative points of view. Indeed, they will most often reject the claims of others. But, as I argued earlier, they must first make an effort to listen to and understand their differences so that they do not interfere arbitrarily with them. In short, they must learn to cast their own interests in a manner that does not dominate others. Essential to this endeavor, then, is an effort to account for and track the interests of others which civic virtue and republican citizenship helps them to do. However, republican citizens must understand that nondomination is not a one-way street.

Citizens who live in a modern republican state characterized by freedom as nondomination will have a duty and responsibility not to interfere arbitrarily with others. If they do, the state's constitutional provisions will ask them to account for their domination and may force sanctions on them if they do not recast their ends in a nondominating manner. There can and will be deep disagreements in a modern republican state, but domination must be minimized. To avoid the sanctions of the state, individuals must learn to account for and track the interests of others and to respond appropriately without dominating them. Modern republican citizenship and the virtues that accompany it help individuals to do this. Not surprisingly, some comprehensive doctrines will fare better than others in a state characterized by republican liberty as nondomination. However, it is only those moral doctrines that seek to dominate others which will be confronted by the constitutional power of nondomination. Thus, all competing ideas of the good are tolerated, allowed access to public forums, and tracked as long as they do not arbitrarily interfere with others. Nondomination will not solve all disagreements, nor does it seek to. Indeed it is likely to cause quite a few as citizens actively engage one another as they, and the state, attempt to account for and track the interests of the many competing conceptions of the good held by those who comprise today's modern polity. Some may argue that the inevitable conflict and discord brought about by a population that is constantly engaging with itself will be a strain on stability and threaten liberty. Modern republicans, however, will disagree because, while internal discord and tumults may be threats to liberty, they can also be crucial components of it. Admittedly, nondomination and the effort to end actual or threatened domination in any form is likely to bring difference and diversity out into the open. But it does so in a nondominating manner. The tumultuous, but yet vibrant, society that emerges from such a project is an important component of republican liberty. In order to explore further how modern republicanism can respond to pluralism in a distinct and compelling fashion, I will now look at how Machiavelli responded to challenges to liberty from the different interests that comprised the Roman republic and the Florentine city-state. In doing so, it is my intent to lay the foundation for a compelling modern republican response to pluralism.

Civil discord and stability: Machiavelli's break with the past

A controversial, but yet significant aspect of classical republican theory has been the enigmatic role assigned to civil discord and its relation to stability and liberty. Many Roman writers believed that one of the keys to maintaining a republic was to ensure that there was internal concord. Cicero's *concordia ordinum* was the basis of the belief that the common good took precedence over factional or selfish interest (Skinner, 1990a: 130). Machiavelli challenged this belief by arguing that one of the keys to maintaining republican liberty was a progressive and inclusive effort to tolerate and institutionalize the inevitable clash of internal divisions found within republics. Building on the republican conception of liberty discussed above, a closer look at this debate will be a useful exercise in light of the deep diversity facing today's modern polity. This section will first look at the role of civil discord in republican thought before exploring republican remedies and technologies that were designed to cope with vastly different interests. At the heart of this issue is Machiavelli's belief in the connection between liberty, good education, and good laws and institutions. Using this as our starting point, it is possible to construct a modern republican response to pluralism.

In the opening chapters of *The Discourses*, Machiavelli recounts how the early tumults of Rome were important to the laws and institutions that ensured republican liberty. Machiavelli believed that Rome's liberty was enhanced by the clashes that resulted from the different dispositions of the upper classes and the populace. It was this type of inevitable conflict that was not only necessary for republics, but a healthy sign of a free and prosperous state.

> Nor can a republic in any way reasonably be called unregulated where there are so many instances of honorable conduct; for these good instances have their origin in good education; good education in good laws; good laws in those dissensions that many thoughtlessly condemn. For anyone who will properly examine their outcome will not find that they produced any exile or violence damaging to the common good, but rather laws and institutions conducive to public liberty. (Machiavelli, 1965: 203)

Central to Machiavelli's understanding of Roman liberty was a belief that, although internal discord and conflict required constant vigilance and attention, the resulting political activity and its subsequent influence on the creation of good laws and institutions designed to accommodate the diversity of interests was a necessary strength of republican government. Importantly, it was Machiavelli's belief that education, civic virtue, and the laws and institutions of the state were not only inextricably connected to and dependent on one another, but to liberty as well. Thus, without sufficient levels of education and virtue, the laws and institutions of the state would suffer, resulting in the loss of liberty. Consequently, in republics the maintenance of liberty as nondomination is directly tied to sufficient levels of education and civic virtue. For Machiavelli, then, tumults and internal conflict are not only unavoidable, but their proper management has important implications for the successful maintenance of republican liberty as nondomination.

Machiavelli's republican contemporaries, however, exalted the stability found in the Venetian republic that accorded with the *concordia ordinum* of Cicero and relied on a mixed constitution that vested political power in the nobility. Against the backdrop of intense civil discord among many of the Italian city-states, Machiavelli's contemporaries celebrated Venice and the harmonious coexistence between the classes that became its hallmark and, subsequently, the characteristic most likely to be coveted by observers. Later republicans, most notably James Harrington, seized on Venice's stable and tranquil image and promoted it as the ideal republican model. In *The Commonwealth of Oceana*, Harrington's treatise on republican government, he advocated an elaborate constitutional mechanism based primarily on the Venetian model that would control men's appetite for corruption and avarice through rotating representative bodies (Harrington, 1992: 33). In this way, private differences were controlled and directed into the common good which resulted in a stable and tranquil environment. The constitution of Oceana sought to balance out private interests so that, in many ways, they cancelled themselves out. Such measures, for Harrington, were aimed at structuring society in a narrow and specific fashion that eliminated the tumults of Rome, and instead emulated tranquil Venice.

However, the question of whether to emulate Rome or Venice amounts to a false choice for modern republicans. Although Machiavelli never explicitly acknowledges the pluralism inherent within his world-view, some commentators have argued that implicit within his thought is the basis for a contemporary republican account of difference and diversity (Berlin, 1981: 75; Garver, 1996: 206; Parel, 1992: 111). Machiavelli challenged the belief that there was only one supreme value system. Machiavelli's world was a complex one in which the various humors that comprised his society were in constant conflict with one another, with sometimes disastrous consequences. However, as I argued above, Machiavelli realized that civil society was comprised of many different and sometimes incompatible values and thus challenged the prevailing wisdom of the consequences of tumults and internal conflict. For Machiavelli, according to Berlin, "society is, normally, a battlefield in which there are conflicts between and within groups. These conflicts can be controlled only by the judicious use of both persuasion and force" (Berlin, 1981: 41). In order to secure liberty, then, Machiavelli embraced the benefits that could come of such conflicts if they were controlled and directed in a distinctive republican fashion. For Garver, "Machiavelli discovers in factions the value of diversity and plurality." Furthermore, Machiavelli advocated a republican model that would incorporate these incompatible ends within itself and navigate around them with delib-eration and activity (Garver, 1996: 206–8). Machiavelli's solution to this dilemma was to use history to learn how to deal positively with difference and diversity without risking the security or liberty of the republic. By contrasting the fortunes of Rome and Florence, Machia-velli developed an account of how to cope with diversity and differ-ence by constructing distinctive republican laws and institutions that would channel the dynamic energy created by an active populace.

Rome vs. Florence

Writing in *The History of Florence*, Machiavelli elaborates on, and in many ways seems to contradict, his earlier affinity for civil conflict and internal discord. Florence, for Machiavelli, was a city that was caught between two extremes: it was not entirely capable of preserv-ing its liberty, while being unable to accept servitude (Machiavelli, 1965: 1128). Instead of creating the conditions that would make Florence great, the tumults and internal conflicts brought about misery and servitude for its inhabitants. Even in *The Discourses* we can see Machiavelli's initial affinity for civil discord begin to wane as he seems to contradict himself by suggesting that the internal power struggle between the *grandi* (nobility) and the *popolo* (people) over the agrarian law was one of the causes of the decline in the Roman republic (Machiavelli, 1965: 272–5, esp. 274). Gisela Bock, however, has argued that these differences are not necessarily contradictory, and instead highlight a much more substantive point about Machia-velli's belief in the necessary connection between education, virtue, and the institutions and laws of the republic (Bock, 1990: 181–201).

In his detailed history of the city-state, Machiavelli recounts how time and time again factions seized power only to be plagued by divisive inner conflict which made them susceptible to being overthrown. The resulting conflicts greatly weakened Florence and created the conditions for the population to become corrupt and to be completely at the mercy of the rulers, regardless of who they were (*The History of Florence*: Machiavelli, 1965: 1031). Casting the struggle for power as not only one between the *grandi* and the *popolo*, but also among these classes themselves, Machiavelli continuously recounts how these power struggles tore Florence apart. In book 3 of *The History of Florence*, Machiavelli directly compares the Florentine situation to that of Rome and concludes that, although both cities were beset with similar internal divisions, the outcomes of such divisions were very different. Thus, even though the tumults in Rome and Florence appeared to be similar, they had very different causes and thus their effect on liberty varied (Bock, 1990: 188). "In the two cities diverse effects were produced, because the enmities that at the outset existed in Rome between the people and the nobles were ended by debating, those in Florence by fighting." Furthermore, "it must be that this difference of effects was caused by the different purposes of the two peoples, for the people of Rome wished to enjoy supreme honors along with the nobles; the people of Florence fought to be alone in the government, without any participation in it by the nobles" (*The History of Florence*: Machiavelli, 1965: 1140).

For Machiavelli, then, the civil discord found in Rome differed from that found in Florence because in the case of the former, the resulting remedies – good laws and institutions – were the very strengths and hallmarks of republicanism that he celebrated, whereas in the case of Florence, internal discord led only to violence, death, and ultimately servitude and the loss of liberty. Furthermore, the motivations of the citizens were different in each case, with the Florentines desiring power and the Romans liberty. For Machiavelli, Florence went from slavery not to republican freedom, as the Romans did, but to unrestrained liberty or *licenza* (Parel, 1992: 140–1). It is important to note how differently the Florentines and the Romans conceived their self-interests and the effects this had on their liberty. For the Romans, self-interest was tied to a larger concern for the common good, whereas the Florentines held a narrow and atomistic conception of self-interest that directly contributed to their inability to construct a true republican state characterized by liberty as non-domination. Thus, in Florence, the different groups were always at odds with one another because each pursued its own narrow self-interest without any regard for the interests of the whole (Parel, 1992: 108). Without proper motivation, then, groups became factions and threatened the security of liberty and the maintenance of the republic.

In addition to their different motivations, another key reason for the failure of the Florentine republic, for Machiavelli, was that in Rome suitable institutions were set up to give reasonable expositions of internal conflict so that the diversity and difference found in the citizenry had suitable public outlets. In *The Discourses* Machiavelli argues that essential to the stability of republics are the many public forums and institutions which provide proper outlets for disagreements and differences between the various humors that comprise the republic (Machiavelli, 1965: 211).[1] That Florence lacked proper republican institutions was, for Machiavelli, a key reason for its inability to be free. The lack of appropriate outlets for the disagreements and differences within and among the many factions found within Florence resulted in the uncontrollable and ultimately destructive civil discord that prevented liberty from being realized. In Florence, the constitution and law became the primary instruments of factional conflict, whereas in Rome they became the means of controlling the tumults and calumnies of group conflict (Parel, 1992: 108). The conflicts in Florence also resulted in many citizens becoming disillusioned with the ability of the state to secure liberty and caused them to pursue self-interest and power instead. Thus Machiavelli believed that, in order to maintain liberty, proper republican institutions were essential. Furthermore, if these institutions were to support liberty, they necessarily had to be inclusive and open to the many different interests found within the republic so that vibrant public debates could take place. If republican institutions did secure liberty, Machiavelli believed that individuals would be less likely to pursue their own private self-serving interests, and more likely to respect the common good. An example of Machiavelli's belief in proper public forums and inclusionary government is his prescription for Florence in the *Discourse on Remodeling the Government of Florence*. In this short work, Machiavelli stresses the need for inclusive public bodies comprised of representatives from the various classes and guilds found in Florence (Machiavelli, 1965: 101–15). For Machiavelli, it was important that proper republican institutions were available to the various humors found in Florence because an inclusive and open government would secure the necessary conditions for republican liberty and free the people of Florence from their self-inflicted servitude.

Important for our purposes here is a closer look at how Machiavelli characterizes the different interests and humors that contributed to the conflict in Rome and later in Florence. In light of the many interests that comprise the modern polity, it will be important to ask ourselves if any parallels can be found between the conflicts described in Machiavelli's work and the conflicts found today. Machiavelli often wrote of how the *umori*, or main social groups – the *grandi*, the *popolo*, and sometimes the *plebs* – struggled against one another for power. Indeed, it is this example that he relies on early in *The Discourses* as he celebrates the internal tumults found in Rome between the Senate and the *plebs*, and how the resulting laws and institutions served as the foundation and protector of Roman liberty (Machiavelli, 1965: 202–4). Later in *The Discourses*, Machiavelli further explains the differences between the two groups by stating that the *grandi* have a longing to dominate and the *popolo* a desire to be free from domination (Machiavelli, 1965: 204). Bock maintains that, even in Machiavelli's use of language, we can discern just how his varied view of civil discord manifested itself in his writings and whether or not he was expressing positive or negative opinions:

> The variegated vocabulary he uses in this connection would not seem to leave any doubt as to the negativity of the phenomenon: *discordia* (*civile*), *divisione, odio, inimicizie, disunione, disordine, disparere, parti, sètte* and occasionally, *fazioni* and *contenzioni*. On the other side, to the vision of a well-ordered city he applies a vocabulary that includes such terms as *unione, amicizia, quiete, pace, stabilità, amore* or *amore della patria*. (Bock, 1990: 182–3)

An example of this can be found in the later books of *The History of Florence* where Machiavelli's language turns decidedly negative as he explicitly recounts how the different factions began to divide among themselves, resulting in great tumult and pain to the citizens of Florence. In book 7, Machiavelli expresses disgust at how the *sètte* (sects, factions) began to cause Florence new and more serious problems than the earlier tumults caused by the struggle between the *grandi*, the *popolo*, and the *plebs*. Importantly, the *sètte* were quite distinct from the differences found in the *umori* that had occupied much of Machiavelli's attention in *The Discourses* and earlier parts of *The History of Florence*. According to Bock, "the divisions [were] not between the horizontal class-like *umori*, but between vertical groups such as families (*case*), clans, client groups, [and] patronage systems" (Bock, 1990: 196–7). Machiavelli is careful to point out that the *umori* were unavoidable, naturally occurring groupings that could be controlled by proper laws and institutions. The *sètte*, however, presented a more serious and often fatal problem for republics and needed constant attention (Bock, 1990: 196–7).[2] According to Machiavelli, these types of private and unnatural divisions represented a real threat to liberty and were to be avoided. *Sètte*, or factions which sought power to dominate others and to promote their own private good above the common good, were fatal for republics and resulted in the loss of liberty and thus servitude. It followed that it was only those factions that had a narrow conception of self-interest and sought to dominate others that were a real danger to the republic.

Legitimate difference and diversity

That Machiavelli believed that factions should be avoided does not, however, mean that republicans do not look favorably on diversity and difference. Importantly, it should be remembered that despite the language Machiavelli employed to describe the various interests and differences found within the community, certain conclusions remained constant and are extremely useful for addressing the problems facing a modern polity characterized by deep moral pluralism. For Machiavelli, legitimate difference and diversity were naturally occurring phenomena and the only way to cope appropriately with them was to tolerate and institutionalize them within a true republican constitutional framework that sought to secure and promote liberty (Bock, 1990: 201). An important distinction for Machiavelli was the origin and motivation of the different humors found in the republic, and which kind could legitimately make public claims. For Machiavelli, factions were selfish and unnatural groups who sought to subjugate others to their own private interests and thus represented a real threat to liberty which should be opposed. Different in nature to factions, however, legitimate claims of diversity and difference do not necessarily represent a threat to liberty. Machiavelli believed that internal tumults were inevitable given the different dispositions of the many divisions found within republics. Because such divisions could be fatal to liberty, Machiavelli argued that the best course of action was for the republic to give them appropriate public outlets where their competing interests could find meaningful expression. Additionally, the effects of such an inclusionary government would strengthen the republic because a republic that progressively responded to the challenges presented to it by diversity and difference was one that was the most likely to secure and enhance liberty for its citizens. And it was only in an ideal republic that the different dispositions of the citizenry could find their proper public expositions without threatening liberty. To be sure, difference and diversity are, for Machiavelli, real and constant threats to liberty. However, despite the inherent risks associated with a diverse citizenry, difference and diversity help to form crucial components of republican liberty. "They are both the life and the death of the republic" (Bock, 1990: 201).

Thus, factions brought on by legitimate and naturally occurring difference and diversity can have inherent value for republicans. Machiavelli believed that by bringing competition out into the open so that it could be observed and checked, republics would contain the necessary flexibility and energy to secure republican liberty. For Machiavelli, the Romans found, albeit by accident, "the right means for safely using the energy factions supply" (Garver, 1996: 206). While the aim of some factions may be the promotion of their own narrow self-interests, the result of the activity generated by them can help support the common good when combined with proper republican institutions and laws (Garver, 1996: 207). According to Machiavelli:

Thence it comes that a republic, being able to adapt herself, by means of the diversity among her body of citizens, to a diversity of temporal conditions better than a prince can, is of greater duration than a princedom and has good fortune longer. (*The Discourses*: Machiavelli, 1965: 453)

By factoring in the given nature of diversity and difference, republics have increased flexibility when it comes to securing liberty for their citizens (Garver, 1996: 209). Factions may cause republics to be unstable at times, but they require individuals to keep maximum vigilance and attention, which leads to the creation of good laws and institutions that can offer innovative solutions to the often complex problems brought about by a population defined by difference and diversity.

Good laws and institutions

From the threats to liberty caused by discord and conflict emerge necessary, but yet dynamic, laws and institutions that secure and enhance freedom for republican citizens. The content and forms of these laws and institutions are aimed at preserving the common good and not promoting any private or factional interests (*The History of Florence*: Machiavelli, 1965: 1145–8, esp. 1146). Furthermore, good laws and institutions will affect republican citizens in a positive manner by educating them in the ways of nondomination. Important in Machiavelli's belief in the rule of law is an understanding that no one is exempt from it and that all those who stand before it do so as equals.[3] Echoing Cicero, Machiavelli believed that civic inequality created very dangerous conditions for republics because it resulted in unmanageable conflict (Viroli, 1990: 153). Without civic equality, then, it is easy to see how republican liberty is lost because corrupt factions place their own narrow interests above those of the community (*The Discourses*: Machiavelli, 1965: 306–10, esp. 310). Another important feature of Machiavelli's strong belief in equality is his insistence that all citizens have access to public offices. Without open public access, some citizens may lose faith in the laws and institutions of the republic because they do not see them promoting the common good, but rather believe that they are being used for private gain (*The Discourses*: Machiavelli, 1965: 242). The resulting damage to the republic is twofold. First, the republic loses access to a wide range of good ideas and potentially virtuous citizens, and, second, citizens are denied proper avenues to make demands on the state, which may result in them seeking satisfaction through their own narrow self-interests at the expense of the common good. Returning to the *Discourse on Remodeling the Government of Florence*, Machiavelli argues that, unless public offices are open to the most qualified, and not just those from certain groups or classes, many virtuous and intelligent citizens will be alienated from the government, which may force some to seek power through subversive factions (Machiavelli, 1965: 101–15). Furthermore, in *The Discourses* Machiavelli argues that one of the reasons that the Roman republic survived as long as it did was the openness of public offices regardless of income or group membership. All citizens, rich or poor, were able to make demands on the state to register their interests.

Machiavelli argues that the only positive way to deal with the prevalent difference and diversity found within society is to incorporate all groups into the political system so that they can use republican citizenship and technology to resolve their differences without threatening liberty. To support this claim, Parel maintains that, in a properly constituted republic, diverse social groups can resolve their differences "through the medium of the constitution and the law... so that no group can dominate public affairs or put their own narrow self-interest forward as the only way" (Parel, 1992: 107). In this way, the diverse groups share power and serve as a check on each other. This opens up the possibility that the republic as a whole can provide for the satisfaction of all the relevant groups that constitute it. To this end, the republic encourages the development of citizens from as many different backgrounds and beliefs as possible within the larger scope of republican liberty (Parel, 1992: 107–8). Thus, citizenship, civic virtue, and education all play essential roles in republican government and in the lives of republican citizens. Without widespread civic virtue and citizenship, the laws and institutions of the republic will inevitably be driven by private self-serving interests, and therefore dominate some individuals or groups. The necessary engagement in the machineries of government, in whatever form, ensures that narrow self-serving private interests do not rise to the level of domination and that the common good prevails. Because Machiavelli's faith in the goodness of people was limited, he believed that, unless proper republican institutions were in place, some individuals would seek to promote their own private interests and dominate others, causing liberty to be lost.[4] Isaiah Berlin has argued that Machiavelli believed that "only [an] adequate education can make [citizens] physically and mentally sturdy, vigorous, ambitious and energetic enough for effective cooperation in the pursuit of order, power, glory and success" (Berlin, 1981: 40). Furthermore, certain traits of character are necessary for republics to develop in order to secure republican liberty; these were, for Berlin, not purely instrumental, but moral and ultimate (Berlin, 1981: 57). That is, these values were not merely a means to ensure the state's survival; they were goods themselves and had inherent value since they were related to a citizen's well-being. Thus, within Machiavelli's thought, republics had good and compelling reasons not only to tolerate the diversity found within society, but to develop and exploit the benefits brought on by such differences in order to secure liberty. As in the case of Rome, Machiavelli believed that the various dispositions of the groups that constituted society, when combined with strong and just laws and institutions, yielded a stable yet fluid balance that secured liberty and maintained the vitality of the republic.

Furthermore, as discussed above, Machiavelli envisioned a close and intimate relationship between the laws and institutions of a republic and the citizens that comprised it (*The Discourses*: Machiavelli, 1965: 486). For Machiavelli, an important interdependent relationship existed between the governed and the rules that governed them. Because of this interdependent and intimate relationship, republican institutions and the laws that emerge from them are directly related to the level of education and virtue found in the citizenry and vice versa (*The Discourses*: Machiavelli, 1965: 241). The higher the quality of debate and deliberation, the higher the quality of the law, with respect to republican liberty, that will follow. To this end, the inevitable internal tumults and conflicts that emerge from a population defined by difference and diversity must be channeled by republican institutions into appropriate outlets to produce successful policies that secure liberty and do not dominate while at the same time promoting the common good over private interests (*The Discourses*: Machiavelli, 1965: 421). A tumultuous populace, for Machiavelli, was the logical extension of an active citizenry and thus a manifestation of civic virtue (Skinner, 1978: 181). Thus, republican institutions and laws need virtuous citizens, just as virtuous citizens need good laws and institutions to protect and enhance their freedom. And as discussed earlier, Machiavelli directly correlates the relative goodness of people to the quality of laws and institutions and to the maintenance and security of liberty.

> A Tribune, and any other citizen whatever, had the right to propose a law to the people; on this every citizen was permitted to speak, either for or against, before it was decided. This custom was good when the citizens were good, because it has always been desirable that each one who thinks of something of benefit to the public should have the right to propose it. And it is good that each one should be permitted to state his opinion on it, in order that the people, having heard each, may

choose the better. But when the citizens became wicked, such a basic custom became very bad, because only the powerful proposed laws, not for the common liberty but for their own power, and for fear of such men no one dared to speak against those laws. Thus, the people were either deceived or forced into decreeing their own ruin. (*The Discourses*: Machiavelli, 1965: 242)

Thus, republican institutions and laws are a reflection of the level of virtue found in the population and vice versa. Proper republican institutions and laws help to channel the conflicting interests of the different and diverse humors found among the population while at the same time rendering a free and open society secure in its freedom. A modern republican state characterized by liberty as nondomination is not hostile to pluralism. In fact, it relies on the energy generated by a healthy and diverse population to secure important components of republican liberty. It does so in a distinct yet compelling manner, that not only expects the inevitable clashes of diversity and difference in republican forums, but also in many ways relies on them to help secure republican liberty.

Education and civic virtue form important components of republican versions of citizenship that are directly linked to the quality of institutions and laws that emerge from an active and diverse population. Because certain inherent conflicts and tumults are inevitable, republicans believe that good institutions and laws are essential to the maintenance of liberty. If individuals want security and liberty, given the diversity inherent within society, they need a well-ordered republic to help them achieve them (Parel, 1992: 140). Republicans understand that diversity and difference are real threats to liberty, but they also believe that they play important roles in securing liberty as nondomination. Respecting individuals as citizens, modern republicans believe that appropriate public forums and outlets help channel the dynamic energy of the various humors found within the republic. Because the success or failure of republican laws and institutions is directly related to the cultivation of civic virtue through particular versions of republican citizenship, a rigorous public effort is necessary. Liberty can be threatened by difference and diversity, but it can also be secured by it.

Coping with pluralism

In the section above, I have attempted to outline just how Machiavelli responded to the challenges to liberty caused by the difference and diversity found in ancient Rome and later in Florence. I have argued that important lessons can be learned from exploring how Machiavelli responded to difference and diversity, and that the republican tradition can be helpful in addressing contemporary concerns by stressing the intimate connection between liberty as nondomination, civic virtue, citizenship, and good laws and institutions. In this section I want to build on the lessons of Machiavelli's historical account to provide a firm foundation to the contemporary claims of modern republicanism as a public philosophy. While Machiavelli's experiences with difference and diversity cannot be said to be of the same kind as the radical and deep diversity comprising the modern polity, it is my belief that we can take the main thrust of his thoughts and construct a compelling modern republican account of pluralism. This section seeks to bring Machiavelli's remedies to difference and diversity out of the history of ideas to construct the foundation for a distinctive modern republican account of pluralism.

Lessons from Machiavelli

Modern republicanism takes a different approach to pluralism than liberal accounts by starting with a conception of liberty that conceives freedom as the absence of domination. Accompanying this alternative conception of liberty are necessary and substantive ideals and institutions that constitute republican freedom. In light of its alternative approach, there are three main lessons for modern republicans to take from Machiavelli's experiences with difference and diversity. The first lesson is that modern republicans must not only accept the inevitability of pluralism, but also seek to harness and utilize the dynamic energy created by difference and diversity to help secure and enhance liberty. Just as Machiavelli accepted as given that some individuals and groups hold different, and sometimes incompatible, value systems, a modern republican account of pluralism must also use this as its starting point. By accepting this fact, a modern republican state does not seek to deny the pluralism present in today's society: it accepts it for what it is.

The second lesson that modern republicans must take from Machiavelli's account is that motivations matter. When individuals or groups form factions to promote their own private self-serving ends above those of the community, inevitably domination will rise and should be confronted by the republic. However, this does not mean that modern republicanism opposes legitimate difference and diversity. For example, non-liberal moral doctrines will be able to exist within the republic and participate freely in its forums and help shape the laws and institutions, but only if their non-liberalness does not require the domination of others. If it does, they will be challenged by the state and may legitimately be challenged by others. Individuals and groups within a republican state can be non-liberals, but they cannot be dominators.[5] Those citizens whose ends arbitrarily interfere with others will first be asked to be a part of the deliberation so that all parties to the issue can register their interests with the caveat that their dominating ends are recast before they can proceed. Second, they will be asked to approve and identify with the method and manner in which decisions are made so that they can see that their interests have been tracked, even if they have not been adopted (Pettit, 1997: 198). They will be asked to participate actively in the process so that their interests are fairly and openly registered before being considered along with everyone else's. The state and others will then appropriately respond to their demands and the burden will be on them to explain how their ends are nondominating ones. Furthermore, if they object to the options being considered as dominating ones, they must be prepared to explain why to others and engage in efforts of negotiation to overcome their objections. Individuals and groups who refuse to recast their ends into ones that do not arbitrarily interfere with others will risk encountering either the domination of those they arbitrarily interfere with, or confrontation with the state, which may force sanctions on them if they do not cease to express their ends in a dominating fashion.

The final lesson that modern republicans can take from Machiavelli is that properly constituted institutions can harness the activity and energy created by a population constantly engaging with itself to help maintain and enhance liberty. Thus, modern republicans believe that, given the pluralism present in today's society, a well-constituted republic characterized by liberty as nondomination is the best way forward. For modern republicans, the choice is stark. We can either go down the path taken by Florence: hold a strictly negative conception of liberty, allow individuals or groups to develop into factions by promoting their own narrow self-interest, and thus risk losing liberty as nondomination. Or we can let Rome serve as our model and seek to accommodate a wide range of possible final ends within the scope of nondomination by combining a rich account of citizenship with strong and robust institutions and laws. Furthermore, by understanding and incorporating the intimate and interdependent connection between education, civic virtue, good laws and institutions, and liberty, a modern polity characterized by liberty as nondomination must seek to allow its diverse groups and individuals both the opportunity and access to publicize their interests so that the arbitrary interference can be minimized.

Taken together, these lessons manifest themselves in two main areas. In the first area, on a more nonpolitical and social level, republican liberty as nondomination requires that citizens acquire certain character traits and values through specific forms of citizenship that will assist them not only in their own nondomination, but in their ability to cast their ends in a nondominating fashion. To support the intimate relationship between good citizens and good laws and institutions, the republican approach must contain a robust account of citizenship. These values will help them acquire specific forms of civic virtue that will help them to cast their own life choices in a manner that does not arbitrarily interfere with others. In each of these areas, the pre-modern image of republican citizenship and virtue must be brought into line to reflect the needs and capacities of today's plural populations.

By teaching citizens how to articulate and effectively publicize their interests through distinctive forms of republican citizenship, the republican state does not ask individuals and groups to bracket off their comprehensive identities like political liberalism when determining matters of basic justice. Furthermore, by maintaining that citizens' life choices must not dominate others, the republican state moves beyond comprehensive liberals' insistence on toleration and mutual respect. To be sure, modern republican forms of citizenship rely on more than the mere tolerance of or respect for another's life choices. Republicanism teaches the necessary values and virtues that help individuals and groups ensure that their life choices do not arbitrarily interfere with others, just as it teaches others how not to dominate them in return. Thus, the primary goal of republican citizenship is the inculcation of civic virtue and values aimed at teaching individuals the necessary skills of nondomination and how to cast and express their ends in a nondominating fashion. A republican state characterized by liberty as nondomination requires that individuals not dominate others, just as it requires that the state itself should not be a dominator. In this way, modern republicanism can facilitate alternative power relationships based on nondomination. Individuals and groups must be willing and able to make an effort to discover just what each other's interests actually are. And to do this, all parties to the issue must be willing to sit down, listen, and attempt to understand each other. As stated above, republicans attempt to solve disputes and arrive at mutual understandings in a conversational manner that stresses listening to the other side. Such an effort will help raise the level of trust and increase the amount of civility present within society. For the state, and the citizens that comprise it, to not be dominators they must track the interests of others in society.

However, this does not mean that diverse interests always get their way, or that their wishes or desires are followed blindly. No state could operate in that manner. To track someone's interests, rather, means that their demands must be evaluated and responded to in an appropriate manner that considers just what their interests are in light of the greater republican commitment to nondomination.

In the second area, republican liberty as nondomination requires that fair and strong forms of laws and institutions are available so that the diverse populace has inclusive, open, and nondominating public forums. Inspired by what Machiavelli believed made Rome more successful than Florence, modern republicans maintain that if we are to harness properly the power of diversity and difference and use it to secure and enhance liberty as nondomination, we must have a strong and properly constituted system of fair and just laws and institutions. That is, if we are to harness and channel the energy created by an active citizenry characterized by difference and diversity, a modern republican state must have a well-ordered system of public forums and other governmental institutions available to individuals and groups where they can publicize their interests so that they can then be tracked. Republican institutions must be able to accommodate the various methods and ways in which individuals communicate with one another and must be designed to ensure that all points of view are able to be presented, no matter how encumbered they may be. The ability of the republican state to minimize arbitrary interference in the lives of individuals is dependent on both the laws and institutions and the level of citizenship and civic virtue found in the citizenry. With the goal of ending domination, a modern republican state must have distinct inclusive and open public forums that allow demands from any particular comprehensive moral doctrine. Separating those demands that come from factions from those that come from legitimate diverse moral traditions, the public forums of the republic help to form the common good and secure those individuals and communities from any actual or threatened domination.

Where liberals use mutual respect, toleration, and reasonableness as their regulative values, the republican state uses nondomination. In this way, the modern republican approach is further distinguished from liberalism because it requires more than mutual respect and toleration, and does not limit participation to those who are considered to be "reasonable." As we saw earlier, for some liberals, only those doctrines which can be said to be reasonable can be allowed access to public forums and help determine matters of basic justice. Alternatively, modern republicanism does not seek to limit participation by excluding some members of society who may hold unpopular or controversial views unless these views dominate some individuals' or communities' beliefs. Unlike liberals, then, republicans insist that citizens employ the tracking value of nondomination. In other words, the type of public justification that republicans prefer moves beyond whether or not a belief can be said to be reasonable, to whether or not a belief can be said to be dominating. To help add weight to my claims, in the next section I want to address several complaints about republicanism in light of the pluralism that characterizes many of today's polities.

Is a modern republican account of pluralism possible?

Liberals often complain about republicanism in both its neo-Roman and neo-Athenian forms. As I argued earlier, some liberals, such as Alan Patten, charge that neo-Roman republicanism adds nothing to the liberal state because its values and ideals are instrumental in nature and not obviously more attractive than liberal ones. The thought is that republicans place too much emphasis on active, and thus intrusive, versions of citizenship that may unnecessarily restrict liberty (Patten, 1996: 26, 36 esp. n. 41). This sentiment is echoed by others such as Stephen Macedo and William Galston, who both believe that republicanism's focus on activity is too intrusive into each individual's personal sphere and results in unwarranted interference in their conception of the good (Galston, 1991: 225; Macedo, 1990: 99). Even John Rawls, as I argued in chapter 4, believes that the republican commitment to activity can be troubling, especially if it falls outside of the basic structure of society. My response to this type of criticism has been to demonstrate that the modern republican commitment to activity does not cause the un-freedom of individuals by interfering in their personal identity. Because modern republicans do not see non-arbitrary interference as a restriction of freedom, the real question is not about whether or not this activity is interference. The crucial question for modern republicans is whether or not this activity is arbitrary. And in response to this question, modern republicans would argue that this interference is not arbitrary if it tracks the interests of the people while securing the conditions for them to pursue their chosen ends, as long as those ends are nondominating. The modern republican commitment to activity is centered on the republican belief that citizens wish to be free from mastery to pursue their chosen ends. In other words, they desire freedom as nondomination, and to achieve this they must be willing to be active in letting their interests be known so that the state, and other citizens, can track and appropriately respond to their demands. And, as I argued earlier, this process is best fulfilled by certain republican technologies and a strong commitment to republican versions of civic virtue and citizenship. This highlights the modern republican interdependent relationship between liberty as nondomination, good laws and institutions, and civic virtue and citizenship. With the goal of ending domination, a modern republican state needs to have distinct inclusive and open public forums that allow demands from any particular comprehensive moral doctrine. By separating those demands that come from factions from those that come from legitimate diverse moral traditions, the public forums of a modern republic can help to form the common good and secure those individuals and communities from domination. Moreover, a modern republican state must rely on the dynamic energy created by its diverse communities to help secure and enhance liberty as nondomination.

Another common complaint from liberals is that republicanism has not only an overly narrow definition of civic virtue and citizenship, but also one that is fundamentally biased with respect to cultural minorities and women. Donald Moon has charged that republicanism's versions of civic virtue and citizenship are too stringent because they rely on a strong commitment that not everyone can achieve (Moon, 1993: 148). Furthermore, Moon charges that republicanism relies on versions of civic virtue and citizenship that are rooted in ancient and exclusionary values that carry an inherent bias. Thus, for Moon, republican virtue and citizenship contribute to a privileged status that in its very essence excludes women and minority groups because its fundamental ideals are based on values that are inherently biased. There is no doubt that Moon has a point: the classical republican image of virtue and citizenship was focused on ideals that were inherently biased toward men. Moreover, some republican constitutional mechanisms favored the wealthy aristocracy of a privileged few and sought to protect their status as full citizens while the rest of society existed at a far lower level. For example, the Machiavellian image of virtue is inherently tied to his view of military discipline and the willingness to take up arms to protect the beloved *patria*. Women and minority groups did not figure in the ancient republican image of the citizen.

Moon's complaint ties into another one I touched on in the last chapter. There is, according to Anne Phillips, a widespread belief that the classical version of republicanism "is far from woman friendly" and seems to be one of the worst traditions when it comes to allaying the fears of feminists (Phillips, 2000: 279). The thought goes that classical versions of republicanism reinforced the rigid separation between the public and private spheres. In these accounts, the public sphere was dominated by land-owning males and issues that occurred in the private sphere, such as domestic chores and homely matters, were feminized and denigrated. There is no doubt that all of these images must be taken seriously and emphatically jettisoned if modern republicanism is to be a viable contemporary public philosophy.

But I think that modern republican liberty as nondomination as a foundational objective for a contemporary public philosophy requires as much. Modern republicanism has no time for exclusive elitist approaches to government that limit citizenship and subject large segments of the population to the interests of the few (Pettit, 1997: 96). A modern republican state characterized by nondomination must be one that takes seriously the troubling historical and present realities of the shortcomings of equal treatment of cultural minorities and women. Indeed, the modern republican state must actively seek to address these complaints and redress past injustices of domination. According to Pettit, even though historically freedom as nondomination was only accessible to privileged males, its principles are culture- and gender-free. In short, nondomination makes sense for all individuals, regardless of background or gender. In order to move beyond the pre-modern republican image of civic virtue and citizenship as the privileged domain of propertied males, modern republicanism must progressively seek to end the domination of women and cultural minorities by actively fighting their subjugation (Pettit, 1997: 139–46).

In spite of its pre-modern image of bias, one important contribution modern republicanism can make in seeking to redress its history is to embrace the emphasis on power relationships and recognition that liberty as nondomination requires. Anne Phillips argues that a modern republican approach is something that feminists should take a close look at in terms of furthering their commitment to participatory democracy (Phillips, 2000: 280). Joan Landes makes a similar point when suggesting that feminists should not back away from public participation and that republicanism is a potential ally (Landes, 1998: 2). Thus, for some feminists, the modern republican emphasis on removing domination and dependency via the empowerment of individuals both constitutionally and reciprocally offers hope and a potential way forward. This is especially important given the recent focus on political activity in the public sphere by women and minorities in light of the dominant position held by white men (Fraser, 1998: 331–2). The stress on inclusion, accommodation, and open modern republican forums and institutions will also be attractive to many feminists.

My argument here also ties in with my discussion of Habermas in the last chapter, since modern republicanism shares a similar structural image of the public/private split. However, an important difference is that, with the focus on domination and increasing the power available to vulnerable agents, the traditional image of this division needs to be redrawn to better reflect a public sphere free from domination. However, as Duncan Ivison points out, such moves are possible when we consider the republican focus on the

> maintenance of the maximum amount of space and opportunity for individuals and groups to question and challenge any aspect of institutional, cultural and social life. Public life is thus politicized, made heterogeneous and open to difference and otherness uninhibited by constraints of liberal reasonableness. It follows, importantly, that previously private (or at least nonpublic) realms are subject to political intervention and modification. (Ivison, 1997: 9)

Those who argue that there is a danger that the content and forms of the public sphere and republican institutions will still retain an overly "male" bias have a valid point (Phillips, 2000: 291). It is not simply a matter of reinvigorating the traditional content and space of the public sphere, especially if there is a widespread belief that the traditional notion of the public sphere is inherently biased. Chantal Mouffe makes a similar point in arguing that the prevailing distinction between the public and private needs to be reformulated to better suit the needs of modern democracy (Mouffe, 1993: 83). But with its focus on power relationships and its goal of transforming the public sphere into one where domination is minimized, modern republicanism holds out the possibility of coping with such challenges. As Pettit states, "the republican state will be charged with putting such restrictions on private power that so far as possible . . . people will be able to live in situations where others do not have arbitrary power over them" (Pettit, 2000: 152). In this regard, I believe that modern republicanism can break down the traditional distinction between the public and private to recast political debates into ones that countenance the two powers that accompany nondomination. The key, then, is in stressing nondominating power relationships between not only men and women, but also all members of society, and the importance of respecting the "other." I turn to this issue next.

Respecting the "other"

Responding to Michael Sandel's claims in *Democracy's Discontent*, Charles Taylor has recently suggested that much of the discontent in today's modern liberal polity does not necessarily come from the actual measures put forth by the liberal state, but from what individuals see as the motivation behind these measures (Taylor, 1998: 216). In other words, liberal remedies to the problems facing the modern polity are not necessarily problematic in themselves; it is the motivation behind them that causes some in society to withdraw from politics and heap disdain on the liberal state. Because the liberal state has asked them to bracket off their own personal value systems in light of a liberal commitment to reasonable agreement, those who disagree are branded unreasonable. Taylor's fear is that the liberal state's definition of reasonableness is too stringent and that by labeling unreasonable those who do not, or cannot, bracket their own value systems, the liberal state exacerbates the conditions for fundamental conflict among those groups and communities that comprise it. Instead, he argues, the liberal state should be less concerned with having recourse to fundamental expressions of justice through procedural claims and more concerned with doing what is right to the "other."

To illustrate his point, Taylor uses a hypothetical example of Christian parents advocating school prayer in the state school system to argue that the liberal state undermines its own position by unnecessarily degrading those who disagree with its policies. Liberals, he argues, have two broad ways in which they can react to demands for Christian prayer in schools. On the one hand, they can deny these demands by asking the Christian parents to consider the feelings of those in the school who do not share their belief in Christianity. The upshot of this approach is that all those who are party to the decision, and the comprehensive doctrines that motivate them, are recognized as making legitimate demands on the state. This public recognition lets them know that they have a place in the deliberative community, and that their value system is at least respected, if not officially adopted. For Taylor, because an individual's identity can be conditioned by recognition or its absence, non-recognition can be considered by some to be oppressive (Taylor, 1994: 25). On the other hand, the state could deny the request by stressing how these demands are inconsistent with the latent moral principles of the modern liberal polity because they violate fundamental procedures – in this case the separation between church and state (Taylor, 1998: 217). This denial, the kind of denial that Taylor believes liberals often opt for, would have the effect of demonstrating that these values are inconsistent with principles that we all reasonably could agree upon. Thus, instead of recognizing the value that these ideals have to their adherents, these ideals and the lifestyles that promote them are deemed unreasonable. Taylor argues that liberals need to find an alternative way of framing the debate that does not give precedence to procedural principles, but rather gives each identity and value a fair hearing in light of the circumstances present (Taylor, 1998: 218). The liberal reply to this, according to Taylor, is to promote equal respect and fair procedures that adjudicate according to the principles that reasonable comprehensive doctrines can accept. But, for Taylor, "we are left with the paradox, that a theory which is meant to be based on equal respect ends up offering what many supposed beneficiaries cannot help seeing as the very opposite of respect" (Taylor, 1998: 219). Taylor's solution is to adopt an approach that puts consideration of the "other" to the fore instead of procedural values. He advocates a deliberative process that asks all those involved to listen and try to understand the demands of others in the deliberative community. However, this system cannot exist on its own: it must embody a strong commitment from those who participate in it in order to maintain itself and function properly. Like Sandel, Taylor favors forms of neo-Athenian republicanism to ensure that there is proper allegiance to and participation in the deliberative process. And, like Miller, Taylor believes that those who do participate in the process should not be asked to bracket off their comprehensive identities in order to participate (Taylor, 1998: 221). Taylor's complaint is that liberals unnecessarily start a cultural war based on difference and diversity by branding many valid and important beliefs unreasonable.

Now I have some sympathy with Taylor on this issue. And while my solution is quite different from his, it is one that I believe he would have good reasons to accept. As I argued in chapter 4, Miller (1995) is right to maintain that liberal attempts to deal with diversity and difference by asking individuals to bracket off their comprehensive identities are impossible in light of the deep pluralism in the modern polity. Furthermore, as I have argued above, liberal attempts to cope with diversity and difference by resorting to strict liberal neutrality and equal respect are also deeply troubling. But the solution is not to embrace the human flourishing of the civic humanist approach. Rather, I believe that modern republicanism can help solve this problem without deeply offending either civic humanists or liberals. As I outlined in the second section of this chapter, Machiavelli, and those later neo-Roman republicans who followed him, did not have a singular supreme version of human flourishing. What they did have was a belief that liberty as nondomination had to be a key organizing principle in constituting a republic. Additionally, instances of difference and diversity had to be tolerated and institutionalized within the technology of the state so that no one was subject to actual or threatened domination. The interdependent connection between liberty, good laws and institutions, and civic virtue and citizenship was important, but not because it embraced a singular version of human flourishing as civic humanists would have it.

This intimate connection is important to republicans because it maintains and enhances liberty as nondomination and thus secures individuals and communities from domination. Moreover, it gives republican citizens an opportunity to embrace certain goods that help them to do well and enrich their lives. Without completely undermining many of the key ideals of the civic humanist version of republicanism, modern republicanism retains a strong commitment to citizenship and civic virtue that Sandel, Taylor, and Miller advocate. Likewise, it would abandon strict state neutrality in favor of a distinctive republican bias that countenanced liberty as the absence of mastery. It would strive for a vibrant public culture of civil society where political activity was cherished. So how would modern republicanism cope with Taylor's hypothetical example, and how is it different from liberal approaches?

By starting with a conception of liberty that sees freedom as the absence of domination, modern republicanism satisfies Taylor's call to focus on the "other" when faced with deep divisions, but without a singular version of human flourishing. A republican state characterized by nondomination requires that individuals not dominate others, just as it requires that the state itself should not be a dominator. What this requires is an effort to discover just what individuals' and communities' interests actually are. And to do this, all parties to the issue must be willing to sit down and listen and attempt to understand what each other's interests actually are. For the state, and the citizens that comprise it, to not be dominators they must track the interests of the "other." Iris Marion Young makes a similar point when she argues that when "people stand in interdependent relationships with others . . . they cannot ignore the claims and interests of those others when the former's actions potentially affect the latter" (Young, 2000: 259). However, as discussed above, this does not mean that diverse interests always get their way, or that their wishes or desires are followed blindly. No state could operate in that manner. To track someone's interest, rather, means that their demands must be evaluated and responded to in an appropriate manner that considers just what their interests are in light of nondomination. It means that the state, and those individuals who are party to the issue at hand, must account for and then appropriately respond to the demands being made in light of the greater republican commitment to nondomination. So, in Taylor's hypothetical example of the case of school prayer, a modern republican state would need to have institutionalized and inclusive procedures that encouraged each party to engage one another in an open and public forum using the language of civic virtue and citizenship. Knowledge would be gained not only from their own experiences and particular socializing agents, but also from the modern republican state's own distinct civic education in virtue and citizenship. Ideally the decision being made would take all opinions and values of the participants into account before an appropriate, and, most importantly, nondominating decision was reached.

The point to make here is that within modern republicanism participants stand before the forum as equals while their comprehensive or encumbered identity receives proper recognition by the state as a legitimate nondominating value system (if indeed it is nondominating). It is this that opens up the possibility that modern republicanism can make a positive contribution to what is known in contemporary discourse as "the politics of recognition" (Taylor, 1994). Taylor points out that there is a widespread belief that "our identity is partly shaped by recognition or its absence, often by the misrecognition of others." Moreover, "non-recognition or misrecognition can inflict harm, can be a form of oppression, imprisoning someone in a false, distorted and reduced mode of being" (Taylor, 1994: 25). In accounting for the politics of recognition, nondomination as a public philosophy countenances the importance of agents being accepted for who they are and how they choose to present themselves. Along with the equal footing that agents stand on, they know that if they want their interests tracked they must cast their ends in a nondominating manner. To track someone's interests means to engage them and find out just what their interests are. In other words, it means recognizing who they are and accounting for them before acting. Thus, each is asked to consider the "other" and how their decision might impact on the many incompatible, but equally legitimate, value systems found in the polity.

There is no doubt that there will be difficult cases in terms of minimizing nondomination. In these cases, the key word for a modern republican state must be accommodation. Shelly Burtt has argued that the modern polity must be prepared to accommodate wide-ranging dissension from those individuals and groups whose final ends are in conflict with the state, especially over forms of state education (Burtt, 1994: 51–70; also see Burtt, 1996). A modern republican state has a responsibility to ensure that both proponents and opponents of school prayer in Taylor's hypothetical example mentioned above can register their interests in a fair and meaningful manner so that each party's interests can be tracked and responded to appropriately. A modern republican state will seek to minimize, to the extent possible without sacrificing its larger commitment to nondomination, the arbitrariness of its decisions by accommodating a wide range of comprehensive moral doctrines and by finding compromise solutions that ensure that no party to the dispute is subjected to arbitrary interference. Thus, Taylor's concerns are met, but without relying on a singular conception of the good that contains a thick version of human flourishing.

Conclusion

A modern republican state that is characterized by liberty as nondomination can cope with the deep moral pluralism found in the modern polity. It can do so without endorsing a singular version of human flourishing, and without sacrificing several important liberal goals. By illustrating how Machiavelli responded to the challenges brought about by his experiences with difference and diversity, modern republicans can use his solutions as the foundation of their contemporary remedies. By stressing the interdependent relationship between liberty as nondomination, good laws and institutions, and civic virtue and citizenship, a modern republican state can cope with moral pluralism. Moreover, by tolerating and institutionalizing the moral pluralism found within the modern polity, a modern republican state uses the dynamic energy and activity generated by difference and diversity to secure and enhance liberty as nondomination. Individuals and groups are free to pursue their own final ends, as long as those ends do not seek to dominate others. A modern republican polity will be characterized by strong versions of civic virtue and citizenship that will help ensure that no one group or community is subject to the domination of another. Citizens will engage each other in the inclusive and public forums of the republic using nondomination as their supreme tracking value to construct fair laws and institutions and to deal with each other in a nondominating public sphere. The next chapter will explore just what these distinctive modern republican institutions might look like.

6

Modern Republicanism and Democratic Contestatory Institutions

Introduction

In a way that respects concerns for diversity, I argued in the last chapter that a republican state characterized by liberty as nondomination can cope with the deep moral pluralism found in the modern polity. It does so in a manner that does not endorse a singular version of human flourishing and secures individuals from arbitrary interference. By stressing the interdependent relationship between liberty as nondomination, good laws and institutions, and civic virtue and citizenship, a modern republican state holds out the promise of securing individuals and groups from arbitrary interference. In moving the modern polity in this direction, a very real worry concerning the scope of state activity comes to the fore that must be adequately addressed.

This is especially so since in earlier chapters I have argued that a modern republican state is likely to be an active presence in the lives of individuals and groups in today's polity. I also argued that modern republican citizens will be less likely to object to state intervention and activity than liberal citizens who cherish liberty as non-interference, since whatever interference they experience tracks their interests and is not arbitrary (Pettit, 1997: 148). The upshot is that if this interference is not arbitrary, then a modern republican state's activities might be better placed to address many of the problems faced by today's polities with greater vigor than a liberal state without restricting the liberty of its citizens. Moreover, it follows that a modern republican state will be an active force in the lives of individuals and will affect them in both their political and nonpolitical lives. The risk is that if the state itself becomes a dominator then it becomes a powerful source of un-freedom (Pettit, 1997: 171). Admittedly, a modern republican state will coercively interfere in the lives of its citizens by imposing laws in common upon them. According to Pettit,

> the agencies of the state, including the state that is devoted to republican causes and policies, interfere systematically in people's lives: they coerce the people as a whole through imposing laws in common upon them, and they coerce different individuals among the populace in the course of administering that law and applying legal sanctions. (Pettit, 1997: 171)

If there are real risks of the state itself becoming a dominator, any viable modern republican approach must account for this risk and offer safeguards to minimize it. Furthermore, if a modern republican state must track the citizenry's interests, its activities and processes cannot be seen as denying citizens' interests with impunity. To perform this important task, a modern republican state must find a way to inject a healthy amount of citizen involvement into political matters so that the collective interests of the people can be accounted for and then tracked. Such moves will rely on the citizenry to provide a check on the power of the state with the goal of minimizing arbitrary interference. The key of doing this is contestability, and in particular democratic contestability. If the modern republican approach I have been developing can demonstrate that enough safeguards are in place to minimize the risk of any dominating state activity, then we can focus on the positive benefits of such activity.

For republicans, the coercive power of the state can appear in two different forms. The first obvious form comes from what classical republicans referred to as the *imperium* of the state. The thought is that the state itself can become a dominating force subjecting the citizenry to arbitrary interference. This threat is made even more extreme if the state, as I argued earlier, is to abandon liberal neutrality and instead promote certain substantive ideals that regulate individuals and groups in a distinctive republican manner. Many will be concerned with the implications my argument has in light of the power of a modern republican state and its influence on individuals' and groups' conceptions of the good. They will argue that, since I have already admitted that liberal neutrality must be abandoned in favor of certain distinctive modern republican ideals concerning the regulation of how individuals cast their interests in light of nondomination, a modern republican state can easily fall into the role of dominator itself. For if modern republicanism is to be taken seriously as an attractive and achievable public philosophy, I must demonstrate that the power and influence of the state can be effectively checked to ensure that arbitrary interference is minimized. Put simply, I must demonstrate that the state itself does not become a dominator by subjecting its citizens to its own *arbitrium*. Another form of coercive power that can appear in modern states is closely related to many issues raised in the last chapter, where I argued that some may feel that the threat posed to liberty by difference and diversity in today's polity may lead to factional conflict of the kind feared by Publius and the American founders (Hamilton, Madison, and Jay, 1961). The thought is that narrow self-interest – what classical republicans refer to as *dominium* – will drive people away from commonly held values. Instead, we are left with divisive and polarized political conversations that actually increase the amount of arbitrary interference present both in the political system and in people's everyday lives.[1]

In confronting these issues, throughout my argument I have maintained that modern republicans must take their cue from the way Machiavelli responded to the difference and diversity of his time. Exceptionally, Machiavelli's solutions represented a decisive break from his neo-Roman republican contemporaries in that, as Duncan Ivison has argued, "the values of security and civil discord sit together uncomfortably at the center of the classical republican tradition" (Ivison, 1997: 53). As we have seen, although difference and diversity represent a serious risk to liberty, they can also be an important component of ensuring that domination is minimized. The key is to harness and channel the energy created by the many interests that comprise the modern polity and subject them to public forums where open and inclusive contestation can occur. By accepting and institutionalizing the plural nature of present-day society, a modern republican approach can use difference and diversity to help secure republican liberty. By establishing distinctive republican institutions that seek to accept the forces of difference and diversity for what they are and incorporate them within the institutional and technological structure of the modern republican state, arbitrary interference of both the *dominium* and *imperium* forms can be minimized.

In this chapter I want to take a closer look at just how the formal institutions of the republic are shaped by the constitutional power of nondomination to guard against arbitrary interference. To this end, I will explore the various technologies available to the modern polity in light of republican liberty as nondomination. In doing so I will argue that modern republicanism draws on both classical republican institutional design and on existing institutions. I want to offer real ideas that demonstrate not only that modern republicanism is an attractive approach, but that it is also one that represents achievable ends that enhance the modern polity's ability to minimize arbitrary interference. In considering these issues, three interdependent distinctive republican forms emerge that I have termed the pillars of modern republicanism: democratic contestatory institutions, robust forms of civic education (formal and informal), and modern republican social norms. Each of these three pillars has an important role in providing a modern republican state with enough support to maintain nondomination. If there is weakness in any or all of the pillars, either individually or together, the structure of the whole modern republican project will be undermined. Collectively these pillars interact with individuals and groups to minimize arbitrary interference and transmit the necessary virtues that help to maintain and enhance republican liberty as nondomination. I will set aside my discussion of modern republican forms of civic education and social norms until the next chapter. In this chapter I will concentrate solely on the first pillar, modern republican democratic contestatory institutions.

In pursuing my argument, a secondary, but no less important, goal of this chapter is to try and "cash out" some of the republican ideas put forth earlier. To this end, in what follows below I provide a rough sketch of some key areas that modern republican ideals and values can enhance with a view toward minimizing the extent of arbitrary interference. What I have not done below is to offer rock-solid policy recommendations, something for which I hope I will be forgiven. The main reason why it is impossible to offer such concrete measures lies in the fact that modern republicanism is a fluid public philosophy that, as I hope this chapter proves, relies on substantial inputs from the citizenry in light of specific situations and issues tailor-made to the location and extent of the problems. Thus, for me to offer ready-made policy prescriptions could actually be a case of domination itself since these measures have not come up from the people in a manner with which they identify, or via a method that ensures that their interests have been fairly registered and accounted for in a way of which they approve. Instead, what I have tried to do below is to look at how modern republicanism can improve existing policy-making processes and institutions so that the constitutional and reciprocal powers of nondomination can help minimize arbitrary interference and provide a robust check on the power of the state. In focusing on these concerns, I first look at the connection between democracy and classical and modern republican technologies. I then develop a modern republican democratic contestatory model before defending it against possible objections.

Democracy and republican technology

Not surprisingly, as earlier chapters have suggested, and as those who are familiar with the tradition will know, democracy plays a key role in republican thought (Held, 1996). Insofar as modern republicanism is an ideal inspired by classical forms of republicanism, it too must countenance the important role of democracy in fulfilling its public philosophy. When speaking of modern forms of democracy, I am referring to the general ideal of a constitutional polity that embodies a fair amount of citizen participation through periodic elections and one where power is dispersed throughout a range of institutions. Furthermore, I am speaking of such an ideal that countenances certain basic civil rights and protections supported by the rule of law. In giving shape to a modern republican ideal of contestatory democracy it will be important to consider what else can be added to the modern democratic model to further the cause of liberty as nondomination. This is especially pressing since throughout my argument I have stressed not only the constitutional power of nondomination, but also the reciprocal power as it relates to individuals and groups interacting on a personal level. In each of these forms of power, dialogue and conversation act as the model for resolving differences and approving actions. In responding to the dangers from both *imperium* and *dominium* forms of power, this section takes a hard look at the constitutional power of nondomination and the role of active and inclusive democratic contestatory institutions that will necessarily accompany a modern republican state.

According to David Held, there were two fundamental reasons in classical republican thought behind the idea of incorporating the rule of the people within the state (Held, 1996: 44–5). As we saw earlier, the first, associated with the neo-Athenian republicans, was the belief in the essential value of self-government. This model held that political participation was an ultimate good and that, in acting together in a political society, citizens were engaging "in a shared enterprise orientated towards the realization of the common good" (Held, 1996: 49). This strong version of republicanism was, however, thought to lead to a breakdown of political order due to the lack of sufficient checks on the power of the state as different classes sought to dominate others. The second reason that some classical republicans embraced the democratic model was the great fear of tyranny and the subsequent domination brought about by monarchial forms of government. However, the fear of domination by a tyrant or king was tempered by the realization that any form of government that vested too much power in one institution or class would result in the same risk of domination. Just as a monarch could dominate the people, a political system based on an aristocracy or democracy could prove to be dominating as well. The thought was that each class, or a division of a class, might seek to promote its own narrow, self-serving interests by using the oppressive power of the state, resulting in an increase of domination.

In seeking to tame the extreme nature of classical democracy in moving away from the neo-Athenian model of republicanism, the Roman writers, and subsequently the neo-Roman writers, stressed the need for institutional limitations on the power of both the state and the people. The point was to harness the power of the people without letting that power harness the people. The broad outlines of this move took the form of certain constitutional arrangements that gave priority to the rule of law; the dispersion of power across legislative, administrative, and judicial bodies; open and inclusive representative bodies that were made up of members from the range of social classes; and term limitation (including the rotation of offices) of public officials (Pettit, 1999: 284). The thought was to bring in as many people as possible, set down firm rules of conduct, and strongly constrain the scope of their power, all the while subjecting each official and their office to public scrutiny so that no individual or group could subvert the common good. Citizen activity, and in particular political participation, was deemed necessary to the successful functioning of the neo-Roman model. This was not because this would necessarily lead the individual to a higher state of well-being or flourishing. To be sure, some goods, such as civic virtue or honor and glory, were associated with citizen activity. However, along with these goods, political participation became an essential component of republican government because it could guarantee liberty so that no one group or institution could subject others to its will with impunity. Certain technological features were designed to help bring people out into the political environment so that political power could be dispersed and thus checked. Insofar as I have rejected the neo-Athenian model and aligned modern republicanism with its neo-Roman rival, it will be important to consider in more detail how these writers sought to check the dangers of democracy to minimize the risks of domination.

Neo-Roman republican technology: classical and modern

It was, perhaps, in Montesquieu's seminal work *The Spirit of the Laws* that the technological features of classical republicanism were consolidated into a coherent and feasible blueprint for the modern nation-state

(Montesquieu, 1989). As Judith Shklar has pointed out, Montesquieu firmly believed that the only way to rescue the modern state from monarchy was to "demonstrate that republican virtue was possible only in genuinely popular non-monarchical republican regimes" (Shklar, 1990: 266). Moreover, Shklar argues that one of Montesquieu's main purposes in *The Spirit of the Laws* was to assess the successes and failures of various regimes and from their experiences "construct a comprehensive theory of comparative law" (Shklar, 1990: 268). By contrasting ancient and modern regimes alike, Montesquieu sought to demonstrate certain timeless principles that, if incorporated correctly in the laws and institutions of the modern polity, would create a permanent new republican ideal based on separation of powers and democracy. The novel technological advent of checks and balances was crucial to classical republican thought for two main, but differing, reasons. First, for Machiavelli, checks and balances were essential to republican government because they represented the only way to combat the evil of corruption brought on by narrow, self-interested individuals that characterized his view of a tumultuous population. Machiavelli believed that open and inclusive representative bodies could, in their debates and deliberations, minimize the influence of individual self-interest and promote those goods that benefited the citizenry as whole. Second, for other classical republicans like James Harrington, the separation of powers and checks and balances were the best ways to ensure that domestic tranquility and concord character-ized the collective effort to secure liberty. For these republicans, the key to having such a society lay in the ability of the polity to institute a mixed constitution based on checks and balances. The thought was that while the reins of power were better placed with the people, certain institutional counter-balances needed to be in place to prevent the domination of any individual or group. This allowed self-interest to play a decisive role in governing by bringing it out into the open and letting each interested party participate in the maintenance of liberty while fully acknowledging its own narrow self-interests.

Despite their various reasons for advocating a mixed constitution that sought to balance the competing interests of the citizenry, these republican writers wanted to ensure that liberty was safeguarded by injecting as many interests as possible into the public debate. The thought was to rely on the political activity of the citizenry to check the power of not only the state, but each other. The key to doing this was to ensure that the people not only had the ability to contest the government and each other, but also the necessary institutions through which to do so. As Pettit states, "the republican rationale for dispersing power is, other things being equal, to increase the non-manipulability of the law and to guard against government exercising sway over others" (Pettit, 1997: 178). Such moves are illustrated clearly in Publius's *Federalist Papers* (Hamilton, Madison, and Jay, 1961). In *Federalist* 10 and later in *Federalist* 47–51, Publius argued that the only way to safeguard liberty in the face of the many different competing interests that had emerged in the drive for American independence was to counteract their debilitating effects by ensuring that the republic was comprised of a federal representative system made up of as many interests as possible. Moreover, it would institute a system of overlapping power so that each branch would closely watch the others (Manin, 1994: 47). Such a system would seek to ensure that no one faction or group gained too much influence without being exposed as doing so. This would safeguard the republic by diffusing power among the various self-interested factions so that each one provided a check and balance on the other (Hamilton, Madison, and Jay, 1961: 83). Furthermore, these writers advocated institutions that were democratic in nature so the citizenry became the ultimate check on the power of the state.

For our purposes here, the point to take from the above discussion is that, although democracy was seen as an important component of free government, it carried with it certain risks that, left unchecked, could bring about tyranny in the guise of the majority. Thus, certain neo-Roman technologies such as checks and balances and the rule of law were designed to curb the excesses of Athenian democracy and limit the risk of domination by the majority or by any other group. This point also ties into my earlier discussions about Machiavelli's advocacy of certain properly constituted republican institutions in light of the conflictual nature of maintaining liberty. Three key points emerge from this discussion. The first is that a form of democratic government was essential in guarding against the domination of a monarch. The second is that, although democracy was essential in guarding against domination in the form of a monarchy, it was itself a risky system of government when it came to maintaining liberty and securing the people from excessive power. Experience had taught classical republicans that inevitably some individuals or groups will be stronger in pressing home their point of view and thus the threat of domination remained, albeit in a different form. For these republicans, there was little difference between a tyrant and a tyranny of the majority since both ruled by dominating others. In seeking to limit the extremes of democracies, the final point to make is that these republicans believed that if the energy and commitment from the people could be harnessed and channeled in a distinctive manner by certain technologies, the risk to liberty could be minimized.

It is upon this realization that the contemporary claims of modern republicanism as a compelling and relevant modern public philosophy rest. And it is upon this foundation that the constitutional power of nondomination establishes itself in the modern republic. Earlier, I pointed out that not only does the constitutional power of nondomination seek to deny those who seek to dominate the necessary power to interfere arbitrarily with others (*dominium*), it also must contain provisions which ensure that the state itself does not become a dominator (*imperium*). In other words, the constitutional power of nondomination not only provides a framework to prevent arbitrary interference in the realm of everyday life among individuals and groups, it also must ensure that there are sufficient checks on the power of the state to minimize the risk of it becoming a dominator. The key questions here are just how the constitutional power of nondomination accomplishes this task and where in the state it manifests itself.

The short answer is that the constitutional power of nondomination manifests itself in not only the legal and institutional structure of the state, but also its policy processes. Moreover, the constitutional power of nondomination is better realized in a vibrant democratic culture that, as we saw earlier, stresses citizen participation and spreads power across a range of agencies. This is because a modern republican state must encourage individuals and groups to play the necessary active role in their own nondomination, which in turn helps to ensure that the state itself does not encroach upon their liberty. This aspect of modern republicanism connects to Madison's contention in the *Federalist Papers* that the people themselves are the ultimate check on the power of the state. But it is also tempered by the realization that certain institutions and ideals are a necessary part of democratic government that must limit the risk of domination (Hamilton, Madison, and Jay, 1961: 324). The upshot is this: on the one hand, the constitutional power of nondomination needs the active involvement of the citizenry at large to guard not only against *dominium* forms of domination, but also against *imperium* domination. On the other hand, this must be considered in light of the criticisms of Athenian-style democracy by the neo-Roman republicans highlighted above. Thus, it is necessary for me to argue for a contemporary model of republican institutions and processes that are firmly neo-Roman, but ones that also take into account the dynamics of today's society in light of the difference and diversity discussed in the last chapter. I turn to this task in the next section.

Modern republican democratic contestation

To further the cause of republican liberty, I have argued that certain technological features such as checks and balances were designed to temper the extremes of democratic government. I have also argued that modern republicans strive to solve disputes in a conversational manner that endeavors to accommodate "the other." In making these moves, I believe that the modern republican approach that I advocate is not hostile to other recent developments in contemporary political discourse such as deliberative democracy. As we saw in chapter 4, deliberative democracy is generally a situation in which members of a political community settle political issues by deliberating with each other (Cohen, 1989). Thus, the crude democratic ideal of interest aggregation (with majority victory) is altered to place certain requirements on citizens in terms of their participatory commitments to the state and to each other. A deliberative democracy requires that citizens not simply follow their gut instincts when expressing their interests. Instead it seeks to bring them out into the public arena and asks them to justify their position by giving and taking reasons that others can accept. The upshot of the deliberative approach is that it overcomes the weaknesses associated with other collective decision-making processes that rely on bargaining or the mere aggregation of narrow self-interest (Cohen, 1989: 17–18). In this section I will explore this issue further while also developing a modern republican democratic contestatory model that can contribute to and deepen our understanding of the deliberative process and promote republican liberty. I outline five key steps that rely on democratic contestation to minimize domination. I then consider two likely objections to my argument.

Nondomination and contestation

In identifying the areas most likely to be affected by contemporary republican processes and policy, Pettit argues that these institutions must guard against what he calls the "false negative" and the "false positive." False negatives, for Pettit, are oversights that lead to common interests being ignored, whereas false positives are instances where special interests are mistakenly taken to be ones held in common. The fear is that contestatory republican institutions may force some into a position of domination by faulty processes of interest aggregation or by institutions that may produce policies that do not track the "common avowable interests" of the people (Pettit,

1999: 293, 2001: 159–61). The risk comes from several different sources, including corrupt officials who may act out of their own narrow self-interests without tracking others' interests. It may come from certain rules and regulations that do not take into consideration the various ways in which members of today's modern society communicate. It may also, for example, come from agencies that fail to account for the importance of family life by not scheduling hearings or other official meetings at alternative times so that there are ample opportunities for citizens to participate. Wherever the risk comes from, one thing is certain: modern republicanism must seek to make both the policy and processes of democratic contestation nondominating and participator-friendly.

The task is made even more complex by the realization that processes that are nondominating can produce policies that are dominating. In meeting this challenge modern republicanism has several classically inspired technologies upon which to draw. Pettit's solution to this problem is to argue that democratic contestatory institutions are the best available safeguard. In both the interest-identification and policy processes, an effort must be made to minimize the amount of domination so that any emerging policy tracks the interests of the people. For Pettit, certain safeguards in the form of contestation must appear in each step of these processes. In this manner contestation provides an opportunity for the people to challenge and question both the issues raised and their potential or actual impact on society (Pettit, 2001: 160–7). I accept Pettit's point here but want to explore and develop this idea further. In discussing this issue, I want to revisit my earlier claim that certain ideals and institutions constitute or help to constitute modern republican liberty. I want to argue that contestatory democracy is an essential feature of modern republicanism, but not something that reduces it to civic humanism.

Before proceeding, however, I need to stress one important point. No public philosophy is going to get it right all of the time, especially given the degree of social and moral pluralism I discussed in the last chapter. It is unreasonable to expect that every policy that emerges from a modern republic will be completely nondominating. Instead, I think the point that must be made here is that if modern republicans accept that no policy will be 100 percent nondominating, the key to ensuring that domination is kept to a minimum is to ensure that the policy processes are resilient enough to withstand spirited challenges and considerable dissent. As Pettit points out, the threats of false positives and false negatives are real, and any public philosophy must be on guard against domination brought about by this realization. The key to doing this for modern republican institutions and processes is to ensure that they are strong and meaningful enough to withstand the dynamic energy created by an active democratic populace seeking to identify common interests. At the same time, however, they must also be malleable enough to change course when necessary without causing a loss of faith in and allegiance to their foundations and belief in their capacity to do better the next time around. Thus, the institutional scope and procedural outputs of contestatory democracy must be subject to an inbuilt review that relies on the resilience of modern republican institutions with the hope of strengthening their accuracy. The point I want to emphasize here is that, in trying to minimize the risk of domination, modern republicans need to stress the capacity of the institutions and policy processes to revise and reconsider issues that, for whatever reason, have not furthered the cause of nondomination. So, in terms of Pettit's concerns with false positives and negatives, at this theoretical stage the important thing to stress is the processes and not necessarily the end product. This point is similar to one put forth by Jürgen Habermas, who claims that it is not always possible to arrive at a consensus since there is widespread disagreement on certain basic moral norms. However, what we can do in the face of such a challenge is to strive to stress "shared orientations" and arrive at agreements on how we will resolve certain difficult questions that cannot be universally agreed upon (Habermas, 1996a: 366–9, 1996b: 353; also see Leet, 1998: 84). Thus, if the process is truly nondominating, then any end product that turns out to be one that dominates can be addressed in the normal course of government by institutions constituted to do this very thing. With this in mind, modern republicans do not expect complete agreement with the policies that emerge from democratic contestatory institutions. Rather, the expectation is on reducing the citizenry's exposure to arbitrary interference in the form of dominating institutions, processes, or policies.

In the spirit of the *Federalist Papers*, in guarding against arbitrary power it is likely that a modern republican state will disperse power over a wide range of levels to, in the words of Pettit, "increase the non-manipulability of the law and to guard against the government exercising arbitrary sway over others" (Pettit, 1997: 178). Not surprisingly then, modern republicans can embrace the division of the constitutional power of nondomination into judicial, executive, and legislative branches of the state. Furthermore, it is possible to envisage that within these branches there will be further divisions to minimize the risk of arbitrary power. For example, bicameral legislative branches or policy ombudsman agencies within the executive branch are some examples that seem likely to increase the contestatory nature of modern republicanism (Pettit, 2001: 168–72). But the dispersion of power should not be restricted to branches or agencies of the state. To ensure the maximization of nondomination, it makes sense that each of these areas should be supported and checked by open, inclusive, and meaningful public forums and institutions that are constituted by and for the diverse interests that make up the modern polity. To get an idea of just how modern republican democratic contestation can contribute to the maximization of nondomination, I will outline in the next section five ideas that are available to today's polities.

Nondominating processes and outcomes: democratic contestation

To demonstrate just how modern republican institutions might take shape, below I have identified five ideas or steps that represent a way to bolster the processes of today's polities in light of the democratic contestatory nature of modern republicanism to ensure that domination is minimized. However, a quick word about the makeup of these institutions is necessary. Before any policy-making process can begin, the first move must be to ensure that republican institutions are open and inclusive in the manner that I described in the last chapter. If the point of modern republican institutions is to bring in individuals and groups to solicit their interests and opinions so that they can be tracked, the republic must make it possible for them to do so. Again, the point here is that for the state to be a nondominating one, it must track the interests of the citizenry. Two things are central to this effort.

The first is that the institutions must make it possible for the citizenry to effectively participate in this effort. This means that a variety of locations and mechanisms must be used so that all have the opportunity to register their interests and participate in the policy-making process. These public forums must stretch the imagination about the various manners in which individuals and groups communicate with each another, and accept the different forms and methods which some citizens use and which may be inherently tied to their conception of the good. In this way, the republican state can overcome the objections of some that the ways and means of republican government are too narrow and overly prescriptive (Moon, 1993; Young, 1990). Thus, as mentioned earlier, modern republican institutions must be open to all and not, like some rival liberal approaches, ask those engaging with them to bracket off their comprehensive moral doctrines. This may involve exploiting new technologies such as the Internet or video-conferencing. Or it may involve utilizing more traditional methods of citizen solicitation such as the town hall meeting or neighborhood advisory committees. It might also involve ensuring that an extraordinary effort is undertaken to guarantee the participation of certain traditionally under-represented groups or individuals. The overriding point is that there must be a range of ways and means for citizens to register their interests and participate in the democratic contestatory institutions of the modern republic. To over-specify these at the theoretical level may be an exercise in domination on my part. So whatever shape these institutions take or whatever technology they employ should be a decision that is based on the interests of the particular citizens involved. Thus, the five steps in what follows are offered as one possible way of achieving modern republican contestatory processes and institutions – doubtless there are others. The second point is that, if modern republicanism can identify the right mix of interest solicitation that identifies the proper nondominating aims of the state, it follows that the state must ensure that the actual policy-making process runs smoothly and is itself subject to scrutiny through effective contestation. In both of these areas, any modern republican democratic contestatory institution or process must itself conform to the ideal of nondomination to ensure that arbitrary interference is minimized and that the interests of the citizenry are tracked.

With both of these points in mind, I now turn to the five steps I want to highlight along the policy-making process that modern republics can utilize to minimize the threat to liberty from domination. The first key step is in identifying legitimate issues for the state to address. The first thing that must be said is that whatever issues are ultimately identified must be of the kind I highlighted in chapter 2 when I discussed the types of interests that are of legitimate concern for modern republicans. This point also ties into Pettit's discussion of common avowable interests that I mentioned earlier (Pettit, 2001: 156–8). Within many modern democratic polities there is a wide range of ways in which issues are identified for policy action. Elected representatives, public officials, special or public interest groups, and individuals all have an important role to play in identifying these key areas by participating in this step. Other methods of interest solicitation and consultation, such as the system of Green Papers in the United Kingdom, are at least theoretically consistent with the goals of modern republicanism. Such moves are admirable since they involve government agencies speaking to the people not in bureaucrat-speak, but in a way that facilitates dialogue and helps create lasting conversations between not only the government and the citizenry, but also members of the citizenry themselves. These moves help to establish group-level commitments and reduce the space between governors and governed.

It is no surprise, then, that in looking at the processes that currently exist, there is no need for a wholesale shift away from traditional practices currently employed, especially since many of these may have their basis in classical republican technology or are consistent with the aims of modern republicanism. Such measures as the principle of checks and balances can be seen in the work of Publius as highlighted above or in the US Constitution. Admittedly, in some cases the types of proposals that I am suggesting are not going to be of the kind that focuses on wholesale changes to existing practices. Some might suggest that this realization limits the appeal of modern republicanism since, at least superficially, it does not seem to be offering anything "new." It may be that this is due to classical republicanism's contribution to the practices of the modern nation-state or it may be due to chance. However, I do not think that such criticisms are entirely valid. I want to suggest that modern republicanism does offer something "new" since, at a deeper and more fundamental level, modern republicanism seeks to alter how public decisions are made so that the interests of the people are tracked and domination is reduced. Not only does modern republicanism seek to promote institutions and processes that can realize the constitutional power of nondomination, it also seeks to change the way individuals and groups relate to each other so that the reciprocal power of nondomination can be realized as well. It seeks to alter the intersubjective relationship we have with each other and the state. Put another way, modern republicanism seeks to draw individuals and groups out of their narrow, self-interested ways so that they themselves make the necessary contribution to their own nondomination. So under a modern republican polity we may not get a state that looks on the surface that different from the state that we currently have. But we are likely to get a state that is qualitatively better equipped to counter the threats from domination while enhancing and empowering the position of the citizenry.

Another side of this argument is that since in some cases modern republicanism is not likely to offer wholesale changes to certain existing practices, it is more likely to be an accepted and effective public philosophy. The point here is to stress how modern republicanism can enhance the current system so that problem issues can be identified more easily by empowering individuals and groups so that they have a more effective say in the direction of policy. To accomplish this, a greater effort to bring in citizen input is necessary, as is better communication between the governed and governors. It is not enough to simply rely on the people to express their preferences in periodic elections. Moreover, it may not be enough for the state to simply sit back and wait for the people to bring issues its way. A modern republican state is likely to be active in seeking out individuals and groups to consult them to discover what their interests are. If this activity is legitimated by its nondominating nature, then it cannot be said that it represents an invasion of the state into the realm of the social or private sphere.

The second key step is in the formulation of a reasonable and measured legislative or executive response to the identified and legitimate issues raised by the processes in step one. This process will need to involve not only legislative and executive officials, but also a solicitation of opinions from interested parties. Again, at least superficially, there is nothing new in this point and many contemporary democratic approaches would offer similar prescriptions. However, in differentiating modern republicanism from its rivals it must be stressed that, during this process, the principles of nondomination must be observed. Therefore, these debates must be subjected to open and inclusive forums where various proposals can be put forth among the interested parties so that lively and reasoned discussions can occur that are consistent with nondomination. This point ties into one I discussed earlier, that properly constituted republican institutions have a positive effect on the populace by bringing self-interest out into the open and exposing it to other ideas and interests. There are likely to be further benefits of the open and inclusive nature of modern republican institutions, in that individuals and groups will not only be exposed to other interests and ways of life, but also educated in the ways and means of modern republican ideals as they interact with each other and the state. In this respect, they will not only be exposed to the more formal constitutional power of nondomination as they engage in the formal, open, and inclusive institutions of the state. They will also be exposed to the more informal reciprocal power of nondomination as they develop intersubjective relationships with other individuals and groups within the open and inclusive institutions. When registering their interests with the state and others they will engage in conversations with these others and the state, and be required to cast their ends as nondominating ones. These conversations are likely to be a key feature in establishing such social norms as trust and civility as individuals and groups establish relationships with each other and the state. I will discuss this idea further in the next chapter.

The third step occurs once a legislative or executive remedy has come out of the formative and deliberative phase of the earlier steps. This step would require that the proposed policies are subjected to a public review period, both to allow interested parties another chance to study what has been proposed, and to give society as a whole an opportunity to consider the potential ramifications of the proposed policy remedy away from the rough and tumble environment of legislative battles. There may be those who, for whatever reason, did not or could not enter the debate in the earlier stages and now wish to consider what their position will be in light of what has been proposed. Moreover, there may be some who believed that they had no real interest in the earlier issue, and thus did not wish to get involved in those debates, but have now reconsidered their position.

An example of one way to guarantee democratic contestation is to build on certain features in the United States, where most pieces of legislation emerge from the Congress as detailed outlines of policy prescriptions. The actual implementation of such prescriptions is, constitutionally, the purview of the executive branch, which includes the government departments and agencies and the White House. Once government agencies have written the regulations for the enactment of the policy, these are normally published in the Federal Register and in some cases a public comment period opens for 30, 60, or 90 days depending on what the Congress has specified. On paper, the idea sounds good, but the execution of the public review period means that many miss out on the opportunity presented to them to register their interests and to contest the policy proposals if so desired. I would suggest that the current process be supplemented with an effort to take the policy regulations to the people, especially to those who are likely to be affected, instead of relying on the people to seek them out. However, at present in many cases very few actually register their interest in the public comment period. This may be due in part to the process being carried on beyond their understanding in an undecipherable language of legalese and perhaps even "spin." Another possible reason may be that some feel that the process is stacked against them because there is no real effort to take their opinions into account once the public comment period is up. There is rarely an effort to explain why such opinions were not taken into account. Others may not get involved because they do not know they can or do not know how to do so. Whatever the reasons, there are concrete avenues of improvement open to modern republicans. These can range from a simple publicity effort to ensure that interested parties are legally required to be informed of the new policy regulations and of the comment period to other, more complex solutions which might involve citizen-led committees whose sole remit is to oversee the public comment period to ensure that all interested parties are given the opportunity to register their interests and that their comments must be formally addressed before the final regulations are issued. Whichever path is taken, the point is this – citizens need to see just what has emerged from the executive or administrative branch in a language that they can understand and in processes that allow their interests to be registered and addressed.

An example of this type of thinking can be found in Norway, where government agencies are required by the law regulating public administration (*forvaltningsloven*) to notify affected individuals and groups before the full implementation of public policy (NOU, 1967 [amended 1998]: ch. 7, section 37). According to Johan P. Olsen, for the Norwegian government,

> it has been [an] explicit policy to increase the proportion of women on public committees; females have increased their participation in political parties, the Storting and local councils, and more women are recruited to higher positions in the civil service. The tendency is that groups which so far have been absent from, or marginal in, the corporative-functional system are coopted: artists, pensioned people, Lapps, the handicapped and so on...The...law on public administration [*forvaltningsloven*] also states that affected groups should be heard before policies are set. (Olsen, 1983: 209–10)

In keeping with the spirit of the last chapter, a modern republic can take steps along these lines to make sure that interested parties are brought into the policy-making process. Requiring that certain groups are coopted might be one way to ensure that their interests are being tracked by making them aware of policy changes. However, as Olsen points out, cooptation is no "miracle cure" and can only be effective if certain other conditions, such as a willingness to solve problems through such mechanisms and widespread government legitimacy, are satisfied (Olsen, 1983: 210–11). However, there is no reason why a modern republican state cannot take such moves seriously since cooptation would simply be one step among many to ensure that the interests of the people were indeed being tracked by public policy and domination was minimized. Such moves, while not enough on their own, can help to form important components of modern republican liberty as nondomination.

The fourth step is that policy solutions that actually make it onto the ground and begin to operate must be subjected to periodic reviews to ensure that they are fulfilling their intended goals. Moreover, they need to be subjected to scrutiny to ensure that there are no unforeseen consequences that may cause some to be subjected to arbitrary interference. Finally, unsuspecting individuals and groups must have an opportunity to register their interest if they so desire in light of the functioning of the new policy. The point is to make sure that any enacted policy remedies are not seen as absolutes without any scope for objections or revisions. Moreover, the point of this step is to give those who may not have had any opportunity to register their interests earlier a platform and forum upon which to do so now. Again, both new and old technologies such as the Internet or town hall meetings can be utilized to ensure that enacted policies are effectively addressing the problems they were designed for and guarding against unforeseen consequences. There are a number of methods that states can employ to ensure that public policy is both effective and consistent with the minimization of domination. Without being exhaustive, an example might be independent review committees that consist of citizens, government officials, and other interested parties that are impaneled to produce review reports to be considered by the legislative or executive branch. Such committees or panels could actively seek out the opinions of those most affected by certain government programs while at the same time balancing out the interests of others more indirectly affected. The overall point is to subject government policy to some type of review period where individuals and groups have an opportunity to contest the program and suggest changes to bring it more in line with their needs. Any recommendations or policy proposals to grow out of the review would then trigger the whole process to start up again so that new and more effective policies could then be formulated.

The fifth and final step is perhaps the most straightforward and pedestrian of them all. Nevertheless, in many ways this final step is the most important to the ultimate success or failure of the democratic contestatory institutions of modern republicanism. Beyond each of the four other steps must be periodic, meaningful, fair, and open elections in which officials and their performance are subjected to the ultimate democratic contestatory exercise. To some, this may seem like the most simplistic of issues and one that is already well catered for in other contemporary approaches. This issue is made even more pressing in light of recent trends that suggest that electoral participation is dropping as more citizens tune out. How, then, can this final step be enhanced by modern republicanism? To be sure, modern republicanism offers no one silver bullet that will single-handedly solve the problems associated with growing voter apathy. Moreover, it is not clear what is actually causing the decline in electoral participation and whether or not this represents a real threat to the modern polity (Axford et al., 1997: 129–30). However, in the case of the United States a good start would be to change the way campaigns are financed to ensure that arbitrary interference in the electoral process is minimized. The present system does not ensure that individuals and groups are not dominated; instead it seems to reinforce domination, which ultimately forces some out of the political process and corrupts the whole political system. Keeping the present system in place would likely have an adverse effect on how well a modern republic could solicit the interests and ideas of the citizenry before acting by interfering with them in a non-arbitrary manner. Thus, one idea would be to have a good hard look at public financing that takes place in an atmosphere of nondominating principles by a wide-ranging commission or committee that actively seeks the opinions and interests of the populace in much the same way as laid out above. Widening our focus to include other modern polities, term limits may be another way to ensure that the state seeks to minimize domination by bringing in new individuals with new ideas. Some will argue that forcing politicians out of office may itself be domination. Others might say that these politicians are already subjected to term limits in the form of being forced to run for re-election. While I cannot offer a definitive answer to this issue since I do not know the interests of all involved, I can raise two issues that I think would have a determinate bearing on whether or not term limits could be construed as domination. First, I would point to my discussion of what constitutes legitimate interests and ask whether the anti-term-limit politician was really acting in the public interest or in their own. Next, I would have to have a good look at the type of electoral financing in place to ensure that all candidates are given their due in competing for the office. If such measures were subjected to the type of democratic contestatory processes outlined above then any policy outcome could be thought to be nondominating.

Another possible way to enhance present democratic practices would be to institute a program of mandatory voting. While such a move may at first seem overly controversial and a prime example of the type of unrestrained state coercion that many liberal approaches oppose (Patten, 1996: 36), a closer look reveals that such moves may in fact be entirely consistent with modern republicanism. The basis of my argument here ties in to the point I made earlier that, under a system characterized by nondomination and the ideals and values of modern republicanism, state activity (and coercion) is more readily accepted insofar as that activity tracks the interests of the citizenry. Thus, a prescription such as mandatory voting may be an avenue that a modern republic might employ to enhance the democratic contestatory nature of their institutions. Then again, it may not be something that is consistent with the common good and thus cannot be instituted because it may be construed as state domination. The point is that these concrete decisions must take place on the ground level and be subjected to high levels of contestation before becoming official policy, and then be subject to periodic and meaningful review after implementation. In this case, a citizen who is coerced by a modern republican state to vote must be given a meaningful opportunity at each step of the policy-making process to participate fully and register her interests (whatever they are) on the matters at hand. As we saw above, the decision must go through several different layers of contestation and be subjected to periodic review and reconsideration. Again, at each step along the way, the citizen who opposes mandatory voting must be given the opportunity to register her objection. Finally, certain considerations may be made to ensure voters may check a "None of the Above" box on their ballot or that they can have an alternative ballot that simply registers their attendance and not their preference.

Overriding each of these steps is the realization that, if legitimate issues are identified for action, the polity must act on them. Not surprisingly, along the way difficult decisions will have to be made and some may not agree with the end product. Modern republicans are under no illusions that a state can rule by unanimous agreement. The fact is that, whatever decisions are made, not everyone will get their way and have their self-serving preferences satisfied fully. But this line of thinking misses the point. As I have pointed out above, and throughout my argument, individuals and groups will be affected in different ways by the scope and modes of modern republicanism. Not everyone will agree with all decisions or policy prescriptions of a modern republic. Instead, what modern republicans can expect widespread agreement on is the institutions and the processes of decision-making and policy creation that minimize the risk of domination because the public forums are open and inclusive and decisions are always subjected to contestation. Along the way, active citizen involvement and input is not only encouraged, but also necessary to ensure that domination is minimized. Such efforts will likely involve a range of methods and seek to reach out to those who have traditionally been excluded from such discussions. If an agent feels that a decision has gone against her, it is not necessarily because she has been treated unfairly or subjected to domination. If she has been given ample opportunity to register her interests in light of the high degree of democratic contestation that characterizes a modern republic, she has not been subjected to domination. As Pettit points out, in an ideal republic agents who feel that they have not gotten their way may point to bad luck that their point of view did not carry the day (Pettit,

2001: 170). This point goes back to the issue of micro- versus macro-level interests discussed in chapter 2. Thus, in my example if there is widespread agreement that something must be done to increase meaningful electoral participation (macro-level interest) then someone who happens to oppose the solution (micro-level interest) because she does not favor the remedy is not being dominated when she is coerced by the state. She has had ample opportunity to participate actively in the debates and to contest the interests of others. Finally, as I mentioned earlier, she can feel satisfied that there can be no final, ultimate solutions in modern republicanism. If her opposition to such measures remains, she can feel at ease that there will be other days to challenge the policies and to propose those that she favors.

In each of these steps, the overriding point must be this: modern republican democratic contestation is an attractive way to minimize domination in both its *imperium* and *dominium* forms. Admittedly, modern republicanism does not seek to offer "right" or "true" answers as neo-Athenian republicanism might. But this is one of the key reasons it is an attractive approach suitable for the modern polity. The *imperium* of the state is subjected to robust and spirited contestation from not only the constituent parts that comprise the polity through checks and balances, but from the people who act as the ultimate check and balance on its powers. Furthermore, private *dominium* is rigorously confronted by strong institutions and by a robust belief in the rule of law and democratic contestatory procedures. Beyond the ideals and values that support nondomination and help to sustain and nourish the modern republic, there are few absolutes. This feature helps to ensure that the modern republican state can react to the changing nature of the world as a whole, and its own citizenry.

Before concluding this section, a quick word about the role of the judiciary is necessary. Earlier I mentioned that the constitutional power of nondomination could also appear in the form of a judiciary. Furthermore, as mentioned above, such constitutional provisions as the separation of powers, including judicial review, are wholly consistent with modern republicanism and support the principle of contestation. Such a branch of government will likely play a key role in minimizing not only state domination, but also domination that occurs below the level of the state. Individuals and groups will have the ability to petition the courts to raise issues or instances of possible arbitrary interference and the courts will have the ability to order the other branches to revise measures that are dominating. The courts will also have an oversight function to ensure that the proper rules and procedures are being followed at each of the policy-making steps listed below. Moreover, a nondominating judiciary has a role in ensuring that the policy-making steps themselves do not become instances of domination. Another role the judiciary might play is in combating corruption by ensuring that public officials are held to the highest standards of public ethics. Finally, the judiciary may have an important role in ensuring that issues that make it through the aggregation stage and into the policy processes outlined below are legitimate, are aimed at the common good, and are consistent with the specific constitutional principles of the state. All in all, the point here is that a strong judiciary will have an important role in minimizing domination and ensuring that the contestatory nature of the other two branches of government does not become dominating itself. And, like the other branches and levels of government, it too will be subjected to contestation to ensure that it does not become a dominator itself.

Objections to modern republican democratic contestation

I believe that any objections to what I have argued for above will come in two broad forms: the procedural and the substantive. The procedural objection is likely to come from those critics who believe that the measures set out above would create intractable gridlock. The thought is that those procedures would force issue identification and policy-making to grind to a halt while countless objections and opinions are considered so that they can be tracked and accounted for before any resolution progresses to the next step. If such a resolution could, in the end, be found, a related objection would be that the measure itself would probably be so watered down through compromises that the end result would be an overly weak and ill-suited public policy. To be fair, I think that these are certainly legitimate concerns and ones that a modern republic would have to take seriously. In reply, there are three points that I would like to raise. My first comment is that such criticisms are only likely to be true in certain cases where policies are, for what may be good reasons, very controversial or difficult to resolve. No contemporary approach escapes the reality of the fact that there are difficult issues that must be dealt with effectively. Not all of these issues are dealt with in a timely manner, but it is not always down to a lack of trying or will to do so. It is simply because the issues involved are complex and thus the remedial policies must be thoroughly considered and measured to fit. Doing so may take time and involve difficult decisions that lead to compromises. However, the point is not to rush through policy remedies or to shy away from tough issues. The point must be to set up fair procedures that track the interests of the people to cope with these difficult issues, which, if the procedures laid out above are being followed, have been identified by the people as legitimate issues to pursue. So yes, some issues may need more time to be resolved than others, which leads me to my second reply to this type of criticism.

Nothing that I have said above implicitly rejects measures that can be taken to speed up the resolution of some issues as long as those measures do not themselves constitute domination. For example, pre-agreed time limits can be imposed on the various steps above or, in some cases, interim measures can be put into place while certain parts of the process are still considering the final resolution of the issues. Moreover, in genuine cases of emergency or crisis, certain procedural measures can and should be in place to increase the ability of one or more of the branches or parts of government to react as long as those measures themselves are not dominating and are subjected to contestation to ensure that they are being exercised in the way that is intended. The bottom line is this: some of these measures may increase the amount of time some debates take; but while they are taking place, the nondominating procedures and institutions of the state should be functioning to ensure that liberty is maintained and that individuals and groups are secured from arbitrary interference. The final reply I have to the type of criticism aimed at the procedures of modern republicanism is that the people themselves represent the ultimate check on the power of the state. Thus, if the people collectively object to the amount of time taken by, or the functioning of, modern republican institutions and procedures they retain the power to change them to better address legitimate issues in a more timely manner if they so desire. If the amount of time or the difficulty involved in getting measures through modern republican institutions becomes a case of domination itself, then it must be challenged by the people who collectively are empowered to do so since any modern republican state has to track their interests and must be challenged if it is thought to not be doing so.

The second possible objection to the democratic contestatory process outlined above is more substantive in nature and is aimed at criticizing the types of skills and character traits that modern republicanism is likely to require. Like my response to the first objection, I think that this is an issue that modern republicans must take seriously. Broadly, my reply to this objection ties in to my earlier discussions regarding the nature of civility, civic virtue, and citizenship within modern republicanism. Specifically, in chapter 2 I argued that within both the reciprocal and constitutional powers of nondomination resided certain ideals and institutions that constitute modern republican liberty. To support these two forms of power, modern republicanism is likely to require distinctive and substantive virtues and values that will positively interact with some individuals' conceptions of the good. Moreover, the institutions and ideals of the modern republican state will regulate the availability of some ways of life. Not surprisingly, some will object to these moves. But I think that this can be defended, and in each step of my argument I have tried to do so. These concerns are real, especially when the difficult cases of cultural minorities or other traditionally disadvantaged groups, including women, are involved. However, as I have tried to demonstrate throughout my argument, modern republicanism can cope with these difficult questions, and can do so in a compelling and attractive manner. This is due to the substantial benefits in acquiring the types of character traits that accompany the ideals and values that support republican liberty as nondomination discussed in chapter 2. Briefly, the first benefit is that agents are secured from any anxiety or uncertainty they may experience from those who seek to interfere arbitrarily with them. The second benefit is that nondomination reduces the degree to which agents have to be prepared to defend themselves against arbitrary interference. The third benefit is that agents who experience a decrease in their vulnerability to arbitrary interference from others will also experience subjective and intersubjective benefits.

But that is not all that is available to republican citizens. I also identified other benefits available to agents who live in a system characterized by republican liberty as nondomination, such as the increased and institutionalized recognition they will receive from others and the state in pursuing their nondominating final ends. Due to their empowered status and the demands of civility, they will be able to be accepted for who they are and have equal standing with others in the open and inclusive forums of a modern republican state. Moreover, they will not be asked to bracket off their comprehensive identities or final ends nor will they be labeled unreasonable and thus lose their standing. These agents will be more or less on an equal footing with one another when it comes to the amount of freedom they enjoy and this will be common knowledge between them (Pettit, 1997: 87). They will feel confident of their status and thus be able to extend a degree of trust and civility toward other nondominating agents who they know to be on an equal footing with themselves. Enhancing the position of agents by legitimizing their standing before the open and inclusive institutions of the state will likely result in an increase in the range of options available for the republic to pursue. This point ties in to a similar one made by Machiavelli, where he argued that properly constituted republican institutions contributed to an increase in the range of options available to pursue because of the increased participation of citizens, who brought with them an injection of new ideas and points of view. Throughout each of the five steps outlined above, citizens will be exposed to a range of views, some of which will introduce them to new ideas and ways of thinking. Moreover, Machiavelli believed that the resulting civic activity helped to secure liberty by exposing the myriad interests in the republic to other ideas and opinions and the ideals and values of the state (*The Discourses*: Machiavelli, 1965: 329). Thus, while the modern republican democratic contestation will increase the amount of scrutiny policy prescriptions are subject to and may result in some issues taking more time to be resolved, there are certain offsetting benefits as the citizenry seeks to identify areas of legitimate common interests that should be addressed by the state.

In each of these areas, a modern republican state will provide a rich conception of citizenship and civic virtue that will aim at instilling the necessary ideals and values that support the republican conception of liberty. These ideals and values – such as listening to the other side; respecting the "other"; solving matters in a conversational manner; and being able to accept decisions that one is opposed to with the understanding that they do not constitute arbitrary interference (if, in fact, they do not) – all help to make modern republicanism an attractive contemporary public philosophy. Moreover, republican forms of citizenship and institutions combine to secure individuals from arbitrary interference. These institutions, then, are valuable to republican citizens because they themselves are not only the guarantors of their freedom, but also constitute a part of their freedom. Thus, republican citizens who cherish their freedom will also cherish the institutions that maintain and secure their freedom. This account of freedom differs from the liberal account in that individuals do not view the necessary interferences that the modern state must have as a restriction of their liberty. Many citizens will view these "interferences" as an enhancement of their freedom. They will know that they are not going to be subject to the arbitrary will of others or the state as long as their ends do not require the domination of others. Thus, the constitutive nature of the necessary ideals and institutions that accompany liberty as nondomination means that republican citizens will have a more intimate and close relationship with those ideals and institutions. The nondomination that individuals enjoy in the republican state is realized in the presence of certain ideals and institutions that form component parts of their overall conception of liberty. Institutions or ideals that track their interests are not seen as restrictions of their liberty. Rather, as Pettit argues, they are viewed as the reality of their freedom (Pettit, 1997: 108).

Conclusion

In this chapter I have argued that modern republicanism needs a robust account of democratic contestatory institutions and processes so that arbitrary interference, in both the *imperium* and *dominium*, can be minimized. I pointed out that such institutions are inspired by neo-Roman republican institutions that sought to balance out the role that narrow self-interest played in public policy. These institutions were also designed to limit the power of the state so that no one branch or office could force its will on the people. Additionally, we saw how neo-Roman republicans believed that the people represented the ultimate check on the power of the state and that any modern version of republicanism had to be based on an account of democratic theory. Modern republicanism, then, stresses the need for an active populace so that domination can be minimized. The constitutional power of nondomination manifests itself in certain distinctive republican institutions and ideals that are spread across a range of public offices and processes. This power of nondomination inspires the actual constitution of government and is embedded within the institutions and laws that are created by the general citizenry in accordance with rules and regulations that all have been offered the opportunity to help construct. While domination will never be totally eliminated, the resilience of modern republican institutions and processes will ensure that domination is kept to a minimum and that the state is kept in check to prevent it from becoming a source of arbitrary interference. However, I noted that some will object to the demanding nature of modern republican policy institutions and policy-making processes, and that others might object to the demanding nature of modern republican citizenship and civic virtue.

Some will argue that modern republicanism will lead to a kind of institutional and/or procedural gridlock. This objection holds that modern republican procedures would force issue identification and policy-making to grind to a halt while interests are being accounted for and tracked to minimize domination. In reply I countered that some policies may take longer to emerge but that this is not something that should cause too much concern. I pointed out that some issues are so complex that to rush through them might be a source of un-freedom itself. Moreover, I noted that the speed and accuracy of these policy-making processes in large part depends on the people themselves and how well they utilize the republican resources at their disposal. Others might argue that the types of skills and character traits that modern republican democratic contestation is likely to require are overly prescriptive and may clash with some individuals' or groups' conception of the good. My reply was to point out that modern republicanism does contain a rich ideal of citizenship and a robust account of civic virtue. However, in instilling the ideals and values of modern republicanism, certain attractive benefits become available. Each of these benefits provides agents with certain resources that make their lives go well while increasing the range of nondominating actions that they can pursue. They become secure in their position in life and empowered to make decisions about their final ends without arbitrary interference from the state or others.

However, democratic contestatory institutions and processes are not enough to sustain modern republicanism. Instead, I believe that the success or failure of modern republicanism as a public philosophy in large part relies on the strength or weakness of each of the three republican pillars I mentioned above, not on whether or not democratic contestatory institutions will single-handedly solve the problems of the modern nation-state. Thus, democratic contestatory institutions and processes cannot exist in a vacuum and must be supported fully by both strong forms of civic education and modern republican social norms. Admittedly, at this stage in my argument, some critics may not be convinced of the viability or attractiveness of modern republicanism as a public philosophy for today's world. To complete my discussion, the next chapter will look at the need for robust forms of both formal and informal civic education and the need for distinctive modern republican social norms.

7

Modern Republican Civic Education and Social Norms

Introduction

Without a purposeful and resolute effort by not only the state, but also the citizenry, republican liberty as nondomination is unattainable. As Pettit has pointed out, if republicanism is to breathe and live as a real force, its ideals and institutions must become resident in the habits and hearts of the citizenry. That is, if individuals and groups are to live their lives free from arbitrary interference, the ideals and institutions of republicanism must take residence in their habits and be embedded in the norms of civil society (Pettit, 1997: 241). I have suggested that three interdependent pillars support the modern republican project: democratic contestatory institutions, robust forms of civic education, and prevailing social norms. We spent the last chapter looking at modern republican democratic contestatory institutions and how a contemporary polity might supplement its existing institutions to minimize arbitrary interference. It is now time to explore the other two pillars of modern republicanism in an effort to clarify just what its contribution to public philosophy might be.

This chapter will first explore the distinctive and vigorous educative effort that supports and enhances republican ideals and institutions by teaching citizens not only how not to be dominators, but also how to use both the formal and informal institutional apparatus of the republican state. This section will also explore the important role of political education in keeping the state under control and making sure that it does not become a dominator itself. I will then discuss the powerful role of social norms in the modern republican project and argue that, if this project is to succeed, these norms must support liberty as nondomination. In making my argument I will demonstrate the necessary and intimate relationship between each of the three pillars that buttress the whole of the modern republican project.

Educating the republic

Earlier I pointed out the important connection that Machiavelli made between good institutions, good laws, good education, and the maintenance of liberty. I argued that any modern republican approach would have to acknowledge the intimate connection between these principles and seek to instill certain distinctive values and ideals in the citizenry. Moreover, I argued that democratic contestatory institutions would be a prominent feature in any modern republican state because they were well equipped to counter the threat from domination that comes from the state, and from those who seek to promote their narrow self-interests at the expense of the common good. However, I noted that some might object to the highly specialized and demanding skills that would be necessary in a state governed by such contestatory institutions and procedures. In this section, I want to revisit these issues to not only develop a broad outline of a modern republican approach to civic education, but also to consider it in light of rival liberal approaches.

Liberal approaches to civic education

Contemporary liberal theories of civic education argue that certain ideals and values are essential to the survival of the modern democratic state. For many, mutual respect and toleration combine with the essential features of the modern democratic state to ensure that future citizens are prepared to participate fully in today's multicultural and diverse society. The content of this effort, then, is crucial to its success. However, the content of this effort may have negative effects on certain individuals or groups who have heavily encumbered comprehensive identities that are often at odds with liberal ideals and values. Despite the issues raised by this conflict, the prevailing liberal view toward civic education is that the state has compelling reasons to promote certain character traits and values that contribute to the virtues of good citizenship.

Amy Gutmann has put forth an intriguing and systematic account of liberal civic education. Gutmann argues that an essential feature of any liberal democratic state must be the ability to transmit and nurture certain liberal political virtues that ensure a vibrant public culture. Furthermore, this political education "has moral primacy over other purposes of public education in a democratic society. [It] prepares citizens to participate in consciously reproducing their society, and conscious social reproduction is the ideal not only of democratic education but also of democratic politics" (Gutmann, 1987: 287). So that individuals are prepared for the active role they must play in maintaining their own liberty, education must be structured in such a manner that they have access to a common language of citizenship and the capacity to involve themselves actively in public affairs. For Gutmann, then, "democratic education supplies the foundations upon which a democratic society can secure the civil and political freedoms of its adult citizens without placing their welfare or its very survival at great risk" (Gutmann, 1987: 289). Thus, a proper liberal democratic education is essential if individuals are to keep their liberty intact and perpetuate the liberal state. Gutmann believes that the liberal state must embrace and teach certain comprehensive liberal doctrines such as individuality and autonomy, which not only help to support the continuity of the state and secure liberty, but aid in the development of the self. By fostering such values as mutual respect, Gutmann maintains that the liberal approach to civic education will expose individuals to different ways of life and give them the necessary tools with which to evaluate their own choices when it comes to making personal decisions about conceptions of the good (Gutmann, 1995: 564).

The thrust of Gutmann's project is to require that minimum standards of civic education be thoroughly integrated into the state school curriculum regardless of the impact that such an effort might have on individuals whose comprehensive life choices are at odds with liberal ideals. By insisting that citizenship and certain political virtues are essential in the lives of developing citizens, Gutmann argues that the state has a compelling interest in transmitting these values, even when they conflict with individuals' or groups' comprehensive moral doctrines. This robust account of civic education relies on an attempt to foster mutual respect among citizens. Gutmann believes that one of the keys to maintaining and enhancing justice is that individuals respect one another and can find a basis for social cooperation. In order to foster mutual respect, the state legitimately exposes individuals to contested conceptions of the good. For Gutmann, the point is not only to expose individuals to competing conceptions of the good, it is to teach them how to "evaluate different political perspectives that are often associated with different ways of life" (Gutmann, 1995: 577). Gutmann's project is to ensure that individuals have the necessary resources to reflect on and evaluate the various ways of thinking about political issues that accompany the different ways of life found in a society characterized by social diversity. In other words, future citizens need the ability to reflect critically on the many different, and sometimes incompatible, values held by a population defined by diversity.

If today's democratic state is to flourish, for Gutmann, citizens must have the capacity and resources to make informed decisions about complex problems that often lie outside of their own much narrower personal convictions. The teaching of civic virtue helps future citizens to attain the ability to engage in fair and just political reflection that is an intractable feature of today's modern polity. For example, if the state fails to instill in the citizenry a commitment to mutual respect, individuals, and even public servants, cannot be expected to honor certain liberal principles such as non-discrimination, which will in turn undermine equality (Gutmann, 1995: 577–8). Thus, Gutmann's approach cuts deep into the nonpolitical values that individuals hold. Nevertheless, for Gutmann, such a project is necessary and she believes that the public education system is the best vehicle to promote certain liberal virtues and accomplish this important task. For Gutmann, democratic principles, combined with mutual respect and toleration, help to ensure that citizens are prepared to engage positively with one another in the political process. Such a project helps to enlarge future citizens' range of thinking about moral ideals, even in instances where these principles may impinge on their family's deeply held comprehensive doctrines (Gutmann, 1995: 578). For Gutmann, it is essential that the liberal approach to civic education affect individuals' and communities' comprehensive moral doctrines. The upside is that liberal values will enlarge individuals' and groups' range of possibilities when confronting different ways of life.

Similarly, Eamonn Callan (1997) has put forth a conception of civic education based on the ideas found in Rawls's political project. Callan, like Gutmann, maintains that civic education is the key in developing citizenship and the necessary virtues that ensure the survival of the liberal state. Callan argues that education must play an active and vital role in developing the necessary character traits that ensure the vitality of a just political order. According to Callan, "creating virtuous citizens is as necessary an undertaking in a liberal democracy as it is under any other constitution" (Callan, 1997: 3). Callan's conception of an approach to civic education inspired by political liberalism centers around his reformulation of Rawls's political project and the necessary political virtues that must accompany it that I discussed in chapter 4.

Callan's claims center on his belief that Rawls's political virtues that support the fair terms of cooperation in the idea of public reason bring "autonomy through the back door of political liberalism" (Callan, 1997: 40). For Callan, the active acceptance of the demands of reciprocity and the burdens of judgment will necessitate the attainment of certain reflective skills and character traits. This, in turn, requires future citizens to assess critically certain conceptions of the good that lie outside of the basic structure of society. Callan argues that "future citizens must be taught to think in particular ways about doctrines that properly lie outside the scope of public reason: they must become critically attuned to the wide range of reasonable political disagreement within the society they inhabit and to the troubling gap between reasonable agreement and the whole moral truth" (Callan, 1997: 40). In securing active agreement over the fair terms of cooperation, and in accepting the burdens of judgment on a political level with the necessary understanding of reciprocity, individuals' nonpolitical beliefs will be either intentionally or unintentionally affected in a profound manner. By accepting reciprocity and the burdens of judgment, individuals' political life will necessarily affect their view of the good in their nonpolitical life. For Callan, then, individuals who accept the nonpolitical burdens of judgment must also accept a particular version of autonomy that cannot be separate from their nonpolitical beliefs. To accept Rawls's burdens of judgment "enjoins us to be ethically autonomous to a substantial degree and, given the requirement of reciprocity, to respect the autonomy of others when we cooperate politically with them" (Callan, 1997: 41). Furthermore, "learning to accept the burdens of judgment in the sense necessary to political liberalism is conceptually inseparable from what we ordinarily understand as the process of learning to be theoretically (and not just politically) autonomous" (Callan, 1997: 40). The primary goal of liberal versions of civic education, according to Callan, is to develop an idea of the reasonable that contains within it certain informal "cardinal personal virtue[s] of liberal democratic politics" (Callan, 1997: 8).

Freed from Rawls's insistence that the values and virtues of political liberalism must be political in nature and not presuppose any partially or wholly comprehensive goods, Callan argues that any successful liberal approach to civic education must make certain substantive demands on individuals by relying on what he calls "justice as reasonableness":

> Justice as reasonableness devolves into a cluster of mutually supportive habits, desires, emotional propensities and intellectual capacities whose

coordinated activity requires contextually sensitive judgment. Future citizens need to develop some imaginative sympathy for compatriots whose experience and identity incline them to see political questions in ways that differ systematically from their own. A respect for reasonable difference and a concomitant spirit of moderation and compromise has to be nurtured. A vivid awareness of the responsibilities that the rights of others impose on the self, as well as a sense of the dignity that one's own rights secure for the self, must be engendered. (Callan, 1997: 8)

Callan's thought is to exploit the substantive elements of specific forms of liberal virtues by arguing that acceptance of reciprocity and the burdens of judgment would require certain minimum ideals that are liberal and comprehensive in nature. Callan maintains that, in accepting reciprocity and the burdens of judgment, individuals must also accept a degree of ethical autonomy. Importantly, individuals must also accept the autonomy of others under the constraints of reciprocity (Callan, 1997: 41). As stated above, this acceptance of autonomy falls outside of the political sphere and will affect individuals and groups in their nonpolitical lives. Autonomy and individuality, then, are justified in Callan's approach because they help to maintain justice as reasonableness, no matter how they affect those comprehensive views that don't countenance them. That is, for Callan, justice as reasonableness regulates the ends permissible in a liberal state by placing certain substantive requirements on its citizens.

Some elements remain constant in both Callan's and Gutmann's approaches to public civic education. Both theorists maintain that the mere survival of the liberal project demands that some form of substantive, state-driven educative effort take place. Both theorists fill their approaches with certain instrumental liberal goods that may be incompatible with some individuals' or communities' conceptions of the good, but maintain that teaching this minimum level of virtues is both justifiable and necessary. Both theorists advocate a position that puts mutual respect at the center of liberal civic education. Furthermore, both theorists argue that the state should be an active partner in the total educative effort along with other forms of civic education such as the media, industry, and other government institutions. In short, there does not seem to be anything further that a republican focus might add to the above-discussed liberal approaches. Just what, then, can a modern republican approach add to this debate? In the next section, I will broadly outline the form and direction a modern republican account of civic education might take. I will argue that even though both approaches share similar commitments, modern republicanism goes farther because it requires a richer and more robust account of the necessary virtues transmitted by civic education that support liberty as nondomination.

A modern republican approach to civic education

Republicanism has a long and abundant tradition of advocating a complete and pervasive system of civic education to support its distinctive ideals and institutions. Much of this tradition owes its thrust and focus to the neo-Athenian version of republicanism espoused by Aristotle among others and discussed in earlier chapters. In *The Politics*, Aristotle suggests that the provision of a common education helps to foster a sense of unity and togetherness that is essential in constituting a state (Aristotle, 1988: 1263b–1264a; also see Rahe, 1992: 24). This commitment to education, as we have seen in earlier chapters, is aimed at fulfilling a narrow definition of the good and promoting specific forms of *eudaimonia* or human flourishing so that individuals can realize their true self. For neo-Roman writers, such as Machiavelli, who did not define a singular notion of the good, education has a slightly different focus (Rahe, 1992: 266). Nevertheless, the importance of a complete and compelling notion of civic education remains intact in the neo-Roman version of republicanism that I advocate. This is especially true when it comes to the contemporary public philosophy developed by Pettit and Skinner, who advocate the neo-Roman republican conception of liberty as nondomination. As I argued earlier, for Machiavelli, education, virtue, and the laws and institutions of the state were not only inextricably connected to one another, but to liberty as well. Although Machiavelli does not offer a specific republican account of civic education, it is clear that he saw a strong educative effort as a necessary feature of a properly constituted republic. For example, Machiavelli equates corrupt cities with those "where education has not produced any goodness in [individuals]" (*The Discourses*: Machiavelli, 1965: 496). It follows that if the republic was to stave off corruption, it was essential that the state be filled with sufficient levels of education and virtue which in turn would support the laws and institutions of the state (*The Discourses*: Machiavelli, 1965: 202). In this section, I will argue that in republics the maintenance of liberty as nondomination is directly tied to sufficient levels of education and civic virtue that helps form important components of republican versions of citizenship. Furthermore, I will argue that, without sufficient levels of education and virtue, the laws and institutions of the republic suffer, resulting in the rise of corruption and the loss of liberty. The upshot of my argument is that, in modern republics, an important feature in the maintenance of liberty as nondomination is its direct link to sufficient levels of education and civic virtue.

Machiavelli tells us that the failure of republican versions of citizenship and civic virtue in this educative effort will have a negative effect on the laws and institutions of the state and liberty will be at risk. Without widespread civic virtue and citizenship, the laws and institutions of the republic will inevitably be driven by corruption and private interests and the risk of domination will rise. As I argued earlier, corruption occurs in republics when some individuals seek to promote their own private interests and dominate others, which puts liberty at great risk. In chapter 5, I discussed how Isaiah Berlin maintained that Machiavelli believed that only a thorough and robust civic education could prepare citizens to play the necessary active role in the maintenance of republican liberty (Berlin, 1981: 40). According to Berlin, the republican approach to civic education must inculcate certain virtues and develop "certain faculties in [citizens] of inner moral strength, magnanimity, vigor, vitality, generosity, loyalty, above all public spirit, civic sense, [and a] dedication to the security, power, glory, [and] expansion of the *patria*" (Berlin, 1981: 43–4). To this end, it is necessary for modern republican citizens to develop certain substantive character traits so that liberty as nondomination can be secured. Furthermore, I also argued that Machiavelli believed that the republic necessarily had to "educate the desires" of its citizenry (Burtt, 1990: 28). This effort would not only secure republican liberty, it was also the only way for individuals to do well by themselves. Citizenship, civic virtue, and education all play essential roles in republican government, and in the lives of republican citizens. Without widespread civic virtue and citizenship, there is a risk that individuals who promote their own private interests at the expense of the common good will inevitably drive the instruments of state power. Taking a cue from the classical republican approach, a modern republican state must play an active role in the content of public education by educating its citizens in the substance and forms of nondomination, and the necessary values and virtues that accompany it. In doing so, a modern republic hopes to cultivate certain types of individuals who locate their good with that of the greater community to foster group-level commitments that will reduce the amount of arbitrary interference within society.

First and foremost, modern republican civic education must begin with the distinct conception of liberty as nondomination. Certain substantive quasi-perfectionist virtues and values, such as the ones mentioned above, are crucial to the success of liberty as nondomination, as are the institutions and ideals that accompany the republican conception of liberty outlined in the last chapter. A modern republic will supply certain components of civic education aimed at creating a citizenry characterized by a rich sense of citizenship and civic virtue. Broadly, for modern republicans citizenship consists of two interdependent dimensions. The first dimension is one of status, often a legal one, which grants the holder certain rights that can be political or civil in nature and is likely to be embodied in a constitution or bill of rights. The second dimension, and one that for modern republicans is crucial, concerns citizens' obligations to others and the state. In terms of this second dimension, civic virtue and civility will play a key role. And, as I argued earlier, civic virtue is understood as individuals' ability to cast their ends in a manner that does not interfere arbitrarily with others and an appreciation of how their actions impact the whole of society. In short, it is the ability to treat others with civility.

In order to instill these values in the citizenry, a modern republican state will directly interfere, but not in an arbitrary manner, in the education of citizens. To ensure that this interference is not arbitrary a modern republican state must register the interests of the people in the open and inclusive forums of the state. Once a policy has been subjected to the democratic contestatory institutions of the republic, any emerging policy will be instituted but yet remain open for review in line with the processes I described in the last chapter. Any emerging policy will teach children and adults the virtues that comprise republican versions of citizenship and help individuals not to interfere arbitrarily with others. Moreover, the inculcation of these virtues and values also seeks to orient republican citizens in a particular direction so that their lives are enriched and they can do well by themselves. Crucial, then, to this effort are certain skills and character traits that will not only help citizens treat others without domination, but will also help them to play the active role in their own nondomination. Unless individuals are prepared to play an active role in their own nondomination by letting others and the state become aware of their interests, their interests cannot be registered and responded to in an appropriate manner.

To help individuals with this task, the republican state will play an active role in ensuring that civic education cultivates specific virtues that help them cast their ends in a nondominating fashion and play the active role in articulating their interests so that they are not dominated. First, like the liberal approach, the republican state will demand that the state school curriculum inculcates individuals with the virtues necessary to learn how to tolerate and respect others. It will ask them to listen to the varying demands of individuals and encourage them to engage one another so that each party plays the necessary active role in their own nondomination. But it goes further than many liberal versions of good citizenship in that it asks individuals to not only tolerate and respect others but to engage them, in an effort to discover just what their interests are so that they are registered and then tracked. By engaging others in this manner, individuals are better able to cast their ends in a nondominating manner and treat them with civility in the hope that they will be treated likewise. Again, on this point, this sentiment is associated with the type of Renaissance humanism that influenced republican writers and stressed listening to the other side and engaging with it from an informed position. Because republicans endeavor to find common ground and solve problems in a conversational manner, dialogue and compromise must be a part of any civic education curriculum (Skinner, 1996: 15–16; also see Pettit, 1997: 189). It is important that these skills help individuals find their voice in a language that is both reflective of their own particular experiences and priorities and intelligible to others engaging in the common conversation. These skills also help individuals sharpen their ability to listen to the other side so that they can cast their ends and respond appropriately. This point also ties in with my earlier discussion of modern republican democratic contestatory institutions and the general approach to working through problems.

Importantly, this point also highlights the modern republican priority of asking individuals to respect the "other," and to understand that their own nondomination requires them to attempt to locate their interests within the larger republican effort to secure all individuals from actual or threatened arbitrary interference. It seeks to place their demands on an equal footing with the demands of others so that each party can account for, and then appropriately respond to, one another. It follows that another task of modern republican civic education is to help citizens gain the ability to articulate their interests so that others can track and then respond to them in an appropriate manner. Modern republican civic education must enable and empower individuals to play this necessary active role in their own nondomination. If others are to track their interests, individuals must first let them know what their interests are. However, as we discussed in chapter 3, this effort will not come without a price for some individuals or groups. Liberals like Kymlicka are fearful that such robust requirements will negatively affect minorities and other traditionally disadvantaged groups by forcing them to defend publicly their conceptions of the good. Modern republicans share this fear, but believe that there is a greater good at stake that serves to protect minorities and other traditionally disadvantaged groups by securing them from the arbitrary interference of others. If the successful maximization of republican liberty as nondomination is dependent on communication and dialogue, the republican state must make every effort to develop a language of citizenship that allows a common point of entry and is accessible to all the individuals and groups that comprise the republic.

That these values and virtues have a certain quasi-perfectionist quality to them may be a cause of concern for some. But, as I argued earlier, I think this concern can be dealt with by a modern republican state. As I pointed out, nondomination will inevitably affect certain nonpolitical beliefs and character traits of individuals' nonpolitical comprehensive doctrines. The republican state legitimately promotes those values and virtues that help individuals to publicize their interests, so that they can be tracked. These values and virtues help them to track other individuals' interests so that they can act without dominating them, which in many ways secures them from arbitrary interference. However, because nondomination seeks to secure individuals from any actual or threatened arbitrary interference, it provides them with the security and freedom to pursue their own chosen ends so that they themselves can decide those things that are valuable and those things that are not, as long as their choices do not dominate others. Thus, the quasi-perfectionism within the republican approach educates and inculcates individuals in the substantive virtues that support liberty as nondomination and can bring them some benefits while leaving their ultimate ends open, as long as these ends are cast in a republican manner. While the republican state has a firm idea of what types of ends are acceptable – those that do not dominate – liberty as nondomination secures a wide range of final ends available for individuals to pursue unhindered by the state or others. A modern republican state will not only strive to secure those conditions that allow individuals to determine what is valuable and what is not within a wide range of final ends that cannot be said to dominate others, it will also help individuals to publicize their ends so that they themselves are not dominated. And in doing so, modern republicanism recognizes that certain life choices support nondomination better than others, and thus acts to secure these conditions so that all citizens can live nondominated lives and pursue their own chosen nondominating ends.

Critics may charge that the stress modern republicanism places on its robust version of citizenship may force some to alter or misstate their interests as they publicize them to others and the state. Additionally, some will maintain that the forms and language of republican civic education may undermine some individuals' or communities' traditional methods of communication (Moon, 1993; Young, 1990). These critics charge that the republican effort to regulate life plans is overly prescriptive and may undermine certain cultural or social practices and beliefs. The republican state must be sensitive to this criticism if it is to not allow some individuals or groups, or even itself, to dominate those who object to the form and vehicles of republican civic education. However, any serious public philosophy requires that certain virtues and ways of doing things are essential to the maintenance of liberty. Liberal theories, such as the ones put forth by Kymlicka and Rawls, maintain that civic education must teach individuals liberal virtues and values such as individuality or autonomy (Kymlicka, 1996; Rawls, 1996). Gutmann's liberal theory also maintains that individuals must learn some basic principles that may be in conflict with their own conception of the good. Callan's conception of political liberalism too requires that civic education teaches certain values that may be viewed by some as comprehensive in nature and thus in conflict with their own conception of the good. Modern republicanism is no different from these approaches when it comes to insisting that certain values and ways of doing things are necessary if individuals are to secure their freedom and live nondominated lives.

The real difference that separates these approaches from the modern republican one is the depth and scope of the uniform system of values promoted by the state and the likely effects that such an institutionalized effort is likely to have. As I argued in earlier chapters, liberty as nondomination regulates the acceptable life choices that are permitted in the republican state. Nondomination requires that individuals' and communities' ends be cast in a manner that does not arbitrarily interfere in the lives of others. What nondomination does not require is that individuals or groups adopt each other's ends, or those ends that are fairly and justly translated into matters of basic justice. The regulation inherent within nondomination is about casting certain life choices into ones that track the interests of others and do not require the domination of them. Admittedly, this effort may adversely affect or even cause some individuals' ends to be distorted in a manner to which they may object. This ties in with my discussion in chapter 2 on what can legitimately count as an interest that should be registered and tracked to republicans. Legitimate interests for republicans are ones that, for the most part, take into consideration the interests of others and do not subject others to arbitrary interference (Pettit, 1997: 56, also see p. 198). These interests are often ones that are widely recognized and shared in common with others and do not require the domination of others. For republicans, self-serving preferences are not regarded necessarily as legitimate interests that individuals can demand are tracked, especially if those interests do not respect others and result in dominating them.

Any modern republican account of civic education will teach individuals how to engage constructively with others who have made incompatible life choices and how to attempt to express their ends in a nondominating fashion. As stated above, it does not require that they accept or adopt these alternative ends. What it does require, however, is that they cast their ends in a manner that does not subject others to arbitrary interference. In this way, the republican approach to civic education is not just a repackaging of liberal toleration and mutual respect. To be sure, it is more than the mere tolerance or respect of another's life choices. Modern republican civic education teaches the necessary values and virtues that help individuals and groups to ensure that their life choices do not interfere arbitrarily with others, just as it teaches others how not to dominate their life choices. Thus, the primary goal of a republican approach to civic education is the inculcation of values and virtues aimed at teaching individuals the necessary skills of nondomination and how to cast and express their ends in a nondominating fashion. It also promotes active involvement in problem-solving exercises that are aimed at ensuring that all voices can be heard in the distinctive republican forums that are open to all. Such activity stresses civility and the building of relationships between those engaged in the common project of modern republicanism. Activities such as these will also go toward establishing relationships between individuals and groups within society and can help form the bonds of trust and understanding. I will discuss this issue more in the next section.

A robust form of civic education that is consistent with the theoretical goals of modern republicanism is perhaps best represented by the recent efforts of the British government to formalize taught citizenship modules within the state school system. From 2002 education in citizenship and democracy will be part of the statutory curriculum within secondary schools in England. According to the guidelines, the citizenship curriculum "will play an important role, alongside other aspects of the curriculum and school life, in helping pupils to deal with difficult moral and social questions that arise in their lives and in society" as well as personal, social, and health education (Qualifications and Curriculum Authority, 1999b: 4). The guidelines are the result of an advisory committee set up by the Qualifications and Curriculum Authority chaired by the political philosopher Bernard Crick. They focus on three main areas: becoming informed citizens; developing skills of enquiry and communication; and developing skills of participation and responsible action. In each of these areas, the stress is on political, social, and moral education. Importantly, students are asked to stand back and reflect on not only their own values, but also those of others. In particular, students are asked to acquire the skills necessary for spiritual, moral, social, and cultural development and to "use their imagination to consider other people's experiences and be able to think about, express, explain and critically evaluate views that are not their own" (Qualifications and Curriculum Authority, 1999b: 14). They are asked to develop certain abilities to facilitate their active participation in political and social issues such as communication, problem-solving, and IT skills. Overall, students are not only being asked to learn about their government and how it operates; they are being asked to be able to reflect critically on their own lives and those of others in an effort to promote certain virtues such as mutual respect and toleration. Some may argue that the focus on mutual respect and toleration makes this approach consistent with the broad thrust of the two liberal approaches outlined above. However, I believe that the British approach goes further in asking students to reflect on moral and spiritual issues in the hope that not only will they be able to participate fully in democratic society, but that they will become active agents in their communities or neighborhoods and thus improve the quality of their own lives. Asking them to consider both moral and spiritual issues is in effect asking them to go well beyond the liberal focus on political issues. Moreover, by asking them to consider other people's experiences and to be able to recognize another's interests, it moves in the direction that any modern republican approach to civic education should take.

But what of those citizens who see the modern republican ideals and institutions of citizenship and civic education as a source of domination? How is it that these citizens' interests will be tracked if their comprehensive identities are in fundamental conflict with the necessary virtues and ideals that help to support liberty as nondomination? In most cases, those individuals or groups whose comprehensive identities fall into this category cannot expect the state, or even others, to tolerate or accept their dominating ends. Citizens whose ends arbitrarily interfere with others will be asked first to be a part of the deliberation so that all parties to the issue can register their interests, and second to identify with, and approve of, the method and manner in which decisions are made so that they can see that their interests were tracked, even if they were not adopted (Pettit, 1997: 198). They will be asked to participate actively in the process so that their interests are fairly and openly registered before being considered along with everyone else's. The state and others will then appropriately respond to their demands and the burden will be on them to explain why it is that these ends arbitrarily interfere with them. Individuals and groups who refuse to recast their ends into ones that do not arbitrarily interfere with others will risk encountering either the domination of those they arbitrarily interfere with, or confrontation with the state, which may force sanctions on them if they do not cease to express or act on their ends in a dominating fashion. For those who cannot identify with or accept the open and inclusive procedures or decisions of the state and see this as an explicit form of domination, a modern republican state must be prepared to find a compromise or settlement so that these closely held ends can be accommodated while minimizing the risks to others. The content of this compromise will in large part depend on how extreme these individuals' demands are.

In these difficult cases the key word for the republican state must be accommodation. This point ties in with my argument in the last chapter over Taylor's hypothetical example involving school prayer. According to Shelly Burtt, the modern polity must be prepared to accommodate wide-ranging dissension from those individuals and groups whose final ends are in conflict with the state (Burtt, 1994: 51–70). To further explore this issue, it will be useful to look at an important US court case, *Mozert v. Hawkins County Board of Education*, about public education and the limits of religious freedom. This case centered on a challenge to the state's right to mandate certain facets of public education and involved the failed efforts of fundamentalist Christian families to exempt their children from their school's basic reading curriculum that not only taught reading skills, but also citizenship and the values and virtues that accompany it (*Mozert v. Hawkins*, 1987). The children's parents objected to the reading list because they believed its content was a threat to their chosen way of life as it contradicted their strict religious beliefs (Gutmann, 1995: 565). The court decided that the state had compelling interests in requiring students to obtain a minimum level of civic education and rejected the parents' objection. Many liberals have supported the court's decision by arguing that the state has good reasons to insist that all future adults are educated to at least a minimum standard of civic education that would help prepare them to be fully functional citizens. As I outlined above, the overarching liberal position is that some values and virtues, such as autonomy or individuality, are so important to the maintenance of justice that the state has good reasons to insist that they are actively promoted and integrated into the state school system's basic curriculum (Gutmann, 1995: 567; Macedo, 1995: 470; also see Kymlicka, 1996: 87; Rawls, 1996: 200). Specifically, in this case, these liberals maintain that the court was right to insist that the children in the Mozert case participated in these reading courses despite the effects it might have on their deeply held comprehensive beliefs. As we have seen above, republicans too would argue that the state has good reasons to require certain basic levels of citizenship and actively promote these values and ideals. However, I think that the republican approach would differ from liberalism's in its willingness to find a solution that would track the interests of the parents in the Mozert case, and still teach the children the necessary values and virtues of nondomination.[1]

Analyzing the Mozert case, Burtt maintains that both the state and the parents of the children involved could have found a compromise solution that would have satisfied their competing demands. For Burtt, "when families' religious values clash with the public school curriculum... democratic ideals and practices are in most cases best served by working with parents to minimize their objections." Burtt believes that, by allowing the parents to opt their children out of the substantive elements of the state's citizenship program, the parents could have developed their own curriculum that would have given due consideration to their narrow comprehensive doctrines *and* taught the necessary values and virtues that are essential for members of a modern democratic polity. In placing the burden of finding an acceptable alternative on the parents, it is hard to see how they could have maintained that they were subjected to arbitrary interference from the state. For its part, in accommodating the parents, the state could have fulfilled its duty to ensure that all children are educated to at least a minimum standard of citizenship while minimizing the amount of arbitrary interference to which they believe they are being exposed.

But what if some groups such as indigenous or traditional communities hold intractable values that are fundamentally incompatible with modern republicanism? Again, the guide for modern republicanism must be compromise and accommodation. According to Pettit, an example of this type of compromise is the unique manner in which indigenous people are dealt with in post-colonial society (Pettit, 1997: 200). The thought to convey here is that those individuals who have valid and compelling reasons which warrant special treatment from the state to ensure that they are not the subject of state domination will be given the opportunity, to the extent that is possible, to live their lives according to their dominating ends.[2] The state will seek to ensure that the risks of domination to others are minimized and will only consider such claims in extraordinary circumstances. In such exceptional circumstances, modern republicanism must seek to minimize the exposure of individuals and groups to domination.

Some ways of life cannot be reconciled completely with republican aims and these may cause difficult issues to arise. However, as I have argued elsewhere, I believe that a strength of modern republicanism is its resilience and its ability to constantly reassess such difficult issues through the robust democratic contestatory institutions. In dealing with these difficult issues, the state has two main options. In the first case, in the presence of special circumstances such as those of indigenous populations, the state can allow individuals or groups an exemption from certain substantive requirements with respect to certain practices or beliefs. Or, in the second case, the state can minimize the arbitrariness of the decision by accommodating, to the extent possible, these individuals' and groups' comprehensive doctrines by finding a compromise solution that satisfies both parties. However, as a last resort, if such a compromise cannot be found, then those individuals and groups who insist on interfering arbitrarily with others will be confronted by the republican state. The state must have the right to protect other members of society from their arbitrary interference, even if it leads to confrontation.

Not surprisingly, in addition to the necessary values and virtues that support nondomination, the republican approach to civic education, like the liberal approach, will educate individuals in the institutions and legal framework of the state. If the state is to secure and enhance liberty as nondomination for its citizens by relying on the principles of contestatory democracy, the institutions and legal framework of the state must be a central part of civic education. As we discussed in the last chapter, republican institutions and laws play a central role in securing the conditions of nondomination for the citizenry. These institutions must be inclusive and open to the many different interests found within the republic so that vibrant public debate can take place. Additionally, as we discussed earlier, in many ways these institutions help to constitute the liberty experienced by republican citizens as an important interdependent relationship exists between the governed and the rules that govern them. It was this interdependent and intimate relationship that led Machiavelli to believe that republican institutions and the laws that emerge from them are directly related to the level of education and virtue found in the citizenry and vice versa (*The Discourses*: Machiavelli, 1965: 241). The thought is that the higher the quality of debate and contestation within republican institutions, the higher the quality of laws with respect to nondomination that emerge. It follows that citizens must learn about the substantive nature of the institutions of the republic, how they work, how to use them, and, importantly, how to challenge them. To support the contestatory nature of modern republicanism, it is essential that the citizenry has both the ability and the means to challenge the institutions and laws of the state. Thus, every institution and legal or policy decision made by the state must be open to meaningful challenge and contestation. On this point, a more informal dimension of civic education is highlighted.

In addition to the formal transmission of civic education through the state school system, there must be certain informal mechanisms that operate through the contestatory procedures and institutions of the modern republican state. As citizens engage with the state in its democratic contestatory procedures and institutions, they will inevitably be exposed to certain distinctive republican virtues. In other words, contestation itself helps to educate citizens in the ways of the republic and of nondomination as individuals and groups engage each other and the state to let their interests be known so that they can be tracked. And, as I argued above, this informal source of civic education is not solely limited to learning about the structures and procedures of government. Individuals and groups will also be educated about one another and be challenged to listen to the other side and act appropriately in a nondominating manner when expressing their interests. The reciprocal power of nondomination puts them on an equal footing as others recognize their interests as they publicize them and they can look others in the eye. They will benefit not only from sharing their experiences, but from experiencing the sharing of others as they learn to treat them with civility and respect.

Thus far, I have argued that any modern republican approach to civic education must contain substantive and robust forms of citizenship and civic virtue. The values and virtues that support liberty as nondomination must be integrated into the public or state school curriculum and taught to children who will develop into adults with all the rights and duties that are necessary to maintain the republican state. These substantive forms of republican citizenship will help to prepare citizens to play the necessary active role in the maintenance of liberty, and will also help to prepare citizens to play the necessary active role in their own nondomination. By learning how to cast their final ends in a nondominating fashion, citizens will be free to choose and revise their ends in a manner that is consistent with republican liberty and their position to pursue those chosen ends will be improved. The open and inclusive republican institutions help to secure citizens not only from arbitrary interference from others in society, but from the state as well. As discussed in the last chapter, a high degree of contestability will ensure that the state itself does not become a dominator, and that citizens register their interests with the state and with others. However, good education and good institutions are not enough to sustain the modern republican project. Any modern republican state's success in guaranteeing liberty as nondomination will, in large part, depend on the development of a comprehensive and embedded set of social norms that help to buttress the values and virtues of republican liberty as nondomination, and the ideals and institutions that it supports. The more these ideals and institutions become integrated into the norms of civic society, the less the state has to intervene to protect individuals, and vice versa (Pettit, 1997: 148). In the next section, I will discuss the crucial role and power of social norms and argue that without a robust set of modern republican norms the project that I have been defending is doomed to failure.

Modern republican social norms

If a modern republican state is successfully to secure republican liberty as nondomination for its citizens, the virtues and values that support this conception of liberty must become embedded in the norms of society. This is not something that is necessarily new within the broad spectrum of republican approaches. Earlier, I discussed how Machiavelli believed that the relative success of republican laws and institutions was inextricably tied to the existence of certain norms that would complement these laws and institutions (*The Discourses*: Machiavelli, 1965: 241). There is an intimate and close interdependent relationship between the norms of society and the laws and institutions that constitute the republican state. As outlined above, the modern republican approach to civic education and the distinctive institutions of the republic play a central role in the development and support of these norms. In many ways, modern republican norms must win a place in the habits and hearts of its citizens. According to Pettit, "the laws must be embedded in a network of norms that reign effectively, independently of state coercion, in the realm of civic society" (Pettit, 1997: 241). The three pillars of modern republicanism must work together if the republican state is truly to secure its citizens from arbitrary interference.

Nondomination as a social norm

In its most simple formulation, a norm is a behavioral regularity. Norms are ways of doing and thinking about things that are accepted as general practice and adhered to by individuals and groups, sometimes unconsciously. They help to give depth and character to a society and can be a powerful social force (Pettit, 1997: 243–6). Norms help to shape the different ways in which individuals and groups evaluate their life choices and provide a common tie that binds them together. In many ways, norms are an integral part of the collective identity of a society and represent the preferred way of doing things. The development of norms is a process that is deeply rooted in the traditions and customs of individuals and groups, and their power as a social force is in large part dependent on how closely they track the interests of the people.

Another important factor is the intimate connection between the norms of everyday life and the norms of a state's legal and constitutional system. Jürgen Habermas has pointed out the way in which legal norms help to provide society with reference points by which the members evaluate their own life plans. Moreover, these reference points are mostly seen as having emerged over time in response to various political, cultural, and ethical influences and represent, more or less, a commonality shared, at least in part, by the members of society in general (Habermas, 1994: 124–6). In this manner, legal or political norms permeate the ethical culture of society and provide its members with certain rights and duties that exist alongside their own individual or group identity. Of course the coexistence of political and social norms does not mean either that the political or social norms should not be subjected to scrutiny, or that they will not bring about conflict. However, as I have argued, this is not something to be feared by modern republicans since certain kinds of conflict can play a central role in the maximization of nondomination. Instead, along with democratic contestatory institutions and robust forms of civic education, the sometimes conflictual nature of political and social norms can actually increase the enjoyment of nondomination as arbitrary interference is rooted out and exposed. When conflicts emphasize certain problems and highlight the differences between some members of society, it is important to capitalize on the energy and attention created by such situations. Such moments can serve as catalysts for deep and searching questions about existing practices and norms. The processes and debates surrounding these questions can help to expose domination and minimize arbitrary interference.

For a modern republican state to be successful, norms must play a vital role in ensuring that liberty as nondomination is the prevailing public philosophy. The norms of a society characterized by the republican conception of liberty as nondomination will help to make liberty available to all segments of society, both on an individual and a group level. In many ways, norms serve as a fundamental and rudimentary check on the power of the state and can help keep the state focused on its commitment to prevent arbitrary interference (Pettit, 1997: 247). To this end, the state must use great vigilance not to undermine the important role that norms play in society. However, at the same time the state should not hesitate to challenge those norms that can undermine the nondomination enjoyed by citizens. The state must play an active role in combating this arbitrary interference and will have to take controversial positions because some social norms can ignore the interests of some individuals and groups in society (Pettit, 1997: 255). Throughout my argument I have suggested that a modern republican state is likely to be an activist state and this is also true in terms of challenging prevailing social norms.

For example, consider the United States' current non-recognition of gay and lesbian unions and the effect this has on key areas of their lives, such as health care, taxes, or insurance premiums. Same-sex unions certainly challenge the traditional manner in which many in US society view marriage, and it has become not only a social norm to oppose these types of marriages, but a legal norm as well. As the issue stands now, a modern republican state characterized by liberty as nondomination would have to address this problem on both the legal and social fronts. From a legal standpoint, in an ideal situation, a modern republican state would use its open and inclusive forums and institutions and the five processes outlined in the last chapter to consult with individuals and groups to gauge their interests and opinions. All points of view would be surveyed, and a conversational effort to arrive at a decision would take place. A vibrant debate would help to separate legitimate interests from illegitimate ones and a decision would be made that tracked the interests of the citizenry. For the sake of this example, I will assume that the decision to emerge from the contestatory process ends the legal prohibition on same-sex unions. In response to the decision, a modern republican state would have an important and active role to play in challenging those segments of society who disagreed with the ultimate decision and maintained that the norms of traditional marriage should continue. The state, along with those whose interests are to expand the legal definition of unions, would have to listen to the objections of those who opposed their position and engage in a contestatory and educative campaign to ensure that everyone's interests were being registered and aired in appropriate public forums. In this instance, on both the legal and social fronts, the republican state must play a key role in not only educating those who are opposed to same-sex unions, but in becoming educated itself on why the others oppose such moves so that an appropriate response can be crafted. But what of those who might still maintain that the recognition of same-sex unions dominates them and degrades the institution of marriage?

Some individuals will feel that the (hypothetical) decision to grant legal recognition to same-sex unions is unfair to them. They may argue that such recognition fundamentally undermines the institution of marriage that is closely tied to religious beliefs that are held deeply by many. For these individuals, to challenge their beliefs and conception of the good in this manner is not seen as tracking their interests and represents the arbitrary interference of the state. To these individuals, it may seem that they are being dominated and that they are thus not free. In response to this, there are three important points to make. The first point is that, by consulting the citizenry in open and inclusive contestatory forums, the state has taken the first step to eliminate arbitrary interference. No individuals or groups were asked to bracket off their deeply held beliefs or opinions and all were given equal opportunity to air their concerns and contest the opinions of others in the open and inclusive forums of the republic. The second point is that some objectors may have been expressing illegitimate and misplaced demands in the form of self-serving preferences. In this case, their self-serving preference against gays and lesbians caused the domination of these individuals and groups because it interfered with them in an arbitrary manner at will and with impunity. To be sure, from their point of view, they objected to gay and lesbian marriages because such recognition was not sanctioned by their beliefs. For many, the thought of gay and lesbian marriages is tantamount to blasphemy and is an affront to some of their most deeply held beliefs. It may be that they do not view these beliefs as purely self-serving preferences, but legitimate interests that they believe should be tracked. However, as I argued in earlier chapters, beliefs such as these may not be consistent with republican liberty as non-domination because they seemingly require the domination of others. The third important point is that the state, in recognizing same-sex unions, has not actually forced the objectors to perform same-sex marriages or, for that matter, engage in such practices. Moreover, in this case the republican state has not asked them to alter their procedures or beliefs to allow same-sex marriages in their churches. Instead, the state has held that, from a legal and civil standpoint, gay and lesbian unions should be allowed and recognized. The state has not forced the Church or those opposed to these unions to recognize them as religious marriages or to participate in performing them if they object. Rather, the republican state has sought to accommodate the interests of the citizenry and minimize any arbitrary interference by ensuring that such unions are allowed and bringing to bear the same level of state protection in terms of legal status and benefits. In allowing such unions, the state not only sends an important message about the legal status of the couples involved, but it also promotes and bestows an important label of recognition that will break down dominating attitudes in the whole of society.

In this example, protecting gays and lesbians in a legal manner from arbitrary interference from others is only the first goal that modern republicans want to accomplish. The end goal of this process is the hope that those whose final ends required the domination of others are taught that casting their ends in this manner deprives them of certain benefits and goods. The modern republican hope is that, through the ideals and institutions of the state, individuals will come to understand how their own good can be identified with that of the greater republican community so that corruption is kept at bay, and nondomination maximized. In this manner, the legal recognition of same-sex unions was only the first step for republicans. The second step is to challenge the social norms that caused the domination of same-sex couples and denied them a certain legal status. If modern republican ideals are embedded in a network of prevailing social norms, arbitrary interference will be minimized and individuals and groups will be better able to do well by themselves and enjoy their secure liberty. Aggressively challenging dominating social norms will have a profound effect on the modern republican project. And, as mentioned above, the vibrant and tumultuous environment that is likely to accompany any modern republican state will play a key role not only in challenging dominating social norms, but also in the development and maintenance of nondominating ones. I turn to this issue next.

Conflict and norms

Dominating norms that are not consistent with the republican project must be challenged and modified so that new, nondominating, norms can become a powerful force within society. Discord and tumult can help to challenge and reshape norms so that they have a degree of fluidity and shift to fit the ever-changing circumstances of life in the modern polity (Pettit, 1997: 251). For example, the American civil rights movement of the 1950s and 1960s challenged not only the legal impediments to equality, but also the social hindrances that permeated the wider society. Using the vibrant public forums of the state and wider society, civil rights campaigners had a significant impact on not only the existing political norms, but also on the prevailing social norms that accepted inequality and segregation. The legal impediments were just one of the reasons that civil rights campaigners engaged in this enormous undertaking. Challenging the social norms of inequality and segregation was a primary goal as well. For the civil rights campaigners, the legal and social norms of segregation were inseparable, and both had to be challenged if effective change was to be instituted. This intimate connection is clearly highlighted in the words of Martin Luther King, Jr:

> Through education we seek to change attitudes; through legislation and court orders we seek to regulate behavior. Through education we seek to change internal feelings (prejudice, hate, etc.); through legislation and court orders we seek to control the external effects of those feelings. Through education we seek to break down the spiritual barriers to integration; through legislation we seek to break down the physical barriers to integration. One method is not a substitute for the other, but a meaningful and necessary supplement. Anyone who starts out with the conviction that the road to racial justice is only one lane wide will inevitably create a traffic jam and make the journey infinitely longer. (King, 1987: 40)

It is no mystery that civil rights campaigners in America had to wage their fight for justice and equality on the two fronts mentioned above. On the one hand, they had to fight for just and equal political and legal rights with whites, while on the other hand, for their campaign to succeed, they had to challenge directly the prevailing attitudes and social norms that saw them as second-class citizens. Modern republicans, then, must too recognize the need for a robust set of social norms that reflect republican priorities and help to ensure that arbitrary interference is minimized. However, when such social norms are themselves the source of arbitrary interference, the modern republican state has an important and necessary role in seeking to bring these norms in line with liberty as nondomination.

The important point here is that a modern republican state must actively pursue some ideals that permeate deep into the social fabric of the state. Such a move is similar to one found in Habermas. As Habermas argues, the public sphere must sharpen some social problems into "a consciousness of crisis" so that they can be disrupted politically by the state (Habermas, 1996a: 366–9). At times, this effort will be controversial and may cause a considerable amount of conflict. Admittedly, such moves are likely to prove difficult and may be seen by some as the embodiment of domination itself. As stressed above, great vigilance is required to check the power of the state so that it does not become a dominator itself. When social norms that dominate are challenged, as in the hypothetical example above, some may seem alienated and seek to withdraw so that they can hold on to their cherished, but dominating, ways of life. A modern republican state must be sensitive to this sentiment and seek to accommodate such individuals as far as possible within the constraints of its wider commitment to liberty as nondomination. However, the state's commitment to liberty as nondomination must be resilient to such claims if it is to minimize arbitrary interference. While coping with such dissenters may prove taxing or difficult for a modern republican state, other positive effects can be seen. As I argued earlier, a modern republican state's commitment to civic virtue and civility may fundamentally challenge some individuals' ends and identities by distorting them. Ends that require the domination of others cannot exist within a modern republican state characterized by liberty as nondomination. This may, according to Pettit, help improve the options available to some individuals because there may be some nondominating dimensions of identity that are attractive and compelling that were not available to them under their dominating identity (Pettit, 1997: 257). Furthermore, a widespread commitment to the maintenance of norms which support liberty as nondomination will help to foster group-level points of view and assist individuals as they engage in the formation of the common good. An overriding commitment to group-level identities such as patriotism helps to nurture community and unite individuals and groups from widely varying moral traditions (Pettit, 1997: 257–9; also see Miller, 1995; Oldfield, 1990; Taylor, 1989; Viroli, 1995). This point ties in with Robert Putnam's now famous essay and book on the need for a renewed sense of civic engagement to stem the erosion of social capital (Putnam, 1995: 66; also see Putnam, 2000).

Putnam's research charts the decline of traditional forms of civic engagement and suggests that there has been a corresponding drop in social capital which he takes to be the "features of social organization such as networks, norms and social trust that facilitate coordination and cooperation for mutual benefit" (Putnam, 1995: 66). Noting that several factors related to modernity may be the cause of this erosion, Putnam suggests that we need to find new ways of restoring social capital that fit in with life in the modern, and often hectic, polity. Importantly, his recommendations suggest that preventing the erosion of social capital must be a holistic effort undertaken by society (Putnam, 1995: 75–7). In other words, it is not a problem that politics or the state alone can solve. The solutions to the need for social capital are mostly found outside of the traditional political sphere. Modern republicans too understand the need for civic engagement and social capital since both can contribute to the ideals and institutions associated with, and supported by, nondomination. Furthermore, as I have been arguing in this chapter, it is not something that can be done by government institutions alone, although they have an important role to play. The collective effort that helps to form and support social norms will be an asset to a modern republican state as it tries to minimize its citizens' exposure to arbitrary interference. The strength and viability of the first two pillars of modern republicanism – democratic contestatory institutions and robust forms of civic education – will, to a large extent, rely on the power of social norms to ensure that arbitrary interference is minimized. Robust modern republican social norms will likely require high levels of social capital if they are to be truly effective and help minimize the extent to which individuals and groups are exposed to arbitrary interference.

Here it is necessary to make a further point on modern republicanism that will help to buttress the strength and viability of the three pillars that support liberty as nondomination. For the most part I have discussed modern republicanism in terms of what type of public philosophy a national government should pursue. In doing so I have argued that nondomination and the virtues and values that support it must extend outside of what we take the traditional political sphere to be. However, beyond this I have not explicitly discussed the possibility or even the feasibility of nondomination serving as a public philosophy below the level of national government. This is a controversial issue and is at the center of many current debates between liberals, who are seen as favoring national or federal policies, and communitarians, who are generally taken to favor more locally based policies. I think that this issue is certainly an important one, and one that modern republicans have good reasons to weigh in on. In terms of the approach that I have put forth earlier, and especially the policy prescriptions put forth in the last three chapters, it may seem at first glance that the fight for nondomination must be led by a federal or national state entity. On one level, there is no doubt that if the citizenry is to live under a system characterized by republican liberty, it would follow that nondomination would be a central concern of the state's at a national level. However, I do not think that there is anything within modern republicanism that dictates that this is necessarily the only place in which the fight for nondomination can reside. While in some cases this might be the only feasible place or the only real way to ensure that arbitrary interference is minimized, it is not exclusively so. There is no reason why lesser state institutions or bodies cannot adopt the ideals and institutions of nondomination. Indeed, there are good reasons to expect that state institutions below the national or federal level should adopt a nondominating approach to governing. This point ties into Benjamin Barber's work in *Strong*

Democracy (1984), where he argues that political institutions need to be refocused from the bottom up. The complaint is that the top-level focus of the current systems of democracy tends to put an unhealthy distance between governors and governed. Instead, Barber suggests a model that stresses locally based solutions, including neighborhood assemblies to serve as forums for deliberation and to eventually have certain powers to legislate on local issues (Barber, 1984: 267–73).[3]

This also ties in to the modern republican effort to instill and embed nondomination and the values and virtues that support it as the prevailing social norms that reside in the habits and hearts of the people. Moreover, the more the principles of nondomination can become ordinary functions of modern life, the better the chances of maximizing republican liberty and making real the benefits brought about by republican virtues and enhancing the lives of the people. The point here is that if nondomination is to take residence in the citizenry's hearts and minds as a social norm, then the more it permeates national, state, and local governments the better. But the hope for modern republicans is that these norms will penetrate the realm of civil society and govern interactions outside of the narrow political sphere. To the extent that this is possible, the better chance there is to minimize arbitrary interference in the whole of society, and the more opportunity there is to increase social interaction and promote group-level commitments and raise social capital.

Conclusion

In this chapter I have explored how modern republicanism as a public philosophy is likely to interact with individuals and groups through civic education and social norms. In the first area, a modern republican approach to civic education will contain distinctive and substantive values and virtues that help to support liberty as nondomination and foster a republican spirit among the people. Like liberals, modern republicans believe that the development of certain values and virtues is essential for citizens in the modern polity. Unlike liberals, these goods are substantive in nature and may challenge and even distort some individuals' and groups' comprehensive moral doctrines. However, a modern republican state can justify this by appealing to the value of nondomination and the benefits that accompany it. Ends that explicitly or implicitly arbitrarily interfere with others must be confronted by the republican state. Thus, the modern republican approach to civic education goes well beyond the liberal approach that relies on the principles of toleration and mutual respect. The modern republican approach asks individuals to go further by insisting that they cast their ends in a manner that does not subject others to arbitrary interference. To do this, they must first listen and understand how their differing, and possibly incompatible, ends can be recast into ends that do not arbitrarily interfere in the lives of others. Republican forms of civic virtue require a commitment from all parties to utilize the values and ideals that support liberty as nondomination to act in a manner that tracks the interests of others. Modern republican versions of citizenship will help individuals to use the open and inclusive public forums of the state to register their interests so that they can be tracked.

In the second area, recognizing the powerful force of social norms, both the modern republican approach to civic education and the ideals and institutions that support nondomination and contestation are aimed at fostering a group-level commitment to certain distinctive ways of doing things. Understanding the close and intimate relationship between certain social norms and the success of modern republican laws and institutions, the state must play a very delicate role in maintaining those norms that help to minimize arbitrary interference, and challenging those that undermine the cause of liberty as nondomination. At its most basic, modern republicans understand that nondomination will not be successful in minimizing arbitrary interference unless it becomes an integral part of the public and non-political culture of the many individuals and groups that comprise the modern polity. Modern republicanism, and the virtues and values that accompany it, represent a rich and robust way of thinking about liberty. Without a deep commitment from individuals on a nonpolitical level, nondomination cannot become embedded in the prevailing social norms and overriding public philosophy of the modern state.

Combined with the type of contestatory democratic institutions I discussed in the last chapter, robust forms of civic education and social norms form the three pillars that support the structure of modern republicanism. If liberty as nondomination is to become a meaningful and powerful public philosophy in the modern world, all three of these components are necessary. If one fails, they all fail, as they are completely interdependent and their success or failure depends on how well they are rooted in the foundation of society. Thus, a further requirement is necessary if republican liberty as non-domination is to minimize actual or threatened arbitrary interference. Liberty as nondomination, and the virtues and values that support it, must take root in the habits and hearts of the citizenry and be resilient enough to change with them and react to new challenges or familiar problems. In many ways, the success or failure of modern republicanism will depend on how well democratic contestatory institutions, robust forms of civic education, and social norms perform their overlapping and interdependent roles in developing a distinctive and pervasive republican culture that secures its citizens from domination and allows them to exercise their freedom in a society free from arbitrary interference.

Conclusion

At the start of this book I suggested that political philosophers and politicians were using classical republican themes in a confused and often unhelpful manner. I argued that what was needed was a modern republican account to inspire, inform, and assist a renewed effort to reinvigorate the political ideals and institutions of the modern world. Such an approach can be realized by eschewing the narrow confines of Berlin's famous typology of liberty, and instead following the advice of Constant and learning to realize liberty as a rich, but yet complex, combination of ideals inspired by both ancient and modern writers. In trying to satisfy this requirement, I believe that the neo-Roman republicanism of Machiavelli becomes a key starting point for modern republicans for two important reasons. First, we see the beginnings of a distinctive conception of liberty that emphasized the necessity of strong laws and institutions to ensure that the citizenry was not dependent on others for its liberty. In urging the people of Florence to set aside their narrow self-interests, Machiavelli also argued that certain republican forms of mixed constitutions and other technological devices such as checks and balances and open and inclusive institutions be constituted. Combined with the robust forms of civic virtue and citizenship that had to be cultivated so that citizens could resist corruption and understand their role in creating the common good, these institutions helped to secure liberty. Moreover, these ideals and values had to reflect the intimate interdependent relationship between the citizenry and the laws and institutions that governed it.

The second reason Machiavelli becomes a pivotal figure for modern republicanism is his belief in how conflict could play a central role in the maintenance of liberty. However, as we saw, this conflict was not of the factional kind that was endemic in the Florentine republic of his time and represented the triumph of narrow self-interest over the common good. Rather, this conflict was a naturally occurring consequence of the republic of his day populated by equally legitimate, but yet differently minded, individuals and groups who sought to rule themselves through properly constituted republican institutions. Such beliefs were predicated on the thought that being free of dependency on others would allow individuals and groups to pursue their own objectives as long as the state remained at liberty. By creating balanced laws and institutions that encouraged a life of virtue, the structural foundations of the republic promised individuals security and liberty so that they were left free to pursue their own ends, as long as these ends were consistent with republican liberty. Thus, a modern republican approach must not only look closely at Machiavelli's conception of liberty and the virtues and values that supported it, but also at the important contribution he made to institutional design and the role of conflict in securing the conditions of freedom.

In moving from classical republicanism to modern republicanism I have argued that we must continue in the direction pointed out by Skinner and Pettit. By thinking of liberty as neither solely the absence of interference nor the realization of self-mastery but rather as the absence of mastery, an attractive and compelling modern republican approach can begin to emerge. Modern republican liberty as nondomination allows that certain interferences can have the effect of enhancing liberty and coping with the problems of the modern world. Through fully exploiting the constitutional and reciprocal powers of nondomination, our liberty can become more resilient and secure. The constitutional power of nondomination helps to ensure that the ideas and institutions of the modern republic are properly constituted and that domination is minimized. The reciprocal power of nondomination holds out the promise that certain modern republican virtues will interact on a personal and more intimate level with agents to enrich and deepen their lives while helping to constitute their freedom. Countenancing the intimate and interdependent nature of these two powers, agents who live in a state characterized by modern republicanism will receive certain benefits unavailable to them in systems characterized by non-interference. They will have an increased capacity for choice and will be empowered and secure in making their choices. They will stand on an equal footing with others and be able to look them in the eye as modern republicanism alters the traditional power relationships between competing social agents and insists on recognition and civility.

In the last part of this book, in trying to demonstrate how modern republicanism represents an attractive way forward, I have explored how liberty as nondomination can manifest itself in the modern polity. Indeed, throughout my argument, I have suggested that modern republicanism characterized by liberty as nondomination represents a fresh new approach that can cope with the many problems facing the modern polity. Conflict, citizenship, and civic virtue all play important and interdependent roles to help secure this alternative conception of liberty. By accepting the inevitable clash of difference and diversity, the modern polity can reinvigorate the institutions of the state and secure its citizens from arbitrary interference. It can do so without endorsing a singular version of human flourishing, and without sacrificing several important liberal goals. Such an approach is not neutral in the same way as the liberal neutrality of Kymlicka, nor is it reducible to the political liberalism of Rawls.

A properly constituted modern republic must be characterized by strong laws and institutions that help cultivate certain types of citizens who can identify their own good with that of the community, and thus secure nondomination. Through strong forms of citizenship and civic virtue, a modern republican state helps individuals to mold and cast their ends in a manner that is consistent with republican liberty. Individuals and groups are free to pursue their own final ends, as long as those ends do not seek to dominate others. Any modern republican approach must stress the intimate relationship between liberty as nondomination, good laws and institutions, and civic virtue and citizenship so that the full potential of the constitutional and reciprocal powers can be realized. Furthermore, by tolerating and institutionalizing the pluralism found within the modern polity, a modern republican state can channel the dynamic energy and activity generated by a population defined by difference and diversity to secure and enhance liberty as nondomination. I suggested that a modern republic would strive to create open and inclusive forums in a nondominating public sphere, where citizens could engage each other using nondomination as their supreme tracking value as they constructed fair laws and institutions.

The key to guarding against threats to liberty in both the *imperium* and *dominium* was a robust account of democratic contestatory institutions and processes so that arbitrary interference could be minimized in the whole of society. Such institutions are inspired by neo-Roman republican institutions and seek to balance out the degree to which narrow self-interest and self-serving preferences play in today's public policy. Since modern republicanism connects the maximization of nondomination with an active populace, it is essential that the constitutional power of nondomination manifest itself in certain distinctive institutions and ideals that are spread across a range of public offices and processes. The goal is for the constitutional power of nondomination to become embedded within the institutions and laws that, in turn, are created by the general citizenry in accordance with rules and regulations that all have been offered the opportunity to help construct. The hope is that such institutions will help to check the power of the state while helping to minimize the amount of intersubjective domination that agents are exposed to. There is, however, a realization that domination can never be totally eliminated. The key is to rely on the resilience of modern republican institutions and processes to minimize the risks of arbitrary interference and keep the state from becoming a dominator itself.

Democratic contestatory institutions and processes cannot alone sustain the modern republican project. The success or failure of modern republicanism as a public philosophy will rely on how well democratic contestatory institutions perform their role as one of the three modern republican pillars. I have argued that, if modern republican liberty as nondomination is to become a meaningful and powerful public philosophy, the virtues and values that support it must take root in the habits and hearts of the citizens and change as they change. To support this effort, a modern republican state must actively seek to educate and cultivate individuals of a certain republican character type, who can cast their ends in a nondominating manner. In many ways, the success or failure of republican liberty as nondomination will depend on how well education and institutions can cultivate certain modern republican norms that are embedded within, and reflected by, the attitudes of society as a whole. Thus, the two remaining pillars, robust forms of civic education and social norms, help complete modern republicanism as an attractive public philosophy.

A modern republican approach to civic education will contain distinctive and substantive values and virtues that help to support liberty as nondomination and foster a republican spirit among the people. In coming to know the skills associated with the constitutional and reciprocal powers of nondomination, agents will be in an improved situation to make their mark in the world. A modern republican state justifies this by appealing to the value of nondomination and the benefits that accompany it. A modern republican state must confront those whose ends explicitly or implicitly arbitrarily interfere with others. A modern republican approach to civic education teaches the benefits and skills of civic virtue so that individuals treat each other with civility by casting their ends in a manner that does not subject others to arbitrary interference. Modern republican forms of civic virtue and civility require a commitment from all parties to utilize the values and ideals that support liberty as non-domination so that they can act in a manner that tracks the interests of others. In doing so they will have to learn to listen and understand how their differing, and possibly incompatible, ends can be recast into ends that do not arbitrarily interfere in the lives of others. Moreover, modern republican versions of citizenship help individuals to use the open and inclusive public forums of the state to register their interests so that they can be tracked.

In fostering group-level commitments and certain distinctive ways of doing things, republican social norms complete the pillars that support the modern republican project. In recognizing the close and intimate relationship between certain social norms and the success of modern republican laws and institutions, the modern republic will play a key role in supporting those norms that help to minimize arbitrary interference. The modern republic will also have to play a key role in challenging those norms that undermine the cause of liberty as nondomination. The thought is that the ideals and institutions of nondomination will not be successful in minimizing arbitrary interference unless they become an integral part of the public and nonpolitical culture of the many individuals and groups that comprise the modern polity.

In many ways, the success or failure of modern republicanism will depend on how well democratic contestatory institutions, robust forms of civic education, and social norms perform their overlapping and interdependent roles in developing a distinctive and pervasive republican culture that secures its citizens from domination while allowing them to exercise their freedom in a society free from domination. If liberty as nondomination is to become a meaningful and powerful public philosophy, all three of these pillars are necessary to support the modern republican project. The interdependent nature of these pillars means that if one fails, they all fail and their effectiveness will depend on the strength that all three can muster collectively. Keeping in mind the resilient nature of liberty as nondomination, the ideals and institutions of modern republicanism must be able to change as the people change and react to new challenges when they arise, or to dogged old problems when they cannot be solved easily.

The modern republican approach that I have defended is not something that represents a complete revolution in the way we think about politics, nor is it too radical to be taken seriously. Central to my argument is an understanding that there is an inspirational lineage between modern republicanism and neo-Roman republicans such as Machiavelli and those later writers that he influenced. Even though modern republicanism is grounded in the writings of classical republicans, a central feature of this approach is its ability to change and be adapted to different situations to address a range of problems when they occur in today's world. At the heart of this modern republican approach is its alternative conception of liberty as nondomination and the manner in which its ideals and institutions help to constitute the freedom experienced by its citizens. Although the modern republicanism that I have defended is distinct from its neo-Athenian counterpart and the rival liberal approaches I have discussed, I believe that it is compatible with many of their aims and I have tried to demonstrate that. Modern republican versions of civic virtue and citizenship, when combined with strong institutions and laws, can play the important role of helping redefine how we think about politics so that individuals and groups can better utilize the structures of the state to secure their liberty as nondomination as they take advantage of the constitutional and reciprocal powers of nondomination and the benefits that they receive.

Finally, as I have tried to point out, those who are serious about nondomination must understand and accept that not all problems are purely "political" in nature and thus cannot be solved in the narrow realm of traditional politics. What is needed is a more holistic approach that relies on the fundamental goal of nondomination to secure individuals and groups from arbitrary interference on both a political and a nonpolitical level so that intersubjective relations can also benefit from the modern republican approach. We must change the way we think about our commitments, not only to ourselves, but to each other, and the activity required to ensure that we remain free. The activity that is required by a properly constituted modern republican state does not have to rely on burdensome and time-consuming commitments. Indeed, it is this very activity that enables modern republicanism to offer contemporary polities a way forward. By understanding liberty in this alternative sense, individuals and groups can secure themselves from the domination of others and the state while helping themselves to do well. In presenting my case I hope that I have argued with sufficient vigor that, while the classical republican approach may provide us with certain clues as to how to improve our thinking about politics, we must concentrate on building a coherent modern version that can cope with today's problems. Given the state of modern politics, it is not simply a matter of recovering the ideals and images of classical republicanism. Instead we must look to a modern republican account for inspiration and hope that arbitrary interference can be minimized so that we can live free lives and engage with each other with the civility and respect we all deserve.

Notes

Chapter 1 The Ideal of Polity

1 For a further discussion on Rousseau's republicanism, see Oldfield (1990: 50–77).
2 Skinner specifically refers to Alasdair MacIntyre's work. See MacIntyre (1985: 146–64).
3 For other important critiques of MacCallum, see Oppenheim (1981) and Parent (1974).
4 It is important to note that Machiavelli's equality is not social or economic in nature, but rather legal and political. For further discussion see Bock (1990: 189).
5 Skinner specifically refers to Ronald Dworkin (1977: xi, 170–7).
6 As is well documented, Machiavelli was hostile to some forms of religion, especially Christianity, because he believed that it cultivated the wrong kind of virtues that were incompatible with the necessary requirements of maintaining the republic. Christianity tended to stress ideals that were antagonistic to Machiavelli's own conception of virtue, and he consequently believed that it had weakened the citizens' love of *patria* (Skinner, 1978: 183). Machiavelli maintained that Christianity glorified "humble and contemplative men, rather than men of action. It has assigned as man's highest good humility, abnegation, and contempt for mundane things" (*The Discourses*: Machiavelli, 1965: 331). The difference between Christianity and the civil religion favored by the Romans was that the latter sought to glorify civic virtue and thus nourish political liberty, whereas Christianity had the effect of diverting individuals' purposes away from the virtue necessary to maintain the republic, and instead focusing them on their own lives and on God.
7 For example, according to Pocock *vivere civile* was built primarily from Aristotelian influences which manifested themselves in the citizen's ability to "equate political activity with the practice of virtue and to make the

flow of political and particular events intelligible and justifiable" (Pocock, 1975: 116).

Chapter 2 Modern Republicanism: Liberty as Nondomination

1   To avoid confusion, for the purposes of my argument when I use the term "interest" or "interests" I am not using it to represent what some may see as real or true interests, but rather what individuals perceive to be their interests.

2   As we saw in the last chapter, an obvious reply is that there are alternative conceptions of freedom such as MacCallum's that are less strict than freedom as non-interference. For example, John Gray suggests that liberty should be understood as the non-restriction of options (Gray, 1989: 47). Thus, in response to the threatened restriction of liberty I highlighted above, freedom as the non-restriction of options can be construed in such a manner that non-active interference can be adequately dealt with. An agent subject to this form of un-freedom is seen as someone whose actions have been limited by either real or imagined threats that restrict their options. This challenge to republican liberty as nondomination demonstrates that, as Baldwin has argued, liberty can be conceived on many different levels, each one stressing different aspects of what it means to be free. My point here is that trying to understand the different senses of liberty and how their various components each relate to one another leads to alternative conceptions of liberty, each with its own strengths and weaknesses. To that end, my main objective in this chapter is to highlight the strengths of the republican approach in light of the weaknesses found in the freedom as non-interference approach put forth by Berlin and adopted in part by subsequent liberal theorists. To the extent that other conceptions of liberty are relevant to my argument, I will address these later in this chapter and in subsequent ones.

3   For a wider discussion of nondomination combating uncertainty, anxiety, and fear of subordination see Pettit (1997: 83–90).

4   I will further develop this point in subsequent chapters, especially chapter 5.

5   For a further discussion of how republican ideals and institutions constitute the liberty experienced by republican citizens see Pettit (1997: 106–9, 1998: 86–7).

6   For an excellent collection of articles on liberal neutrality, see Goodin and Reeve (1989). Especially useful is Jones's article "The Ideal of the Neutral State" (1989). Another good article is de Marneffe's "Liberalism, Liberty, and Neutrality" (1990).

7   Kymlicka makes a similar claim by focusing on the reason *why* a particular conception of civic virtue is being promoted by the state (Kymlicka, 1998b: 136). Also consider Kymlicka's views on state neutrality in *Contemporary Political Philosophy: An Introduction* (1990) and in "Liberal

Individualism and Liberal Neutrality" (1992: 165–85). I will fully address both Kymlicka's and Rawls's claims in chapters 3 and 4 respectively.

8   There are many instances in *The Discourses* where Machiavelli discusses the qualities necessary to preserve republican liberty. A good summary of his argument is found in book 1, chapters 50–60 (Machiavelli, 1965: 298–320). Also see Skinner (1984: 208–12) for a further discussion of these qualities.

9   I would like to thank Philip Pettit, Mark Philp, and an anonymous referee for helping me have a deeper understanding of instrumental, intrinsic, and ultimate values.

10 Believing that something has intrinsic value and making a persuasive case for it are separate claims. As I have argued elsewhere (Maynor, 2002b) there is an argument that modern republican goods such as civic virtue and citizenship may indeed be intrinsically valuable. In this chapter I do not intend to pursue this claim. Rather, my goal here is to argue that, even on an instrumental level, there are important and significant differences between liberal and modern republican goods.

Chapter 3 The Challenge of the Cultural Marketplace: Modern Republicanism and the Neutral State

1   See Goodin and Reeve (1989) and de Marneffe (1990) for two very good overviews of liberal neutralism. Also see Dworkin (1975) for another good discussion.

2   For example, Joseph Raz's liberal approach abandons liberal neutrality and advocates state perfectionism (Raz, 1986). For the purposes of this chapter, I will concentrate on liberal neutralists like Kymlicka.

3   For the purposes of this chapter, I will set aside Michael Sandel's republican arguments against liberal neutrality because, as I have argued earlier, I maintain that the modern republican approach that I espouse is fundamentally different from his approach. For a further discussion on these differences see Pettit (1998) and Skinner (1997).

4   I would like to thank Philip Pettit for pointing me in the direction of Korsgaard's work and for helping me to understand this issue further.

5   Although Burtt classifies Machiavelli in a tradition associated solely with the education of desires approach, I understand Machiavelli's account to be closer to that put forth by Quentin Skinner. Skinner maintains that Machiavelli promotes a combination of the accommodation of interests approach and the education of desires approach. See Burtt (1990: 26 n. 9) for further discussion on this point.

6   This point is also made by Machiavelli, who believed that, unless properly constituted, republican institutions would fall into the hands of those who sought to promote their own narrowly tailored private ends above those of the common good. An example of this is

Machiavelli's belief that, when Florence was faced with divisive factions and conflict, instead of using the public institutions to secure the common good for all, individuals sought to promote their own private interests at the expense of other individuals' liberty (*The History of Florence*: Machiavelli, 1965: 1145–8, esp. 1146).

Chapter 4 Without Regret: The Comprehensive Nature of Nondomination

1   Tocqueville's thought is often used by writers in contrasting ways. Bellah, for example, evokes Tocqueville to illustrate the civic humanist foundations of American mores while Macedo takes Tocqueville to be a liberal (Bellah et al., 1985; Macedo, 1988). Most recently, it is interesting to note that one of Rawls's fiercest critics, Michael Sandel, evokes an essentially Tocquevillian republicanism in *Democracy's Discontent* (Sandel, 1996). Sandel's complaint is that the primacy of, and attention to, a Rawlsian system of rights has left America's public philosophy bereft of the reflective and critical capacities necessary for individuals in today's modern polity to flourish (Sandel, 1996: 4). As I outlined earlier, Sandel's solution is to invoke a neo-Athenian version of republicanism that he believes influenced the American founders who espoused a theory of self-government and active participation. These ideals were central to the maintenance of liberty so that citizens have the necessary environment or community to maximize the exploration of their true selves and to flourish as political animals. This neo-Athenian-inspired doctrine not only requires that citizens are taught and encouraged to play active public roles, but also maintains that the government must sacrifice any claims to neutrality among competing ideas of the good. It thus fits more closely with Rawls's definition of civic humanism (Sandel, 1996: 5–6).
2   I would like to thank Mark Philp for bringing this point to my attention.
3   There is a plethora of recent literature on deliberative democracy. In addition to those works mentioned in the text, some that have been useful to me include Benhabib (1996), Bohman and Rehg (1997), Carter and Stokes (1998), Elster (1998), and Gutmann and Thompson (1996).
4   Callan believes that the active engagement in public reason and the acceptance of the burdens of judgment will necessitate the attainment of certain reflective skills and character traits that will require agents to assess critically certain conceptions of the good which lie outside of the basic structure of society. For Callan, "future citizens must be taught to think in particular ways about doctrines that properly lie outside the scope of public reason: they must become critically attuned to the wide range of reasonable political disagreement within the society they inhabit and to the troubling gap between reasonable agreement and the whole moral truth" (Callan, 1997: 40). In other words, in securing active agreement on the fair terms of cooperation, and in accepting the burdens of judgment and the associated

understanding of reciprocity, agents' nonpolitical beliefs will either intentionally or unintentionally be affected in a profound manner by the state. Unlike Rawls, however, Callan views this as being beneficial to individuals (Callan, 1997: 41–51). These benefits concern individuals' ability to develop the virtues associated with autonomy, such as critical reflection, mutual respect, and toleration. In other words, Callan maintains that, under his version of liberal civic education, individuals are exposed to certain (partially) comprehensive goods that have a profound and beneficial effect on their nonpolitical lives.

5   Rawls, however, is right to argue "that the term neutrality is unfortunate [because] some of its connotations are highly misleading [and] others suggest altogether impracticable principles" (Rawls, 1996: 191).

6   As I argued in the last chapter, although Pettit asserts that the republican state reflects a "shared-value" neutrality, I maintain that any element of value violates basic strict neutrality and therefore cannot claim to be neutral. For a further discussion of Pettit's position, see "Reworking Sandel's Republicanism" (Pettit, 1998: 91).

7   Several theorists who work in this area have made similar charges against contemporary liberal approaches. For more information see Landes (1998); Okin (1998); Patemen (1983); Squires (1999); and Young (2000).

8   In discussing this issue I have tried to use the same language as Rawls and thus have followed his terminology since his project is the main topic of the present inquiry. When such language proves misleading and/or burdensome, I will strive to utilize other characterizations of the split such as public/private and note the differences.

9   For an excellent collection of a range of ideas specifically on this topic see Landes (1998).

10   This is not to say that the modern republican project is a perfect fit with Habermas's theory. For the purposes of this chapter I set these questions aside and take them up more fully in the next chapter.

Chapter 5 Factions and Diversity: A Modern Republican Dilemma

1   For a good discussion on the role of humors in Machiavelli's political writings see Ivison (1997: 58–60) and Parel (1992: 101–12, 140–52).

2   For further discussion see Bock (1990: 197–8).

3   As I mentioned in chapter 1, it is important to note that Machiavelli's equality is not social or economic in nature, but rather legal and political. For further discussion see Bock (1990: 189).

4   For a useful discussion on Machiavelli's view of people see Ivison (1997: 65–6). Also see Berlin (1981: 41).

5   An example of this approach can be found in Machiavelli's view of the difficulty republics faced when confronted with the ideals of Christian morality. Machiavelli opposed Christianity on the grounds that its value

system was inconsistent with the secular, and superior, virtues of the value system found in his neo-paganism. For Machiavelli, Christian morality fundamentally undermined the virtues that were needed to secure liberty and nurture the kind of society that would maintain the republic (Berlin, 1981: 45–6; also see Garver, 1996: 197). However, despite believing that Christian morality was incompatible with republican values, Machiavelli maintained that individuals could still subscribe to both, as long as their commitment to liberty was real and strong. For Machiavelli, Christians could come over to republican thinking without having to sacrifice their ultimate ends, whereas republicans could only accept the full thrust of Christian morality by ceasing to be republicans (Garver, 1996: 215).

Chapter 6 Modern Republicanism and Democratic Contestatory Institutions

1   For a further discussion of the dangers of *imperium* and *dominium* forms of power see Pettit (2001: 153–6).

Chapter 7 Modern Republican Civic Education and Social Norms

1   As discussed earlier, Charles Taylor has an alternative approach to these types of divisive issues: see Taylor (1998).
2   In determining who may qualify for this type of treatment, certain considerations must be undertaken by the state in terms of past injustices or extreme cases of domination. Obviously, such cases will be controversial no matter what the ultimate decision is. Any modern republican state would have to be prepared, to the extent possible, to subject these issues to the contestatory institutions and processes of the state.
3   The full program of Barber's project includes other modern republican-friendly policies, such as a nationally led focus on civic education and various other measures to improve citizen participation. For a further discussion of his proposals, see Barber (1984: 261–311).

References

Allen, A. and Regan, M. (eds) (1998), *Debating Democracy's Discontent: Essays on American Politics, Law, and Public Philosophy* (Oxford: Oxford University Press).

Arendt, H. (1958), *The Human Condition* (Chicago: University of Chicago Press).

Aristotle (1988), *The Politics*, ed. S. Everson (Cambridge: Cambridge University Press).

Avineri, S. and de-Shalit, A. (eds) (1992), *Communitarianism and Individualism* (Oxford: Oxford University Press).

Axford, B., Browning, G., Huggins, R., Rosamond, J., and Turner, J. (1997), *Politics: An Introduction* (London: Routledge).

Baldwin, T. (1984), "MacCallum and the Two Concepts of Freedom," *Ratio*, 26: 125–42.

Barber, B. (1984), *Strong Democracy: Participatory Politics for a New Age* (Berkeley, CA: University of California Press).

Bellah, R., Madsen, R., Sullivan, W. M., Swidler, A., and Tipton, S. M. (1985), *Habits of the Heart: Individualism and Commitment in American Life* (New York: Perennial Library).

Benhabib, S. (ed.) (1996), *Democracy and Difference* (Princeton, NJ: Princeton University Press).

Benhabib, S. (1998), "Models of Public Space: Hannah Arendt, the Liberal Tradition, and Jürgen Habermas," in Landes (1998), pp. 65–99.

Benn, S. and Gaus, G. (eds) (1983), *Public and Private in Social Life* (London: Croom Helm).

Berlin, I. (1969), *Four Essays on Liberty* (Oxford: Oxford University Press).

Berlin, I. (1981), *Against the Current: Essays in the History of Ideas* (Oxford: Oxford University Press).

Bock, G. (1990), "Civil Discord in Machiavelli's *Istorie Fiorentine*," in Bock, Skinner, and Viroli (1990), pp. 181–201.

Bock, G., Skinner, Q., and Viroli, M. (eds) (1990), *Machiavelli and Republicanism* (Cambridge: Cambridge University Press).

Bohman, J. and Rehg, W. (eds) (1997), *Deliberative Democracy: Essays on Reason and Politics* (Cambridge, MA: MIT Press).

Brennan, G. and Hamlin, A. (2001), "Republican Liberty and Resilience," *The Monist*, 84(1): 45–59.

Brugger, B. (1999), *Republican Theory in Political Thought: Virtuous or Virtual?* (New York: St Martin's Press).

Burns, J. H. and Goldie, M. (eds) (1991), *The Cambridge History of Political Thought: 1450–1700* (Cambridge: Cambridge University Press).

Burtt, S. (1990), "The Good Citizen's Psyche: On the Psychology of Civic Virtue," *Polity*, 23: 23–38.

Burtt, S. (1992), *Virtue Transformed: Political Argument in England 1688–1740* (Cambridge: Cambridge University Press).

Burtt, S. (1994), "Religious Parents, Secular Schools: A Liberal Defence of an Illiberal Education," *The Review of Politics*, 56: 51–70.

Burtt, S. (1996), "In Defence of *Yoder*: Parental Authority and the Public Schools," in Shapiro and Hardin (1996), pp. 412–37.

Callan, E. (1997), *Creating Citizens: Political Education and Liberal Democracy* (Oxford: Clarendon Press).

Carter, A. and Stokes, G. (eds) (1998), *Liberal Democracy* (Cambridge: Polity).

Christman, J. (1998), "Pettit, P., *Republicanism: A Theory of Freedom and Government*" (book review), *Ethics*, 109(1): 202–6.

Cicero (1991), *On Duties*, ed. M. Griffin and E. Atkins (Cambridge: Cambridge University Press).

Cohen, J. (1989), "Deliberation and Democratic Legitimacy," in Hamlin and Pettit (1989), pp. 17–34.

Constant, B. (1988), *Political Writings*, ed. B. Fontana (Cambridge: Cambridge University Press).

Dagger, R. (1997), *Civic Virtues: Rights, Citizenship, and Republican Liberalism* (Oxford: Oxford University Press).

Daniels, N. (ed.) (1978), *Reading Rawls* (Oxford: Blackwell Publishers).

de Marneffe, P. (1990), "Liberalism, Liberty, and Neutrality," *Philosophy and Public Affairs*, 19: 253–74.

Dworkin, R. (1975), "Non-Neutral Principles," in Daniels (1978), pp. 124–40.

Dworkin, R. (1977), *Taking Rights Seriously* (Cambridge, MA: Harvard University Press).

Elkin, S. E. and Soltan, K. E. (eds) (1993), *A New Constitutionalism: Designing Political Institutions for a Good Society* (Chicago: Chicago University Press).

Elster, J. (ed.) (1998), *Deliberative Democracy* (Cambridge: Cambridge University Press).

Fontana, B. (ed.) (1994), *The Invention of the Modern Republic* (Cambridge: Cambridge University Press).

Fraser, N. (1998), "Sex, Lies, and the Public Sphere," in Landes (1998), pp. 314–37.

Fullinwider, R. K. (1999), "Pettit, P., *Republicanism: A Theory of Freedom and Government*" (book review), *Philosophical Books*, 40: 131–3.

Galston, W. (1991), *Liberal Purposes: Goods, Virtue, and Diversity in the Liberal State* (Cambridge: Cambridge University Press).

Garver, E. (1996), "After Virtù: Rhetoric, Prudence and Moral Pluralism in Machiavelli," *History of Political Thought*, 27: 195–222.

Goodin, R. and Pettit, P. (eds) (1997), *Contemporary Political Philosophy: An Anthology* (Oxford: Blackwell Publishers).

Goodin, R. and Reeve, A. (eds) (1989), *Liberal Neutrality* (London: Routledge).

Gray, J. (1989), *Liberalisms: Essays in Political Philosophy* (London: Routledge).

Gutmann, A. (1987), *Democratic Education* (Princeton, NJ: Princeton University Press).

Gutmann, A. (1995), "Civic Education and Social Diversity," *Ethics*, 105: 557–79.

Gutmann, A. and Thompson, D. (1996), *Democracy and Disagreement* (Cambridge, MA: Harvard University Press).

Habermas, J. (1994), "What is Universal Pragmatics?", in Outhwaite (1996), pp. 118–31.

Habermas, J. (1996a), *Between Facts and Norms: Contributions to a Discourse Theory of Law and Democracy* (Cambridge: Polity).

Habermas, J. (1996b) "On the Cognitive Content of Morality," in *Proceedings of the Aristotelian Society* (London: Aristotelian Society).

Habermas, J. (1997), "The Public Sphere," in Goodin and Pettit (1997), pp. 105–8.

Hamilton, A., Madison, J., and Jay, J. (1961), *The Federalist Papers*, ed. C. Rossiter (New York: Mentor Press).

Hamlin, A. and Pettit, P. (eds) (1989), *The Good Polity: Normative Analysis of the State* (Oxford: Basil Blackwell).

Harrington, J. (1992), *The Commonwealth of Oceana and A System of Politics*, ed. J. G. A. Pocock (Cambridge: Cambridge University Press).

Held, D. (1996), *Models of Democracy*, 2nd edn (Cambridge: Polity).

Herzog, D. (1986), "Some Questions for Republicans," *Political Theory*, 14: 473–93.

Heyd, D. (ed.) (1996), *Toleration: An Elusive Virtue* (Princeton, NJ: Princeton University Press).

Hobbes, T. (1968), *Leviathan*, ed. C. B. MacPherson (Harmondsworth: Penguin).

International Herald Tribune (1995a), "Clinton's New Message: Put Democracy Back to Work," 23 Jan.

International Herald Tribune (1995b), "Clinton Bowing to Political Reality, Models a More Centrist Presidency," 26 Jan.

Ivison, D. (1997), *The Self at Liberty: Political Arguments and the Arts of Government* (Ithaca, NY: Cornell University Press).

Jones, P. (1989), "The Ideal of the Neutral State," in Goodin and Reeve (1989), pp. 9–38.

Kahane, D. (1996), "Cultivating Liberal Values," *Canadian Journal of Political Science*, 29: 699–728.

Kelly, P. J. (2000), "Republican Freedom Reconsidered," presented at the 2000 Annual Meeting of the American Political Science Association, August 31–September 3, 2000.

King, M. L. (1987), *The Words of Martin Luther King, Jr.* (New York: Newmarket Press).

Korsgaard, C. (1993), "Commentary on Cohen and Sen," in Nussbaum and Sen (1993), pp. 54–61.

Kymlicka, W. (1989), *Liberalism, Community, and Culture* (Oxford: Oxford University Press).

Kymlicka, W. (1990), *Contemporary Political Philosophy: An Introduction* (Oxford: Clarendon Press).

Kymlicka, W. (1992), "Liberal Individualism and Liberal Neutrality," in Avineri and de-Shalit (1992), pp. 165–85.

Kymlicka, W. (ed.) (1995), *The Rights of Minority Cultures* (Oxford: Oxford University Press).

Kymlicka, W. (1996), "Two Models of Pluralism and Tolerance," in Heyd (1996), pp. 81–105.

Kymlicka, W. (1998a), *Finding Our Way: Rethinking Ethnocultural Relations in Canada* (Oxford: Oxford University Press).

Kymlicka, W. (1998b), "Liberal Egalitarianism and Civic Republicanism: Friends or Enemies?", in Allen and Regan (1998), pp. 131–48.

Landes, J. B. (ed.) (1998), *Feminism, the Public and the Private* (Oxford: Oxford University Press).

Leet, M. (1998), "Jürgen Habermas," in Carter and Stokes (1998), pp. 77–97.

MacCallum, G. (1991), "Positive and Negative Freedom," in Miller (1991), pp. 100–22.

Macedo, S. (1988), "Capitalism, Citizenship, and Community," *Social Philosophy and Policy*, 6: 113–39.

Macedo, S. (1990), *Liberal Virtues: Citizenship, Virtue, and Community in Liberal Constitutionalism* (Oxford: Clarendon Press).

Macedo, S. (1995), "Liberal Civic Education and Religious Fundamentalism: The Case of God v. John Rawls," *Ethics*, 105: 468–96.

Machiavelli, N. (1965), *The Chief Works and Others*, tr. A. Gilbert, 3 vols (Durham, NC: Duke University Press).

MacIntyre, A. (1985), *After Virtue: A Study in Moral Theory* (London: Duckworth).

Manin, B. (1994), "Checks, Balances and Boundaries," in Fontana (1994), pp. 27–62.

Maynor, J. (2000), "Factions and Diversity: A Republican Dilemma," in Pierson and Tormey (2000), pp. 78–91.

Maynor, J. (2002a), "Without Regret: The Comprehensive Nature of Non-domination," *Politics*, 22: 51–8.

Maynor, J. (2002b), "Another Instrumental Approach," *European Journal of Political Thought*, 1: 71–89.

Miller, D. (ed.) (1987), *The Blackwell Encyclopedia of Political Thought* (Oxford: Blackwell Publishers).

Miller, D. (ed.) (1991), *Liberty* (Oxford: Oxford University Press).

Miller, D. (1995), "Citizenship and Pluralism," *Political Studies*, 43: 432–50.

Montesquieu (1989), *The Spirit of the Laws*, tr. and ed. A. Cohler, B. Miller, and H. Stone (Cambridge: Cambridge University Press).

Moon, D. (1993), *Constructing Community: Moral Pluralism and Tragic Conflicts* (Princeton, NJ: Princeton University Press).

Mouffe, C. (ed.) (1992), *Dimensions of Radical Democracy* (London: Verso Press).

Mouffe, C. (1993), *The Return of the Political* (London: Verso Press).

Mozert v. Hawkins County Board of Education, 827 F.2d 1058 (6th Cir. 1987).

Mulhall, S. and Swift, A. (eds) (1996), *Liberals and Communitarians* (Oxford: Blackwell Publishers).

NOU (1967): Act of 10 February 1967 relating to procedure in cases concerning the public administration with subsequent amendments, most recently by Act of 9 January 1998 No. 5 (short title: Public Administration Act).

Nussbaum, M. and Sen, A. (eds) (1993), *The Quality of Life* (Oxford: Oxford University Press).

Okin, S. M. (1989), *Justice, Gender, and the Family* (New York: Basic Books).

Okin, S. M. (1998), "Gender, the Public and the Private," in Phillips (1998), pp. 116–41.

Oldfield, A. (1990), *Citizenship and Community: Civic Republicanism and the Modern World* (London: Routledge).

Olsen, J. P. (1983), *Organized Democracy: Political Institutions in a Welfare State – the Case of Norway* (Olso: Universitetsforlaget).

Oppenheim, F. (1981), *Political Concepts: A Reconstruction* (Oxford: Blackwell Publishers).

Outhwaite, W. (ed.) (1996), *The Habermas Reader* (Cambridge: Polity).

Pangle, T. (1988), *The Spirit of Modern Republicanism: The Moral Vision of the American Founders and the Philosophy of Locke* (Chicago: University of Chicago Press).

Parekh, B. (2000), *Rethinking Multiculturalism: Cultural Diversity and Political Theory* (Basingstoke: Macmillan).

Parel, A. (1992), *The Machiavellian Cosmos* (New Haven, CT: Yale University Press).

Parent, W. A. (1974), "Some Recent Work on the Concept of Liberty," *American Philosophical Quarterly*, 11: 149–67.

Patemen, C. (1983), "Feminist Critiques of the Public/Private Dichotomy," in Benn and Gaus (1983), pp. 281–303.

Patten, A. (1996), "The Republican Critique of Liberalism," *British Journal of Political Science*, 26: 25–44.

Patten, A. (1998), "Pettit, P., *Republicanism: A Theory of Freedom and Government*" (book review), *Political Studies*, 46: 808–10.

Pettit, P. (1989), "The Freedom of the City: A Republican Ideal," in Hamlin and Pettit (1989), pp. 141–68.

Pettit, P. (1997), *Republicanism: A Theory of Freedom and Government* (Oxford: Oxford University Press).

Pettit, P. (1998), "Reworking Sandel's Republicanism," *The Journal of Philosophy*, 95: 73–96.

Pettit, P. (1999), "Republicanism: Once More with Hindsight," in id., *Republicanism: A Theory of Freedom and Government*, pbk edn (Oxford: Oxford University Press), pp. 283–305.

Pettit, P. (2000), "Democracy, Electoral and Contestory," *Nomos*, 42: 105–44; repr. in Shapiro and Macedo (2000).

Pettit, P. (2001), *A Theory of Freedom: From the Psychology to the Politics of Agency* (Cambridge: Polity).

Phillips, A. (ed.) (1998), *Feminism and Politics*. (Oxford: Oxford University Press).

Phillips, A. (2000), "Survey Article: Feminism and Republicanism: Is This a Plausible Alliance?", *The Journal of Political Philosophy*, 8(2): 279–93.

Pierson, C. and Tormey, S. (eds) (2000), *Politics at the Edge* (Basingstoke: Macmillan).

Pocock, J. G. A. (1975), *The Machiavellian Moment: Florentine Political Thought and the Atlantic Republican Tradition* (Princeton, NJ: Princeton University Press).

Putnam, R. (1995), "Bowling Alone: America's Declining Social Capital," *Journal of Democracy*, 6: 65–78.

Putnam, R. (2000), *Bowling Alone: The Collapse and Revival of American Community* (New York: Simon & Schuster).

Qualifications and Curriculum Authority (1999a), *Citizenship: The Report*, March 29, 1999 (London: HMSO).

Qualifications and Curriculum Authority (1999b), *Citizenship: The National Curriculum for England* (London: HMSO).

Rahe, P. (1992), *Republics Ancient and Modern: Classical Republicanism and the American Revolution* (Chapel Hill, NC: University of North Carolina Press).

Rawls, J. (1971), *A Theory of Justice* (Cambridge, MA: Harvard University Press).

Rawls, J. (1996), *Political Liberalism*, pbk edn (New York: Columbia University Press).

Rawls, J. (1999), *The Law of Peoples with "The Idea of Public Reason Revisited"* (Cambridge, MA: Harvard University Press).

Raz, J. (1986), *The Morality of Freedom* (Oxford: Clarendon Press).

Rorty, R., Schneewind, J., and Skinner, Q. (eds) (1984), *Philosophy in History* (Cambridge: Cambridge University Press).

Rousseau, J.-J. (1978), *The Social Contract*, tr. R. Masters and J. Masters (New York: Hafner Press).

Sandel, M. (1984), "The Procedural Republic and the Unencumbered Self," *Political Theory*, 12: 81–96.

Sandel, M. (1996), *Democracy's Discontent: America in Search of a Public Philosophy* (Cambridge, MA: Belknap Press of Harvard University Press).

Shapiro, I. and Hardin, R. (eds) (1996), *Nomos 38: Political Order* (New York: New York University Press).

Shapiro, I. and Macedo, S. (eds) (2000), *Nomos 42: Designing Democratic Institutions* (New York: New York University Press).

Shklar, J. (1990), "Montesquieu and the New Republicanism," in Bock, Skinner, and Viroli (1990), pp. 265–79.

Sidney, A. (1990), *Discourses Concerning Government*, ed. T. West (Indianapolis, IN: Liberty Fund).

Skinner, Q. (1978), *Foundations of Modern Political Thought*, 2 vols (Cambridge: Cambridge University Press).

Skinner, Q. (1981), *Machiavelli* (Oxford: Oxford University Press).

Skinner, Q. (1983), "Machiavelli on the Maintenance of Liberty," *Politics*, 18: 3–15.

Skinner, Q. (1984), "The Idea of Negative Liberty: Philosophical and Historical Perspectives," in Rorty, Schneewind, and Skinner (1984), pp. 193–221.

Skinner, Q. (1990a), "Machiavelli's *Discorsi* and the Pre-Humanist Origins of Republican Ideas," in Bock, Skinner, and Viroli (1990), pp. 121–41.

Skinner, Q. (1990b), "The Republican Ideal of Political Liberty," in Bock, Skinner, and Viroli (1990), pp. 293–309.

Skinner, Q. (1991), "The Paradoxes of Political Liberty," in Miller (1991), pp. 183–205.

Skinner, Q. (1992), "On Justice, the Common Good and the Priority of Liberty," in Mouffe (1992), pp. 211–24.

Skinner, Q. (1996), *Reason and Rhetoric in the Philosophy of Hobbes* (Cambridge: Cambridge University Press).

Skinner, Q. (1997), *Liberty Before Liberalism* (Cambridge: Cambridge University Press).

Squires, J. (1999), *Gender in Political Theory* (Cambridge: Polity).

Sunstein, Cass (1993) "The Enduring Legacy of Republicanism," in Elkin and Soltan (1993), pp. 174–206.

Swift, A. (2001), *Political Philosophy: A Beginners' Guide for Students and Politicians* (Cambridge: Polity).

Taylor, C. (1989), *Sources of the Self: The Making of Modern Identity* (Cambridge, MA: Harvard University Press).

Taylor, C. (1991), "What's Wrong with Negative Liberty," in Miller (1991), pp. 141–62.

Taylor, C. (1994), "The Politics of Recognition," in Taylor and Gutmann (1994), pp. 25–73.

Taylor, C. (1995), *Philosophical Arguments* (Cambridge, MA: Harvard University Press).

Taylor, C. (1998), "Living with Difference," in Allen and Regan (1998), pp. 212–26.

Taylor, C. and Gutmann, A. (eds) (1994), *Multiculturalism* (Princeton, NJ: Princeton University Press).

Time (1995), "Stuck in the Middle," 30 Jan.

Tocqueville, A. de (1969), *Democracy in America*, ed. J. P. Mayer (New York: Perennial Library).

Tuck, R. (1993), *Philosophy and Government 1572–1651* (Oxford: Oxford University Press).

Viroli, M. (1990), "Machiavelli and the Republican Idea of Politics," in Bock, Skinner, and Viroli (1990), pp. 143–71.

Viroli, M. (1992), *From Politics to Reason of State: The Acquisition and Transformation of the Language of Politics 1250–1600* (Cambridge: Cambridge University Press).

Viroli, M. (1995), *For Love of Country: An Essay on Patriotism and Nationalism* (Oxford: Clarendon Press).

Viroli, M. (1998), *Machiavelli* (Oxford: Oxford University Press).

Washington Post (1995), "At Clinton's Dinner, Ideas were on the Menu: President Invites 'Big Thinkers' to Camp David in Preparation for State of the Union Address," 20 Jan.

Williams, G. (1991), *Political Theory in Retrospect: From the Ancient Greeks to the 20th Century* (Cheltenham, UK: Edward Elgar).

Wootton, D. (ed.) (1994), *Republicanism, Liberty, and Commercial Society, 1649–1776* (Stanford, CA: Stanford University Press).

Worden, B. (1994), "Marchamount Nedham and the Beginnings of English Republicanism, 1649–1656," in Wootton (1994), pp. 45–81.

Young, I. M. (1990), *Justice and the Politics of Difference* (Princeton, NJ: Princeton University Press).

Young, I. M. (2000), *Inclusion and Democracy* (Oxford: Oxford University Press).

Index